FREE

Free Study Tips Videos/DVD

In addition to this guide, we have created a FREE set of videos with helpful study tips. **These FREE videos provide you with top-notch tips to conquer your exam and reach your goals.**

Our simple request is that you give us feedback about the book in exchange for these strategy-packed videos. We would love to hear what you thought about the book, whether positive, negative, or neutral. It is our #1 goal to provide you with quality products and customer service.

To receive your **FREE Study Tips Videos**, scan the QR code or email freevideos@apexprep.com. Please put "FREE Videos" in the subject line and include the following in the email:

    a. The title of the book

    b. Your rating of the book on a scale of 1-5, with 5 being the highest score

    c. Any thoughts or feedback about the book

Thank you!

aPHR Study Guide 2024-2025
5 Practice Tests and aPHR Exam Prep Certification Book
[2nd Edition]

J. M. Lefort

Written and edited by APEX Publishing.

ISBN 13: 9781637752456

APEX Publishing is not connected with or endorsed by any official testing organization. APEX Publishing creates and publishes unofficial educational products. All test and organization names are trademarks of their respective owners.

The material in this publication is included for utilitarian purposes only and does not constitute an endorsement by APEX Publishing of any particular point of view.

For additional information or for bulk orders, contact info@apexprep.com.

Table of Contents

Welcome

Dear Customer,

Congratulations on taking the next step in your educational journey, and thank you for choosing APEX to help you prepare! We are delighted to be by your side, equipping you with the knowledge and skills needed to make this move forward. Your APEX study guide contains helpful tips and quality study material that will contribute to your success. This study guide has been tailored to assist you in passing your chosen exam, but it also includes strategies to conquer any test with ease. Whether your goal is personal growth or acing that big exam to move up in your career, our goal is to leave you with the confidence and ability to reach the top!

We love to hear success stories, so please let us know how you do on your exam. Since we are continually making improvements to our products, we welcome feedback of any sort. Your achievements as well as criticisms can be emailed to info@apexprep.com.

Sincerely,
APEX Team

FREE Videos/DVD OFFER

Achieving a high score on your exam depends on both understanding the content and applying your knowledge. **Because your success is our primary goal, we offer FREE Study Tips Videos, which provide top-notch test taking strategies to help optimize your testing experience.**

Our simple request is that you email us feedback about our book in exchange for the strategy-packed videos.

To receive your **FREE Study Tips Videos**, scan the QR code or email freevideos@apexprep.com. Please put "FREE Videos" in the subject line and include the following in the email:

    a. The title of the book
    b. Your rating of the book on a scale of 1-5, with 5 being the highest score
    c. Any thoughts or feedback about the book

Thank you!

Test Taking Strategies

1. Reading the Whole Question

A popular assumption in Western culture is the idea that we don't have enough time for anything. We speed while driving to work, we want to read an assignment for class as quickly as possible, or we want the line in the supermarket to dwindle faster. However, speeding through such events robs us from being able to thoroughly appreciate and understand what's happening around us. While taking a timed test, the feeling one might have while reading a question is to find the correct answer as quickly as possible. Although pace is important, don't let it deter you from reading the whole question. Test writers know how to subtly change a test question toward the end in various ways, such as adding a negative or changing focus. If the question has a passage, carefully read the whole passage as well before moving on to the questions. This will help you process the information in the passage rather than worrying about the questions you've just read and where to find them. A thorough understanding of the passage or question is an important way for test takers to be able to succeed on an exam.

2. Examining Every Answer Choice

Let's say we're at the market buying apples. The first apple we see on top of the heap may *look* like the best apple, but if we turn it over we can see bruising on the skin. We must examine several apples before deciding which apple is the best. Finding the correct answer choice is like finding the best apple. Although it's tempting to choose an answer that seems correct at first without reading the others, it's important to read each answer choice thoroughly before making a final decision on the answer. The aim of a test writer might be to get as close as possible to the correct answer, so watch out for subtle words that may indicate an answer is incorrect. Once the correct answer choice is selected, read the question again and the answer in response to make sure all your bases are covered.

3. Eliminating Wrong Answer Choices

Sometimes we become paralyzed when we are confronted with too many choices. Which frozen yogurt flavor is the tastiest? Which pair of shoes look the best with this outfit? What type of car will fill my needs as a consumer? If you are unsure of which answer would be the best to choose, it may help to use process of elimination. We use "filtering" all the time on sites such as eBay® or Craigslist® to eliminate the ads that are not right for us. We can do the same thing on an exam. Process of elimination is crossing out the answer choices we know for sure are wrong and leaving the ones that might be correct. It may help to cover up the incorrect answer choice. Covering incorrect choices is a psychological act that alleviates stress due to the brain being exposed to a smaller amount of information. Choosing between two answer choices is much easier than choosing between all of them, and you have a better chance of selecting the correct answer if you have less to focus on.

4. Sticking to the World of the Question

When we are attempting to answer questions, our minds will often wander away from the question and what it is asking. We begin to see answer choices that are true in the real world instead of true in the world of the question. It may be helpful to think of each test question as its own little world. This world may be different from ours. This world may know as a truth that the chicken came before the egg or may assert that two plus two equals five. Remember that, no matter what hypothetical nonsense may be in the question, assume it to be true. If the question states that the chicken came before the egg, then choose

2

your answer based on that truth. Sticking to the world of the question means placing all of our biases and assumptions aside and relying on the question to guide us to the correct answer. If we are simply looking for answers that are correct based on our own judgment, then we may choose incorrectly. Remember an answer that is true does not necessarily answer the question.

5. Key Words

If you come across a complex test question that you have to read over and over again, try pulling out some key words from the question in order to understand what exactly it is asking. Key words may be words that surround the question, such as *main idea, analogous, parallel, resembles, structured,* or *defines.* The question may be asking for the main idea, or it may be asking you to define something. Deconstructing the sentence may also be helpful in making the question simpler before trying to answer it. This means taking the sentence apart and obtaining meaning in pieces, or separating the question from the foundation of the question. For example, let's look at this question:

> Given the author's description of the content of paleontology in the first paragraph, which of the following is most parallel to what it taught?

The question asks which one of the answers most *parallels* the following information: The *description* of paleontology in the first paragraph. The first step would be to see *how* paleontology is described in the first paragraph. Then, we would find an answer choice that parallels that description. The question seems complex at first, but after we deconstruct it, the answer becomes much more attainable.

6. Subtle Negatives

Negative words in question stems will be words such as *not, but, neither,* or *except.* Test writers often use these words in order to trick unsuspecting test takers into selecting the wrong answer—or, at least, to test their reading comprehension of the question. Many exams will feature the negative words in all caps (*which of the following is NOT an example*), but some questions will add the negative word seamlessly into the sentence. The following is an example of a subtle negative used in a question stem:

> According to the passage, which of the following is *not* considered to be an example of paleontology?

If we rush through the exam, we might skip that tiny word, *not,* inside the question, and choose an answer that is opposite of the correct choice. Again, it's important to read the question fully, and double check for any words that may negate the statement in any way.

7. Spotting the Hedges

The word "hedging" refers to language that remains vague or avoids absolute terminology. Absolute terminology consists of words like *always, never, all, every, just, only, none,* and *must.* Hedging refers to words like *seem, tend, might, most, some, sometimes, perhaps, possibly, probability,* and *often.* In some cases, we want to choose answer choices that use hedging and avoid answer choices that use absolute terminology. It's important to pay attention to what subject you are on and adjust your response accordingly.

8. Restating to Understand

Every now and then we come across questions that we don't understand. The language may be too complex, or the question is structured in a way that is meant to confuse the test taker. When you come across a question like this, it may be worth your time to rewrite or restate the question in your own words in order to understand it better. For example, let's look at the following complicated question:

> Which of the following words, if substituted for the word *parochial* in the first paragraph, would LEAST change the meaning of the sentence?

Let's restate the question in order to understand it better. We know that they want the word *parochial* replaced. We also know that this new word would "least" or "not" change the meaning of the sentence. Now let's try the sentence again:

> Which word could we replace with *parochial,* and it would not change the meaning?

Restating it this way, we see that the question is asking for a synonym. Now, let's restate the question so we can answer it better:

> Which word is a synonym for the word *parochial*?

Before we even look at the answer choices, we have a simpler, restated version of a complicated question.

9. Predicting the Answer

After you read the question, try predicting the answer *before* reading the answer choices. By formulating an answer in your mind, you will be less likely to be distracted by any wrong answer choices. Using predictions will also help you feel more confident in the answer choice you select. Once you've chosen your answer, go back and reread the question and answer choices to make sure you have the best fit. If you have no idea what the answer may be for a particular question, forego using this strategy.

10. Avoiding Patterns

One popular myth in grade school relating to standardized testing is that test writers will often put multiple-choice answers in patterns. A runoff example of this kind of thinking is that the most common answer choice is "C," with "B" following close behind. Or, some will advocate certain made-up word patterns that simply do not exist. Test writers do not arrange their correct answer choices in any kind of pattern; their choices are randomized. There may even be times where the correct answer choice will be the same letter for two or three questions in a row, but we have no way of knowing when or if this might happen. Instead of trying to figure out what choice the test writer probably set as being correct, focus on what the *best answer choice* would be out of the answers you are presented with. Use the tips above, general knowledge, and reading comprehension skills in order to best answer the question, rather than looking for patterns that do not exist.

Bonus Content & Audiobook

You can access numerous bonus items online, including all 5 practice tests and the audiobook. Go to apexprep.com/bonus/aphr or scan the QR code below with your phone or tablet.

After you go to the website, you will have to create an account and register as a "new user" and verify your email address before you begin.

If you need any help, please contact us at info@apexprep.com.

Study Prep Plan for the aPHR

 **1 Breathe**

Reducing stress is key when preparing for your test.

 2 Build

Create a study plan to help you stay on track.

 **3 Begin**

Stick with your study plan. You've got this!

1 Week Study Plan

Day 1	Day 2	Day 3	Day 4	Day 5	Day 6	Day 7
Talent Acquisition	Learning and Development	Employee Relations	Compliance and Risk Management	aPHR Practice Test #1	aPHR Practice Test #2	Take Your Exam!

2 Week Study Plan

Day 1	Day 2	Day 3	Day 4	Day 5	Day 6	Day 7
Talent Acquisition	Lifecycle of Hiring and Onboarding Applicants	Learning and Development	Change Management Process	Compensation and Benefits	Wage Statements and Payroll Processing	Employee Relations

Day 8	Day 9	Day 10	Day 11	Day 12	Day 13	Day 14
Workforce Management	Compliance and Risk Management	Laws Related to Workplace Health, Safety, Security, and Privacy	aPHR Practice Test #1	aPHR Practice Test #2	aPHR Practice Tests #3-#5	Take Your Exam!

30 Day Study Plan

Day 1	Day 2	Day 3	Day 4	Day 5	Day 6	Day 7
Talent Acquisition	Talent Sourcing Tools and Techniques	Recruiting, Screening, and Selecting Applicants	Lifecycle of Hiring and Onboarding Applicants	Using Technology for Managing Candidate Data	Learning and Development	Developing an Organizational Learning Strategy

Day 8	Day 9	Day 10	Day 11	Day 12	Day 13	Day 14
Training Formats and Delivery Techniques	Change Management Process	Employee Development and Training	Compensation and Benefits	Health Benefit and Insurance Programs	Wage Statements and Payroll Processing	Final Pay

Day 15	Day 16	Day 17	Day 18	Day 19	Day 20	Day 21
Employee Relations	Organizational Structures	Engaging Employees and Improving Employee Satisfaction	Workforce Management	Diversity and Inclusion Initiatives	Compliance and Risk Management	Laws Related to Employment in Union Environments

Day 22	Day 23	Day 24	Day 25	Day 26	Day 27	Day 28
Laws Related to Workplace Health, Safety, Security, and Privacy	Risk Assessment and Mitigation Techniques	Organizational Restructuring Initiatives	aPHR Practice Test #1	aPHR Practice Test #2	aPHR Practice Test #3	aPHR Practice Test #4

Day 29	Day 30
aPHR Practice Test #5	Take Your Exam!

As you study for your test, we'd like to take the opportunity to remind you that you are capable of great things! With the right tools and dedication, you truly can do anything you set your mind to. The fact that you are holding this book right now shows how committed you are. In case no one has told you lately, you've got this! Our intention behind including this coloring page is to give you the chance to take some time to engage your creative side when you need a little brain-break from studying. As a company, we want to encourage people like you to achieve their dreams by providing good quality study materials for the tests and certifications that improve careers and change lives. As individuals, many of us have taken such tests in our careers, and we know how challenging this process can be. While we can't come alongside you and cheer you on personally, we can offer you the space to recall your purpose, reconnect with your passion, and refresh your brain through an artistic practice. We wish you every success, and happy studying!

9

Introduction to the aPHR

Function of the Test

The Associate Professional in Human Resources® (aPHR) exam is one of the HR Certificate Institute's® (HRCI®) recognized HR credentials. Earning aPHR certification can jumpstart one's human resource career and demonstrate a basic understanding of the skills and knowledge of the technical and operational aspects of HR. The aPHR is a unique human resource certification in that it is intended for two different types of professionals, new human resource professionals and professionals who are not in the HR field but wish to display acumen in that field.

The aPHR exam does not require candidates to have any HR experience to be eligible for the exam. Candidates must have a high school diploma or the equivalent to take the exam and earn the certification.

Test Administration

Candidates must apply to take the aPHR and obtain approval prior to registering for the test. The application fee is $100, and the exam fee is $300. The exam is administered year-round via computer at Pearson VUE testing centers around the United States. International locations are available as well. Exams must be scheduled no later than 180 days from the date of approval from HRCI®. Candidates are required to bring a government-issued ID to their testing appointment. Candidates can also choose to use OnVUE to take the test at home.

Requests for special accommodations are available at the time of registration for test takers with documented disabilities.

Candidates must wait 90 days after an unsuccessful attempt at the exam before they can schedule an appointment to retake the exam. Retakes must be scheduled within the 180-day eligibility timeframe.

Test Format

The aPHR exam contains 65 scored questions and 25 unscored pretest questions mixed in throughout the exam. Test takers will not know which questions count toward their official scores. HRCI® includes the pretest questions to gauge their usefulness as scored questions on future iterations of the aPHR. Test questions are of a variety of formats including standard multiple-choice questions with only one correct response and multiple-choice questions with multiple responses required, fill-in-the-blank questions, drag and drop questions, and scenarios. Test takers are given 1 hour and 45 minutes to complete the exam, and there is an additional 30 minutes of administration time.

There are five main domains of content on the exam, termed "Functional Areas." The topics and breakdown for these functional areas are shown below:

Functional Area	Approximate Percentage of Exam
Compliance and Risk Management	25%
Employee Relations	24%
Talent Acquisition	19%
Compensation and Benefits	17%
Learning and Development	15%

Within each functional area, questions are classified into one of the three cognitive levels listed in order of increasing difficulty: knowledge/comprehension, application/problem solving, or synthesis/evaluation. It should be noted that employment laws are covered on the exam, and candidates are responsible for knowing the most current laws at the time of their exam administration.

Scoring

Unofficial scores are available at the test center upon completion of the exam. Official scores are released 24-48 hours after exam administration.

Minimum passing scores are established based on the modified Angoff method, which involves a team of field experts who determine the difficulty of each question and assign the scaled score of 500 as the cutoff score, indicating a score that corresponds to the lowest score that a candidate possessing the minimally acceptable level of knowledge and skills is likely to achieve. Scaling allows different versions of the exam to be compared.

Upon successfully passing the exam, test takers earn aPHR certification, which is valid for three years. To remain credentialed, either 45 recertification credits must be earned over the three-year period, or the exam must be retaken and passed anew.

Talent Acquisition

Talent Acquisition and Recruitment

Talent acquisition is the strategic process of hiring individuals with specific skills and abilities that will align with the organization's goals. It includes not only filling an open position but also taking a holistic view of the workforce needs, both current and future.

The talent acquisition lifecycle is a multi-step process that begins with a hiring need—usually a job opening—and ends with the hiring and onboarding of an employee. This process should be objective and standardized, ensuring that it is free from discrimination or other unethical and illegal practices.

Recruitment is the tactical process of filling a vacancy. The first step in the recruitment lifecycle is to determine the need of the department. If an organization has an opening due to a resignation, promotion, or transfer, the recruitment need must be evaluated. Once the need has been assessed, a job posting should be created that communicates the job description, company information, employee benefit information, and other information that a prospective employee would need to determine whether to submit an application.

The second step in the process is to source candidates and assess the candidate pool. By utilizing various sourcing methods, such as social media platforms, niche job boards, and other appropriate methods, a robust candidate pool can be gathered for the initial screening review. The initial screening review should group candidates into two basic initial categories—meeting required qualifications and not meeting required qualifications. The third step in the process is to further screen the candidates who have the required qualifications. These candidates should be further screened into such groups as "most qualified" and "least qualified." Then candidates should be selected for invitation to interview for the position. Candidates should be selected on criteria such as education, years of experience, accomplishments in previous positions, and leadership experience.

The fourth step in the process is to assess the most qualified candidates via assessment tests or interviews. Assessment tests should be conducted to determine the validity and strength of the candidates' skills. When candidates are invited to interview with the organization, the interviews should be conducted by individuals who are familiar with conducting interviews. Interviewers should be able to assess responses to score and rank the candidates for the hiring manager to review. Once the initial interviews have been completed, finalists should be selected. Hiring managers should then conduct final interviews with the most qualified candidates to make a final selection to offer the position.

The fifth step in the process consists of the employment offer and orientation. The employment offer should include not only the job title and salary, but also the name of the hiring manager, potential start date, necessary background checks or screening required prior to starting, and any pertinent employee benefit information. Benefit information often makes or breaks an offer, so employment offers should include information regarding vacation time, sick leave time, holiday schedules, medical insurance, (including when coverage starts and whether the organization assists with premiums), and any other pertinent information. If the prospective employee has other needs and wishes to negotiate the terms of the offer, it is appropriate at this point to engage in these conversations.

Relocation expenses, deferred compensation, additional vacation time, and signing bonuses are all potential benefits that a prospective employee could negotiate. Once the offer has officially been accepted; the background, references, or medical screenings have been conducted; and the individual has

13

been cleared to start employment, then an official hire date should be established. Once the new employee has begun working for the organization, it is important to immediately orient the individual to the company culture and procedures such as benefits enrollment, payroll, safety, work-related injuries, union participation, policies and procedures, and any other important information for a new employee to be exposed to.

Identifying Staffing Needs and Guiding Talent Acquisition Efforts

Workforce Planning

Workforce planning is the complete strategic process that forecasts an organization's current and future workforce needs, determines the most effective practices and processes to fill these needs, and implements the plans to deliver results. Workforce planning includes the following components at various stages in the process:

- Forecasting
- Critical skills gap analysis
- Recruitment
- Onboarding
- Succession planning

Human Resources professionals should ensure all parties have a clear understanding of each of these concepts.

Forecasting

Forecasting is the process of deciding which positions must be filled and how to fill them. Forecasting is generally used to determine the overall personnel needs of an organization as well as the applicant pools of both internal and external candidates. Then forecasting is used to implement the appropriate methods to align the personnel needs and the applicant pools. During the forecasting process, it is important to understand company trends such as sales, growth, and market opportunities. If growth is such that additional employees are needed, a recruitment plan may be needed to address this need. Additionally, it is also important to understand current company demographics, such as when employees are eligible for retirement. This information is useful when determining future attrition and the needs of the organization if such attrition is realized.

Job Analysis

To ensure that the results are accurate and appropriate when performing a **job analysis**, it is important to fully understand the tools being applied to evaluate the position. Using multiple tools can also ensure that a holistic review is conducted and no pieces are missing from the analysis. It is vital to ensure that a consistent method is used when reviewing a position. Regardless of the tool(s) used to conduct a job analysis, the core components of a position to be reviewed should include the following:

- Scope of work: exact job duties including an idea of daily, weekly, monthly, and annual assignments and responsibilities

- Impact of work on other positions and the organization

14

- Working conditions: equipment, hazards

- Supervisory role, if any

- Reporting relationships

- Relationships, internal and external

- Leadership role, formal or informal

- Minimum requirements to perform the job: knowledge, skills, abilities

- Minimum qualifications, training, and experience required

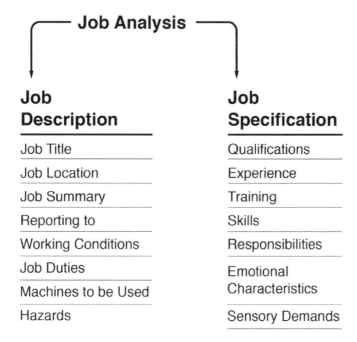

Gaining an understanding of these components can be achieved by having the individual complete a questionnaire and providing information and answers to many questions about what they do. Following up to this questionnaire, interviewing the individual can lead to a deeper understanding of the role. To ensure an understanding of how the position impacts others, it may also be beneficial to interview other employees who may be impacted by this work. Finally, when performing a job analysis, it is helpful to observe the actual work being done. This can provide a deeper understanding of the actual ins and outs of a position.

Job Analysis Method

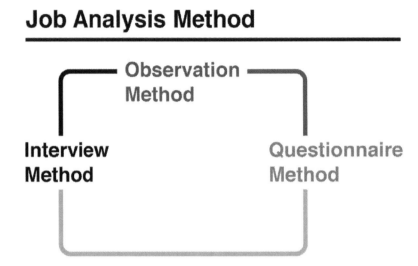

Once the information has been received from the various analysis tools being used, all pertinent data and information should be thoroughly reviewed to determine if the employee is performing work outside of their current job description. If the information from the job analysis does not align with the job description, the Human Resources professional should first work to update the job description with the accurate description of the work being done.

Critical Skills Gap Analysis

A **critical skills gap analysis** is a process by which an organization defines its personnel needs in terms of the skills required to achieve the organization's goals. Having a complete and thorough understanding of the skills available and the skills needed allows an organization to make better decisions in recruitment, training, and succession planning. This analysis also allows employees to understand the skills needed to be successful and to progress within the organization throughout their career. Additionally, critical skills gap analysis can assist in the recruitment process by allowing hiring managers to home in on the required skill sets for applicants. It is also important to thoroughly define a critical skill. A **critical skill** is one that must be present in order to achieve the results necessary. If the critical skill is not present, problems can occur in the completion, accuracy, quality, and other aspects of the task. Critical skills should be identified in the job description and validated through reviewing the work being done on a day-to-day basis.

Job Descriptions

Every position should have **a job description** that reflects the minimum qualifications, specifically the experience and education required to be able to do the job. The salary range should align with these minimum qualifications in that more experienced candidates could earn more within the salary range than less experienced candidates. The job description should accurately describe the work that is expected for that position.

Alternative Staffing Approaches

There are two situations in which staffing alternatives are considered: employee surpluses and employee shortages. Each circumstance has unique challenges, and Human Resources professionals can provide a

Long-term solutions to deal with employee shortages can include the following:

- Issuing recalls or limiting production
- Increasing the recruitment efforts to hire more employees more frequently
- Permanently transferring employees to different positions
- Retraining employees to transfer to the hard-to-fill positions
- Transferring work out of the department

Some solutions for short-term and long-term are the same; they can be implemented for the length of time needed to adjust the employee headcount to the appropriate level. If certain short-term solutions do not achieve the results needed, additional solutions can be implemented or continued until the organization achieves the desired outcome. Human Resources professionals should understand the demographics of the affected employees to propose the best solutions. While certain employees may not respond to a retirement incentive or a vacation buyback program, they may be susceptible to a change in overtime opportunities or a temporary assignment elsewhere in the organization. It may not be feasible to offer multiple solutions, but consideration should be given to offering more than one solution. Each employee is motivated by different factors, and having an understanding of this can assist when determining which options to implement.

Talent Sourcing Tools and Techniques

Recruitment uses sourcing methods to generate a robust, qualified candidate pool. There are numerous ways to source candidates, and some methods may work better for particular positions or markets. Human Resources professionals should understand the positions they are recruiting for and how best to find candidates. Specialized positions in information technology may require postings on a niche IT-focused job board. Positions in maintenance and operations may need online postings in the local newspaper or on Craigslist.com. Each position should be reviewed before advertising so that an appropriate sourcing method can be established to ensure the best possible candidate pool. A sourcing method helps to limit costs and decrease the time needed to build a qualified candidate pool.

Employer Branding

Employee value proposition (EVP) refers to the overall brand that an organization provides to its workforce, both current and future. The EVP answers the question, "What's in it for me?" and allows candidates and employees to have a full understanding of the total rewards that are available as an employee of the organization. Five primary components make up the EVP:

1. Compensation
2. Benefits
3. Career
4. Work Environment
5. Culture

Compensation includes not only the current salary paid but also future salary opportunities such as merit increases, bonuses, and promotions. Compensation should be managed with accuracy, timeliness, and fairness, and it should align with performance. **Benefits** include retirement programs and insurance such as medical, dental, vision, and life; however, benefits also include paid time off, holidays, flexible work schedules, telecommuting options, educational reimbursement, and training opportunities. The **career** component refers to the ability for employees to move within the organization while progressing within their career. Career also includes stability, training, education, coaching, evaluation, and feedback. Employees should know where they stand with their supervisor and within the organization. Encouraging new opportunities to grow and develop, as well as to promote, is vital to supporting the EVP for employees. **Work environment** within the EVP includes recognizing and rewarding outstanding performance, balancing work life and home life, providing challenging and rewarding assignments, and encouraging engagement and involvement at all levels within the organization. Finally, the **culture** component of EVP encourages an understanding throughout the entire organization of the overarching goals and objectives. Culture includes the practice of values such as trust, support, teamwork, collaboration, and social responsibility.

A robust EVP will lead to a higher retention rate of current employees as well as maintain a higher employee satisfaction rate. Employees will trust the organization and its leadership while working hard to accomplish the goals established. A strong EVP will also attract highly talented candidates wanting to join the organization. This will lead to a higher number of qualified job applicants, increased candidate referrals from current employees, improved survey ratings that report the best places to work, fewer vacancies to fill, lower absenteeism rates, and a lower cost per hire.

Social Media

Job boards and social media are among the most common sourcing techniques. Candidates do not generally visit individual company websites to see if there is a hiring opportunity. There are job boards on many social media platforms, and many organizations use targeted advertising on particular sites to appeal to prospective candidates. From LinkedIn to Indeed, job boards can provide a large audience for job opportunities. Organizations also have corporate accounts on Twitter, Facebook, Instagram, and other social media platforms. Having an inviting corporate profile and a list of open job opportunities on a social media platform can increase the number of applicants.

Social media is a great example; recruitment trends in using social media platforms have changed substantially in the past few years. Research shows that in 2011, 56 percent of organizations used social media for recruiting; in 2015, this number increased to almost 90 percent. Organizations that evolve with current trends stay relevant with both passive and active job seekers and are more likely to be seen as potential employers. This is one way for an organization to maintain an active role in the talent pool from which they are sourcing candidates.

Candidate Pipelines

The current market situation and the available talent pool are constantly evolving. Organizations must keep themselves informed about trends in several markets: industry, city, state, and country. Depending on the needs of the organization, it may be necessary to expand recruitment efforts into new markets. Market expansion assists by providing a larger and more diverse applicant pool. Locating qualified candidates is a common concern for any organization. HR professionals can assist with this issue by understanding the immediate surrounding market as well as other opportune markets.

Having knowledge of various educational programs, collegiate and skilled trade, professional associations, and networking affiliations allows recruiters to tap into the most appropriate areas to locate potential candidates. Establishing partnerships with these groups can allow for recruiters to have immediate insight into potential talent pipelines that can directly feed the organization's applicant pools.

19

Organizations that have an available talent pool of candidates have shorter recruitment periods, filling open positions faster. This talent pool can be formed by both internal and external candidates.

Resume Mining

Resume mining is a form of candidate sourcing in which recruiters search resumes for keywords or skills relevant to a specific job or type of work. Mining helps to identify the best candidates for an open position, especially passive ones who aren't actively looking for a new position. A recruiter can perform resume mining manually or with technology like an Applicant Tracking System (ATS), using a string of keywords relevant to the job. When mining passive candidates, recruiters can use resume databases or social media to search for candidates. Recruiters can also search resumes in the system from previous openings to identify candidates who have applied to open positions in the past.

Job Postings

Job postings should include the complete description of work, including the scope, roles, responsibilities, examples of work, and supervisory duties. Additionally, the job posting should indicate required qualifications, preferred qualifications, educational requirements, and previous experience necessary to be qualified for the consideration. Timeframes should be clearly communicated on the job description so that candidates understand when the posting will close.

Job Fairs

Job fairs are events where employers can speak directly to potential employees and distribute information about their company. Job fairs include multiple employers, which allows job seekers to explore companies, connect and network with various businesses, and learn more about the types of jobs available. Job fairs can be virtual, meaning employers use technology to connect with potential employees, or they can be in-person, allowing employers to connect with potential employees face-to-face at a specific location. In talent acquisition, job fairs are a useful way to expand a business's strategy for identifying potential candidates. Employers can also use job fairs to identify candidates for a specific opening or build a talent pool for future openings.

Employee Referrals

Some organizations use an internal program for employee referrals. By entrusting the workforce with referring individuals for open positions, organizations let employees play a part in the hiring initiative. Many programs reward the referring employee with an initial bonus if their referred candidate is hired and then a secondary bonus if their referred candidate remains employed after a certain period of time. This encourages employees to engage with their network and assist in the recruitment process by being ambassadors and champions of the organization. Current employees who are working in the culture and climate of the organization can be the best recruiters.

Recruiting, Screening, and Selecting Applicants

Recruitment

Recruitment refers to the entire process of filling an open position. Because there are various elements to recruitment, it is important to outline and describe each step so that everyone involved understands the overall process, timing, and responsibilities. The recruitment process includes advertising the position;

screening the applicants; setting up interviews; developing the interview questions; selecting the most qualified candidate; negotiating an offer; and completing the background and medical screening, reference checks, and onboarding process. It is important to note that internal recruitments can be substantially different from external recruitments and may require less time to select, hire, and onboard the successful candidate; however, the recruitment should still be outlined thoroughly to ensure complete understanding.

Recruitment Firms/Staffing Agencies

Some positions are harder to fill than others, and in these cases, an executive recruiter may be the most appropriate sourcing option. Executive recruiters can specialize in certain fields, markets, or levels such as executive leadership. While contracting with a recruiter can be an increased cost, it can also serve to fill a position with the best, most qualified candidate who otherwise would not be sourced. Executive recruiters can tap into established networks and passive job seekers, sometimes yielding a candidate pool that an organization would otherwise not be aware of.

Skills Assessments

Many organizations implement testing procedures in the recruitment process to ensure candidates meet the required qualifications for a position. Depending on the position, certain tests may assist the hiring manager in determining which applicant best fits the needs of the organization. There are numerous examinations that an organization can incorporate into the hiring process, including the following:

- General knowledge
- General intelligence or IQ
- Personality
- English proficiency
- Second language proficiency
- Technical or mechanical proficiency
- Cognitive ability
- Reasoning
- Quantitative ability
- Physical ability

The examination selected should be appropriate for the position, such as a typing test for an administrative office position, a personality test for a senior leadership position, or a physical ability test for a law enforcement officer.

A **general knowledge test** shows an applicant's knowledge in certain areas that relate specifically to the open position. A typing test allows applicants to be scored in their specific ability related to their typing skills, such as the number of words per minute, number of errors and time needed to make corrections, and certain formatting techniques. General knowledge tests can also be specific to the subject of the position to ensure the applicants have the knowledge and understanding required of the position. A skills test that shows an applicant's expertise in how to create complete spreadsheets, pivot charts, or formulas would be appropriate for accounting positions that use Microsoft Excel® frequently.

A **general intelligence test**, or IQ test, shows how quickly an applicant can process complex problems with the information provided. These tests can also examine how applicants process available information, determine next steps, gather new information, formulate conclusions, and provide solutions and recommendations.

A **personality test** shows the type of personality of each applicant. The Myers-Briggs Type Indicator (MBTI) is the most common and widely used personality test. It assesses eight dimensions: extroverts or introverts, sensors or intuitives, thinkers or feelers, judgers or perceivers. From these eight dimensions, sixteen separate personality styles emerge in the MBTI method. After answering a series of questions, individuals can be provided with an assessment of their personality, which can be highly useful when constructing a team. This information can assist the team in understanding each other better, resulting in a cohesive, functional team. The MBTI test is an excellent tool to incorporate into the recruitment process when hiring high-level executives, and it can also be an excellent tool to assist current employees in working better within a team.

An **English proficiency test** is one that shows an applicant's knowledge and understanding of the English language. This test is useful for recruitments in communications or marketing as these applicants will be writing, speaking, and communicating on multiple platforms. Assessing applicants in their proficiency of the use of language, grammar, syntax, and parallel writing can be helpful in determining the most qualified candidate for positions that require this skill set. The ability to speak multiple languages is becoming a more sought-after skill set, and if an organization has a need for a second language in particular, it may be appropriate to provide a language proficiency test for the second language.

A **technical or mechanical proficiency test** is one that focuses on an applicant's ability in handling tools, machinery, equipment, or other specialized components. These tests are effective in assessing applicants' ability and knowledge in positions such as maintenance, construction, carpentry, plumbing, or other specialized fields. If a position requires this knowledge, it is appropriate for an organization to initiate a test to score applicants on their knowledge to ensure the most qualified applicant is selected for the opening.

A **cognitive ability test** assesses an applicant's mental abilities in both verbal and non-verbal skills, memory, and speed of processing information. This test includes a series of questions that include puzzles, remembering certain details, and solving complex problems. Applicants receive scores in their ability to reason, solve problems, and learn strategies. These tests are commonly used in standardized testing for students in multiple grades throughout their education experience. These tests are also popping up on social media, encouraging users to complete them and share their scores.

A **reasoning test** allows an organization to assess an applicant pool based on how they determine the right answers to a problem after receiving a situation and a number of certain conditions. Having knowledge of how an applicant thinks allows the hiring manager to understand how the applicant would work through specific issues that they will face in their role.

A **quantitative ability test** specifically assesses an applicant's ability to process numbers. These tests provide applicants with a series of number problems to solve. Some of these tests are timed to determine how quickly applicants process and solve the problems. These tests are excellent sources of information for applicants in areas such as accounting, actuarial, and other math-focused positions.

A **physical ability test** scores applicants based on their physical ability specific to the position. These tests should be standardized with minimum passing requirements. Common elements of a physical ability test include running a mile, sprinting 40 meters, and doing pushups, pull ups, and sit ups in a specific time frame. Generally, each element is given a pass or fail score, and if the candidate fails one element, he or she is dismissed from further consideration. Applicants who pass all elements of the physical ability test will then be ranked based on the best scores in each category. These tests are specific to positions that require physical ability as a qualification for the position. Law enforcement officers, fire fighters, personal trainers, and security officers are examples of positions that should require a physical ability test.

Employment tests must be directly related to the open position. Regardless of the employment test used to assess the knowledge, skills, and abilities of applicants, it is important to have a standardized test that assesses all applicants fairly and equitably.

Interview Techniques and Best Practices

There are various styles and techniques of interviewing. It is important to have an understanding of each type of interview to ensure that the most appropriate can be selected for each open position. Having the best and most appropriate technique applied to the interview process can help enhance the process and provide the hiring manager with the most beneficial insight to the candidates, allowing for the best selection to fill the position. Four common interviewing techniques are focus groups, in-depth interviews, dyads or triads, and paired interviews.

Focus groups are interviews that are primarily discussions, led by a moderator, that focus on the specific work and how this work affects the group present in the discussion. Focus groups are often defined as assessment centers. They generally last one to two hours, with the candidates working with the group to solve real issues and concerns of the job. Candidates are scored on their teamwork, innovation, communication, and other factors which allows the hiring manager to assess the most qualified candidate.

In-depth interviews are formal, one-on-one conversations that can last anywhere from a half hour to two hours or so. In-depth interviews can focus on the scope and range of the position, with questions being either pointed and specific to certain issues the candidate has handled in their previous work or broader in definition as to the work ethic and prioritization of work tasks. In-depth interviews are meant to assess the chemistry and "fit" between the candidates and the hiring managers as well as gain an understanding of the candidate's experience and skills.

Dyads or triads are similar to in-depth interviews but with two or three individuals, respectively. The individuals conducting the interview may be employees who will be working with the new individual. These interviews assess the chemistry and "fit" within the workgroup to gain an understanding of the team dynamic. The in-depth interviews, both with one individual or more, should be structured with the interview questions outlined and discussed prior to conducting the interview. All applicants should receive the same questions and be afforded the same opportunities to discuss their experience and skills.

Paired interviews are consecutive interviews with two employees who will work with the new employee. This interview allows a joint opinion of how the applicant's experience and skills will fit within the process and workflow.

All interview techniques have benefits and drawbacks; Human Resources professionals should review the position to determine which technique is best suited. Ultimately, the interview technique that provides the most accurate information about the most qualified applicant should be the goal. Some recruitment processes incorporate multiple interview techniques. For instance, they may start with an assessment center to narrow down the applicants, move on to a dyad interview with two senior level employees who work within the team, and end with an in-depth interview with the hiring manager. Each interview technique should be implemented in the same way with each applicant. The interview process and questions should be standardized and structured so that all applicants are afforded the same opportunity. Human Resources professionals should work with the hiring manager early in the process to determine what assessments should be made during each step and what the interviewers should be looking for.

Another interviewing technique is to structure the applicant's responses. While many recruiters simply ask a question and allow an applicant to respond however they like, other recruiters provide a framework for each applicant. Applicants are provided with this structure at the beginning of the interview and are scored according to how they answer within this structure. A common interview technique to apply to applicant's responses is the STAR technique. **STAR** stands for Situation, Task, Action, Results. For each question asked, applicants should answer in the following format:

- Situation: provide the context and background of a situation, problem, or issue
- Task: describe the problem and challenges taken on to solve the problem
- Action: discuss and explain the steps taken to implement a solution
- Results: discuss the impact of the action(s) and what was learned

By engaging applicants in this way during the interview, interviewers can better assess the applicants' skills and behaviors. This allows better scoring of applicants, showing which qualified individuals should be forwarded on in the process. The STAR technique is commonly used to assess an applicant's actual behavior when faced with issues and problems. Past performance is an indicator of future performance, and by having applicants answer interview questions in this format, interviewers can gauge the behaviors that the applicant will bring to the table in the new role.

It is extremely important that interviewers be trained in these techniques and understand their role and responsibilities in the interview process. Most organizations request that existing employees participate in the interview process. However, being a subject matter expert may not translate to knowledge of interviewing and applicant scoring. Human Resources professionals should ensure that individuals who conduct the interview receive training—either in house or externally—in the fundamental techniques of interviewing. Interviewers should understand the interview structure and which questions are not allowed during the interview. Human Resources professionals should be present as a participant or as a facilitator to ensure the interviews stay on track relative to time, questions, appropriateness, and structure.

Interviews should be structured so that applicants all receive the same opportunity; however, a recent trend gaining traction is providing applicants an open-ended panel interview. An **open-ended panel interview** is an interview with multiple individuals, such as an entire department or work group, that provides the applicant a certain time period to communicate to the group the reasons that they are the best candidate for the position. While there is no structure to this type of interview, it can be an excellent method to show certain specific skill sets such as quick thinking, communicating a clear message with little time to prepare, communicating to a large group while connecting with each individual, and being

24

able to summarize a large amount of information. Leadership and management positions must have these characteristics, and this interview technique, although new, can be an excellent way to assess an applicant in a different way.

Candidate Experience

Candidate experience refers to the feelings, behaviors, and attitudes a job candidate faces when they interact with a hiring manager and organization during the recruitment process. Candidate experience begins with the organization's webpage, job description, and initial information available to prospective employees.

Studies show that candidate experience is vital to an organization's recruitment efforts. Over 90 percent of candidates are more likely to apply for future positions if they have a positive candidate experience. Almost 100 percent of candidates who had a positive recruitment experience would refer others to apply for employment. Almost 90 percent of candidates with a positive recruitment experience would purchase the products manufactured or sold by the organization. Over 50 percent of candidates with a positive experience would communicate with their social networks about the experience. Even seasoned marketing professionals with a targeted advertising campaign could not have this kind of reach. With potential talent pool shortages and hiring challenges, organizations cannot afford to lose highly qualified applicants due to a bad candidate experience that is announced over a social media platform.

Biases

Biases are a tendency to judge or support a person or thing unfairly based on preconceived notions. Most biases are subconscious, which means individuals don't realize their behavior or attitude is biased. Biases can be detrimental to talent acquisition if candidates are eliminated based on a subjective opinion or first impression. Common biases in talent acquisition include affinity bias, where recruiters or hiring managers tend to select candidates who remind them of themselves, and implicit bias, where candidates are unintentionally judged based on prejudices or stereotypes. To avoid biases in recruiting, businesses must use objective criteria to identify qualified candidates for positions.

Lifecycle of Hiring and Onboarding Applicants

Onboarding

Onboarding is the process of acclimating newly hired employees to an organization. Onboarding introduces employees to several essentials, including the company, culture, and products. Onboarding can last a few hours or a few days and can include introductions with executive leadership and the workgroup. These introductions can then provide new employees with the opportunity to discuss the organization and begin the course of forming strong working relationships.

Reference and Background Checks

Reference and background checks hold significant importance in the process of hiring and onboarding a selected applicant. Reference checks involve contacting individuals who have worked alongside or supervised the candidate to garner insights about their specific qualifications, skills, suitability for the potential role, and overall work ethic. The purpose of these checks is to confirm the accuracy of the candidate's claims and to further assess his or her potential fit within the organization. Background checks are useful in verifying and validating information that has been provided by the candidate. Employment verification, professional certifications, educational qualifications, and criminal history checks are all included in a standard background check. By conducting a comprehensive background check, an HR professional can ensure that the candidate meets or exceeds the requirements of the position while simultaneously maintaining a level of safety and trust within the organization.

Employers should be sure to adhere to federal, state, and local legal guidelines when running both of these checks with a potential employee. The Fair Credit Reporting Act (FCRA) and Equal Employment Opportunity Commission (EEOC) are two examples of laws that guide the processes of reference and background checks and must be abided by. HR professionals must maintain an understanding of these limitations in conjunction with obtaining candidate consent and handling sensitive information with proper care and confidentiality. Employers must also establish consistent processes to effectively execute reference and background checks. Generally, these processes include using reliable resources and diligently verifying a candidate's credentials. By adhering to best practices and strict processes, the risk of potential legal issues can be mitigated, and a fair and consistent evaluation of candidates is maintained. The findings of these checks should align with the overall onboarding program to ensure that the selected applicant can receive the necessary support and guidance needed to transition into a new role.

Offer Letters and Counteroffers

When extending an offer of employment to a candidate, it is important to have as much information available to ensure a complete discussion. A best practice is to have all information available that will be written into the final job offer or contract. Additionally, understanding which items can be negotiated is also important. This allows both parties an understanding of where flexibility is available in the offer. Suppose a particular item is not negotiable, such as when eligibility for health insurance starts. If the candidate asks about negotiating this item, the Human Resources professional can tell them there is no flexibility to negotiate it. This allows for a more efficient and productive conversation about the offer of employment. Extending a verbal offer with these details can allow for discussion and negotiation, resulting in a final and formal offer extension in the form of an offer letter or official contract.

An offer of employment should include the following items, if appropriate based on the position:

- Job title and summary of position
- Base salary and bonus potential
- Fair Labor Standards Act (FLSA) status and overtime eligibility, if applicable
- Benefits, including all insurance offered with eligibility and leave accruals
- Additional benefits if appropriate, including relocation and signing bonus
- Miscellaneous allowances such as car, phone, and clothing
- Probation terms, if any
- Contingency terms such as medical screenings and background checks
- Supervisor and reporting relationships
- Start date, work schedule, and weekly hours
- Location, work environment such as dress code, and company culture
- Growth and professional development opportunities
- Acceptance terms including consideration time and a date to officially accept
- Direct contact for additional questions

Once there is a verbal agreement of the terms and conditions, a formal letter should be prepared to detail all the agreed upon items. It is important to note that some organizations may prefer to prepare an initial offer letter and then rescind and redraft a new, updated offer letter. This new offer letter would include the newly agreed upon terms and conditions after negotiation. Having thorough documentation of the employment terms at each step of the offer and negotiation process may be more appropriate based on the organization and the position.

A common and successful salary negotiation technique is summarized with the five P's: proper preparation prevents poor performance. This technique can be used by the hiring manager and recruiter as well as the candidate to assist with the negotiations process. Being properly prepared for the upcoming negotiations will result in successful outcomes for all parties. Prior to extending the offer of employment, it is important to be prepared with an understanding of why certain terms are being offered, specifically the proposed salary amount. In general, most candidates are interested in this piece of information and will ask questions about how this amount was determined. Having an understanding of the qualifications required for the position, the specific experience of the candidate, and growth opportunity within the position are all excellent pieces of information that can be used to convey how the salary offer was calculated. Additionally, communicating the salary range can allow the candidate insight as to the growth opportunity within this position. This information can also assist the candidate when considering a counteroffer.

The goal in extending employment offers and negotiations is for all parties to be satisfied with the terms. The organization, hiring manager, recruiter, and candidate all have different needs and perspectives regarding what constitutes a successful offer negotiation. Depending on how the discussions progress, however, it may be appropriate to end negotiations and formally rescind the initial offer of employment if the candidate's requests are unreasonable or inappropriate. During these circumstances, understanding which items are negotiable and the flexibility for each can assist in making the decision to end the negotiation discussions. For example, if the candidate requests to negotiate a different job title and responsibilities or a salary outside of the range established for the position, it may be appropriate to end the negotiations. Once an offer of employment has been negotiated and agreed upon by both parties, documents have been updated and signed, and a formal agreement is in place, the organization's focus should shift to an onboarding mentality and bringing in the new employee to the workplace culture and environment.

Employment Contracts

If an employee is receiving an official employment contract, it may be necessary to include additional items. These could include non-compete clauses, confidentiality or non-disclosure agreements, severance terms, copyright and trademark ownership, and other specific terms negotiated between the organization and candidate. Additional items such as the annual calendar showing holidays and days off, company newsletters and articles, health insurance availability, and other information should be provided as well. It is also important to communicate escalating benefits as well. Escalating benefits are benefits that increase over time, based on length of employment time. An example of this would be that a new employee accrues eight hours of paid time off for each month worked; once the employee reaches five years of service, this increases to twelve hours of paid time off.

Offer letters or contracts should be signed by the organization's hiring authority. The offer letter or contract should also include a section indicating that the individual agrees to the terms and conditions of the offer with their signature and date.

Distribution and Collection of Company-Mandated Documents

Human resources basics should also be provided to new employees immediately upon hire. These basics include a complete tour of the corporate intranet. The **corporate intranet** is the internal website provided only to employees; it includes an employee portal for access to information such as medical information and summary plan descriptions, change forms for personal contact information and beneficiaries, policies and procedures, and important information. Some organizations incorporate the payroll portal into the corporate intranet; other organizations maintain a separate payroll portal.

Benefits Paperwork

Employees should also receive all paperwork necessary to enroll in benefits such as health insurance, life insurance, deferred compensation and retirement programs, and union membership if needed. Employees should have a full understanding of the deadlines for returning these documents to ensure enrollments can be completed. Other items such as signing up for direct deposit, finalizing new hire paperwork such as the I-9, and taking a formal picture for the corporate directory should be conducted during onboarding.

Using Technology for Managing Candidate Data

Technology management works to enable access to employee information on numerous levels. From self-service portals and filing electronic documents in the onboarding process to managing recruitments and protecting personal data and information, technology management works to provide a solution for each of these initiatives. A common tool that many employees engage with is the self-service portal. This portal is available through an internal website that requires identification and approved access as an employee. Information such as personnel policies, address change forms, benefits documents for open enrollment, and complaint procedures are made available for employees to access at their convenience. Providing employees with the ability to locate important information when needed is vital to ensuring a positive, open, and empowered workforce. Ensuring that employee data is protected is one of the most important functions of technology management. Information such as social security numbers, birth dates, home addresses, and dependent information including minor children must be protected against hackers and leaks. Enabling the most recent and powerful security protocols and safety features helps to ensure that employees feel secure about the protection of their personal information.

Applicant Tracking Systems

Applicant tracking systems (ATSs) are software applications that manage an organization's recruitment processes. These applications can track various components of the recruitment process, including hiring requests submitted, applications received, interviews scheduled, and offers extended. ATS applications also provide various reports specific to tracking recruitment information. Most organizations utilize an ATS to handle applications, resumes, and candidate data; however, some organizations may use a simple tool such as Microsoft Excel® or Access® to create a customized database. Some companies receive a large number of applications on a daily basis, and an ATS application can provide the capability to manage these applications efficiently. The ATS can perform initial screenings, separate qualified and unqualified candidates, and screen out candidates that do not have the required skill sets.

An ATS provides functionality in multiple areas such as applicant workflow, candidate communications, interview management, skills assessments and tests, background checks, and on-boarding. Human

Resources professionals manage the ATS for the organization, and, through the ATS, provide information specific to the recruitment process. Reports can include information such as how long it takes to fill a position from the initial request to the date of hire, the number of applications received, and the number of qualified candidates for each position. This information can assist in making decisions for future recruitments.

While most ATS applications are customized, the basic structure should incorporate the following:

- Search engine optimization
- Job posting distribution and resume collection
- Advanced candidate search
- Employee referral management
- Integration capabilities
- Robust candidate relationship management
- Advanced reporting and analytics

The ATS application should provide an organization with the specific tools required for their recruitment needs. Most ATS applications can be integrated into an organization's existing website. An example of a widely used ATS that is integrated into corporate websites is Taleo. Taleo offers the ability for the organization to incorporate all recruitment elements into the branding and culture of the organization. Once an organization has determined a recruitment need, the request, often referred to as a **requisition**, is submitted by the hiring department. The requisition is approved, and the job posting is created and managed directly within the ATS.

The ATS will publish the job description to the corporate website, job boards, and other organizations as structured within the ATS platform.

Organizations can also add supplemental questions for candidates to answer as part of the application process. Candidates who are interested in submitting an application are guided through a structured, customized, electronic process in which they can attach additional documentation or other information to be considered. After applications have been submitted, the ATS can be programmed to send out standard communications, such as receipt of the application and next steps. Once the application window has been closed, the ATS can then screen the applications to determine which candidates meet the qualifications and which do not. Their status can then be updated in the ATS, and, again, standard communications can be sent to candidates indicating the status of their application. Throughout all steps of the interview process, the ATS can facilitate screening and communication.

Organizations should implement an ATS that maximizes the recruitment process for the hiring managers, leadership, recruiters, and candidates. ATS applications that provide robust and expansive services offer benefits on a financial, operational, strategic, and technical level.

Financial benefits can include increases in productivity, elimination of manual processes, and freeing up more time to focus on projects that improve profitability and achieving goals. Additionally, positions can typically be filled in less time, which can improve employee morale, customer service, and overall satisfaction. Organizations can see substantial costs when recruiting for and filling an open position. Costs, such as overtime to fill the opening, can add up to much more than anticipated. An effective ATS can assist in decreasing these costs by streamlining the process and reducing the time needed to fill an open position.

Operational benefits can include having a standardized and automated recruitment process, providing advanced reports and statistics, and identifying continuous improvement opportunities. By having a standardized process, organizations implement the same hiring practices across all positions. This is highly recommended by the Equal Employment Opportunity Commission (EEOC) and can dramatically reduce the risk of discrimination in hiring.

Strategic benefits can include improved compliance with regulations; having access to larger, diverse, and highly qualified candidate pools, which results in highly qualified new hires; providing an excellent candidate recruitment experience; and increasing the employment brand with prospective employees.

Technical benefits can include minimizing information technology support when using a web-based system as well as affording unlimited data storage to maintain the records. Additionally, by maximizing the technical capabilities of the ATS application, organizations may see opportunities to re-purpose resources that are now available.

HRIS

A **Human Resource Information System** (HRIS) assists HR with storing information, such as employee documents versus physical paper files, and making effective decisions. This type of system also aids HR personnel with pulling the data needed to compile various reports for federal and state agencies, such as the EEOC. The following is a list of ways a company's HRIS can be used:

- Tracking employees' service awards
- Tracking recruitment efforts
- Allowing for automated benefit administration
- Compliance reporting
- Tracking employees' time and attendance
- Administering training programs
- Eliminating any data entry duplication
- Compensation administration
- Sharing payroll information with the finance group

When selecting and implementing an HRIS, it is important to consider if it will need to be integrated with other company systems and to make decisions as to who will see what information, which determines the number of levels of access.

Data Metrics

Return on Investment (ROI)

Return on investment (ROI) is a way to measure the performance of an initiative or investment. This measure can be expressed as a ratio of the cost of the initial investment compared to the gains associated with the investment. ROI can also be expressed as a percentage and used to measure the return of several initiatives to help determine the comparative overall values.

Cost-Per-Hire

The **cost per hire** is calculated by adding the external and internal recruiting costs and dividing the total by the number of new hires during a specific period of time. Examples of external recruiting costs include items such as advertising a position on job boards, recruitment technology, background checks and drug testing, and pre-hire assessments. Examples of internal recruiting costs include in-house recruiting staff, payment of referral rewards, and internal recruiting systems.

Time-to-Fill

The **time-to-fill** metric lets companies know when their hiring process is taking too long. Time to fill is the number of calendar days it takes a company to fill a position, and the clock may start ticking before a job is posted, such as when HR approves a job opening. Time to fill typically ends when a candidate accepts a job offer. It is important for a company to track the time to fill consistently across various positions.

Time to Hire

The **time to hire** metric lets companies know how quickly they found their best candidate and were able to move them through the hiring process. The time to hire is calculated by subtracting the day the employee (who was eventually hired) entered a job's pipeline from the day they accepted an offer for the position. For example, if a job position is posted on Day 1, a candidate applies for the job on Day 5, and they accept the job offer on Day 12, the time to hire is 12 − 5 = 7.

Attrition Rate

Attrition rate is the percentage of employees that left a business for some reason (i.e., resignation, retirement, or death) and were not replaced during a period of time, typically a calendar or fiscal year. The attrition rate is calculated by dividing the number of employees that left the company during the year by the total number of employees at the beginning of the year and then multiplying that amount by 100. A high attrition rate can serve as a red flag to HR that policies may need to be changed.

Practice Quiz

1. If a job position is posted on Day 1, a candidate applies for the job on Day 7, and she accepts the job offer on Day 15, what is the time to hire?

_____ days

2. Which of the following is a way a company can most effectively utilize a human resource information system (HRIS)?
   a. Providing for duplication of data entry
   b. Restricting payroll information from the finance group
   c. Allowing for only managers to track their attendance
   d. Enabling reporting for compliance purposes

3. Which of the following statements accurately describes sourcing methods in a recruitment process? (Select all answers that apply.)
   a. Sourcing methods should ensure that recruitments are fair and equitable.
   b. Employee referral programs are an excellent way to source candidates and engage current employees in the recruitment process
   c. Job boards and social media platforms are the only method to fully engage potential applicants.
   d. Sourcing methods should afford all qualified candidates the same opportunity for consideration.

4. Arrange the talent acquisition lifecycle steps in the appropriate order:
   a. Assess candidates with tests or interviews   1.
   b. Source candidates and assess the talent pool   2.
   c. Offer employment and orient new employee   3.
   d. Conduct further screening   4.
   e. Determine the hiring needs of the department   5.

5. Match the workforce planning process with its focus:
   a. Forecasting   1. Orient a new employee to the organization
   b. Critical skills gap analysis   2. Determine the positions to be filled and how to fill them
   c. Recruitment   3. Fill an open position
   d. Onboarding   4. Define and refine personnel needs

6. Which component of the employee value proposition (EVP) encourages an understanding throughout the entire organization of the overarching goals and objectives, including trust, support, teamwork, collaboration, and social responsibility?
   a. Culture
   b. Work environment
   c. Career
   d. Benefits

7. Which of the following statements about salary negotiation are true? (Select all answers that apply.)
   a. A common salary negotiation technique is the five P's: proper preparation prevents poor performance.
   b. The goal of salary negotiation is to satisfy the organization's needs.
   c. Salary negotiation is the beginning of the employment relationship.
   d. Four stages of negotiation include preparation, exchanging information, bargaining, and closing and commitment.
   e. Communicating all the various benefits is not necessary during the salary negotiations and can be discussed later in the process.

8. Self-service portals, accessibility to employee information, filing electronic documents, and internal websites are all examples of solutions provided by what?
   a. HR management system
   b. Policies and procedures
   c. Recordkeeping program
   d. Technology management

9. How can an organization help to ensure that employees feel protected regarding their personal information, such as home addresses, social security numbers, and dates of birth?
   a. Allow employees to review their personnel file regularly
   b. Maintain master personnel files off-site at a remote location
   c. Implement a paperless filing system for all employment records
   d. Enable the most recent, powerful security protocols and safety features

10. What does the ROI measure with regards to HR data metrics?
    a. The internal and external recruiting costs
    b. The performance of an initiative or investment
    c. How quickly recruitment led to an employed candidate
    d. The rate at which employees resign or retire

11. Which of the following is described as the tactical process of filling a vacancy?
    a. Recruitment process
    b. Talent acquisition process
    c. Onboarding process
    d. Workforce planning

See answers on the next page.

Answer Explanations

1. 8: The time to hire is calculated by subtracting the day the employee (who was eventually hired) entered a job's pipeline from the day he or she accepted an offer for the position. In this example, a job position was posted on Day 1, a candidate applied for the job on Day 7, and they accepted the job offer on Day 15. Therefore, the time to hire is 15 − 7 = 8 days.

2. D: The following are ways a company can most effectively utilize a human resource information system (HRIS):

- Tracking employees' service awards
- Tracking recruitment efforts
- Allowing for automated benefit administration
- Compliance reporting
- Tracking employees' time and attendance
- Administering training programs
- Eliminating any data entry duplication
- Compensation administration
- Sharing payroll information with the finance group

3. A, B, & D: Sourcing methods should always ensure that recruitments are fair and equitable. Employee referral programs are an excellent way to source candidates while engaging the current workforce in the recruitment process. While job boards and social media platforms are excellent methods to engage potential applicants, there are many other methods that can be effective in sourcing candidates. All sourcing methods used by an organization should ensure all qualified candidates have the same opportunity for consideration.

4. A – 4, B – 2, C – 5, D – 3; & E – 1: The talent lifecycle is a multi-step process that begins with determining the hiring needs of the department. The next steps are sourcing candidates and assessing the talent pool, followed by conducting further screening, and then assessing candidates with tests or interviews. The final step in this process is offering employment and bringing the new employee onboard.

5. A – 2, B – 4, C – 3, D – 1: Forecasting is the process of determining the positions to be filled and how to fill them. Critical skills gap analysis is the process of defining and refining the personnel needs. Recruitment is the process of filling an open position. Onboarding is the process of orienting a new employee to the organization. Succession planning is the process of identifying required critical positions and assessing internal talent pools.

6. A: The culture component of the EVP encourages the entire organization to understand the overarching goals and objectives, including the values of trust, support, teamwork, collaboration, and social responsibility. Choice *B* is incorrect because the work environment component of the EVP includes the recognition of performance, balancing work life and home life, and encouraging engagement and involvement across all levels of the organization. Choice *C* is incorrect because the career component of the EVP includes the stability, training, education, coaching, evaluation, and feedback. Choice *D* is incorrect because the benefits component of the EVP includes the retirement programs, health insurance programs, time off, holiday schedule, telecommuting options, and educational reimbursements.

7. A, C, & D: The five P's—proper preparation prevents poor performance—is a common salary negotiation technique. The employment relationship begins with salary negotiation, which includes four stages: preparation, exchanging information, bargaining, and closing and commitment. The goal of salary negotiation is to satisfy the needs of all parties: the organization, hiring department and manager, and the candidate.

8. D: Technology management is a significant tool that provides numerous solutions to an organization. These solutions can include self-service portals, accessibility to employee information, filing electronic documents, and internal websites. Choice *A* is incorrect because an HR management system is a platform that specifically manages the HR function of an organization. An HR management system is a solution that can be provided by technology management. Choice *B* is incorrect because policies and procedures communicate process, practice, and expectations regarding numerous topics. Choice *C* is inaccurate because a recordkeeping program is a platform that specifically manages the records of an organization such as employee files or payroll. A recordkeeping program is a solution that can be provided by technology management.

9. D: An organization can help ensure that employees feel protected regarding their personal information by enabling the most recent and powerful security protocols and safety features. Personal information such as home addresses, social security numbers, and dates of birth should be protected with the highest level of security as possible. Ensuring that employees know this is also key to making sure there is an awareness of this security. Choice *A* is incorrect because allowing an employee to review their personnel file regularly will not have an impact on the security and protection of the actual file. Choice *B* is incorrect because regardless of where the files are located, the security measures should reflect a high level of protection and confidentiality. If anything, there could be additional security risks in having master personnel files off-site. Choice *C* is incorrect because even with a paperless filing system, appropriate security measures should be put in place.

10. B: The ROI, or return on investment, measures the performance of an initiative or investment. It is often expressed as a ratio of the cost of the initiative compared to the gains associated with it. The internal and external recruiting costs, Choice *A*, are used in calculating the cost per hire. Choice *C* is the time-to-hire data metric, and Choice *D* refers to the attrition rate.

11. A: Recruitment is the tactical process of filling an open position. Recruitment is a component of talent acquisition. Choice *B* is incorrect because talent acquisition is the strategic process that reviews the current and future needs of the workforce to ensure a holistic and complete process is implemented. Choice *C* is incorrect because onboarding is the process of bringing a new employee into the organization and acquainting them with the day-to-day operations, training them in policies such as safety, and finalizing new paperwork. Choice *D* is incorrect because workforce planning is the practice of reviewing all positions within an organization and determining the needs to accomplish the work. Workforce planning feeds the talent acquisition process by identifying the jobs and positions needed first.

Learning and Development

Purpose and Outcomes of Orientation

Employee Orientation

One piece of onboarding is the **new employee orientation (NEO)**. An NEO is the first formal experience that an individual has as an employee with an organization. An NEO is part of the overall onboarding process that is initiated when an employee joins an organization. The NEO can range from a few hours to several days of initiation into the new organization. The NEO includes relaying information to new employees about paychecks, direct deposit, benefits and retirement information, safety and workers' compensation programs, holidays, and other important information that new employees should have after beginning a job with a new organization. Onboarding should also include an opportunity to receive the tools and resources necessary for employees to complete their work. Laptops or desktop computers, phones, printers, and software should be provided with appropriate instruction so that employees can immediately begin to acclimate to the working environment. Studies have shown that when a robust onboarding process is implemented, employees are almost 70 percent more likely to stay with an organization for longer than three years.

Health and safety also constitute an area of focus that should be discussed at length to ensure new employees are aware of and understand the organization's policies and procedures. Health and safety items, including the workers' compensation program, workplace injuries, personal medical leaves, and safety policies, should be reviewed in depth. Procedures such as reporting a workplace injury, applying for a personal medical leave, understanding the safety protocols specific to the organization and the position, and knowing evacuation plans for the location are important pieces of information that all new employees should be aware of. Policies and procedures should be thoroughly reviewed and a copy of the employee handbook provided. Many organizations request employees complete and sign an acknowledgement form to indicate that the handbook has been received, read, and understood. Policies and procedures such as sexual harassment, workplace violence, harassment, performance management, and other significant policies should be discussed at length during the NEO.

If the new employee is a supervisor or manager, additional time should be spent orienting the employee to this specific role. New supervisors should receive an informational report about the employees who will be directly supervised. Standard information such as job title and duties, salary, and seniority can be provided as well. Approving timecards, leave requests, and running reports are standard job responsibilities for supervisors. Performance evaluations are also standard job responsibilities for new supervisors, as are providing an overview of the documents used, timeframes necessary for providing the evaluations, and resources available for performance management.

A new employee needs a lot of information. Therefore, an NEO best practice is to break up the information into blocks or sessions. This allows the employee to absorb the information in a more complete way and ensures a higher retention rate. The four main areas discussed above may be broken down into separate blocks offered on multiple days or provided in one long session. Additionally, new employees should receive a tour of the workplace, including other locations if appropriate; introductions to the team and other employees; and a list of local resources such as local restaurants, coffee shops, post office, banks, gyms, and other amenities. If local businesses offer discounts, specials, or incentives to employees, this information should also be provided.

Finally, it is a best practice for human resources to schedule frequent NEO follow-up discussions with the new employee. Some organizations schedule these discussions for 30 days, 60 days, and 90 days following the start date. These discussions allow for specific questions that a new employee may realize were not addressed during the original NEO. New employees should be aware of the resources available through human resources and the mentor assigned during NEO.

Setting Expectations

Human Resources is responsible for ensuring that employees understand the policies and practices of an organization. HR should ensure that employees understand the expectations regarding behavior, as well as what constitutes an inappropriate action that violates policy. HR should adhere to best practices such as:

- Providing an employee handbook to all new employees during the new hire orientation process

- Displaying labor law posters in break rooms

- Maintaining policies and procedures that are easily accessible to all employees

- Providing training opportunities to ensure that all employees have the knowledge, skills, and understanding to avoid behavior that is inappropriate or illegal

HR should be proactive when coaching and training employees on the policies regarding appropriate behavior. Many organizations react to situations as they occur and provide training only after an issue has been reported. While it is important to address situations as they arise, it is also important to be proactive and work to avoid inappropriate behaviors within an organization. A best practice that can be deployed to ensure proactivity is to require annual regulatory and policy training for all employees. This training can be used as an excellent tool to remind employees of the expectations and requirements, as well as communicate new laws or policies. This type of training also allows an organization to have a record regarding training in the case of audits or lawsuits.

Organizations typically develop a code of conduct and/or a code of ethics to communicate the expectations to their employees. A **code of conduct** details the behaviors a company requires of its employees as well as the behaviors that are prohibited and subsequently result in disciplinary action. A code of ethics details the ideal set of standards a company intends to uphold in its business dealings. The following is a list of sections typically found in a company's code of ethics:

- Confidentiality
- Conflicts of interest
- Gifts, entertainment, and contributions
- Personal use of company assets
- Workplace privacy
- Outside employment
- Ownership of intellectual property
- Fair dealing
- Standards of business conduct
- Reporting code violations

Building Relationships

Some organizations provide a mentor or buddy to new employees during the NEO. The mentor is responsible for going to lunch with the new employee, meeting informally to discuss the organization and answer questions, and being a general resource and friendly face to the new employee. Depending on the working relationship between the new employee and mentor, it may be appropriate for the mentor to bring the new employee along to meetings or other events that would be helpful and informational. Depending on the size of the organization and resources available, multiple mentors may be assigned to allow for various viewpoints. Assigning a mentor from different departments such as payroll, information technology, human resources, customer service, and the hiring department can provide insight to the internal operations, lending to a more informed employee.

Acclimation

All employees should be trained in how the organization's systems work and how they will need to use these systems in their position. From submitting timecards for payroll or approving requisitions and purchase orders, human resources should ensure there is a standard protocol for all employees to be trained on the important systems that will be used in their job. Providing opportunities to expand employee's knowledge of these systems can also open future career opportunities for them. Knowledge really is power, and understanding how to gain this knowledge through data and utilizing the systems and programs available can potentially increase the opportunities available to an employee.

Developing an Organizational Learning Strategy

Elements of Training Programs

Adult learners generally have their own learning styles, and instructors should incorporate the following five elements in all training classes in order to fully engage all participants regardless of their experience:

- Orientation
- Motivation
- Reinforcement
- Retention
- Transference

Orientation is emphasizing to the adult learner what they are going to learn and how they will be able to apply the knowledge to their current work. Adult learners will want to know what the end game is and how they will benefit, both short-term and long-term. **Motivation** is key with adult learners. Some participants will be motivated by the additional knowledge and insights, while others will be motivated by the social interaction with their coworkers. Each individual has a different motivator, and it is important to understand this when preparing a training program. A great way to have a better understanding of what will motivate the class is to review the participants who will be attending and take into account their position, experience, and background. Understanding this information enables the trainer to customize the training plan and include multiple motivators. **Reinforcement** is a successful training technique used when training adult learners. Both positive and negative reinforcement can be appropriate depending on the circumstances and the course material.

Retention is a vital component to any training program. If participants are not retaining what they learned, then the class was ineffective and ultimately a waste of time, resources, cost, and more. Practicing new skills, challenging ideas, and ensuring various ways of presenting the course material will help participants retain the knowledge and information. Transference is one of the most important elements and refers to how participants understand the material and information in relation to their job. **Transference** is understanding what was learned and applying it to everyday life and work. The more connections that an instructor can help participants make in this area, the more successful the training program will be for the adult learners. Incorporating these five elements can enable maximum participation and effectiveness of training programs with all learners, including adult learners.

KSAs

Knowledge, Skills, and Abilities (KSAs) are the attributes or qualifications necessary to perform a specific job. Employees can build KSAs through training and development. **Knowledge** refers to the information required to do the job—that is, understanding concepts from data, facts, or other information used to perform various duties. Knowledge does not require applying information but does entail background in and understanding of a concept or idea. Knowledge-building activities include classroom instruction, reading, or any other activity that develops an understanding of a process or idea. **Skills** are an employee's capabilities from training or knowledge in work experiences. Skills include either hard or soft skills. Hard skills are those used for job-specific abilities or responsibilities, whereas soft skills are the interpersonal capabilities that affect how employees work or interact with others. Either quantitative or qualitative performance metrics can test and measure skill levels. Skills are built through training, on-the-job experience, or any activity that requires the application of a concept or idea. **Abilities** are the capacity to perform a job-related action. Abilities differ from skills in that they focus on an employee's aptitude, or natural tendency to be able to do something. Abilities are typically innate, not developed from experience but from natural inclination.

ADDIE Model

Instructional design is a multi-step process to create and deliver an effective training program. While there are many different structures available to work through, a frequently used design model is the **"ADDIE" model**. This model is a generic instructional design model that can be used for various subject matters in multiple fields. Each step builds on the previous one; because of the simplicity, this model can eliminate wasted time, money, and work. This model is generally seen as the foundation for other instructional design models and is easily adaptable to most training program needs. The ADDIE model follows these steps in the design of a training program:

- Analyze
- Design
- Develop
- Implement
- Evaluate

Each step is vital to the success of a training program and should be conducted thoroughly before moving to the next step. The ADDIE process is linear, meaning that before moving to step 2, step 1 must be completed. If changes occur in the timetable, content, or organizational need during step 3, the process must be started over again at step 1.

ADDIE

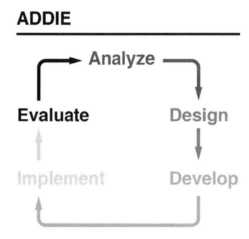

Analysis is the first step; it focuses on what is needed. A needs assessment should be conducted to determine the needs of the organization, departments, teams, and individuals before designing or delivering any training program. The analysis step determines the organization's needs and skills gaps. Having an understanding of who will be in the training is important. Defining the "audience" will help structure the training program in later steps. Additionally, understanding the goal and objectives of the training is vital to having a relevant and respected training program. Aligning training with an organization's overall goals will help employees understand their purpose in the larger organization and how their contributions affect the company.

Design is the second step; it focuses on what should be included. This step also focuses on the audience—who this training program will be delivered to and who will be learning—as well as the instructor who will be delivering this program. Design is the sketched-out plan for the program. Understanding the characteristics of the audience and instructor can help to define how the materials and course should be structured, the learning techniques applied, and how issues such as resistance to training should be addressed. During this step, course content is identified, lessons are structured, tools are selected, and assessment options are reviewed. Storyboards are a great way to visually show the training program to ensure the flow is steady and maintainable.

Development is the third step; it focuses on the actual content and materials. Development consists of the actual deliverable training program that will be implemented, including the visual tools such as PowerPoint® presentations, handouts, lecture notes, tests and quizzes, resource material, and assessments such as discussion questions and group exercises. This step uses the information gathered in the analysis and design steps to create the actual program. Development can also include running trial sessions to determine if there are issues to resolve before delivering the training to participants.

Implementation is the fourth step; it focuses on delivery of the training program. Conducting the training session is the culmination of the first three steps. Preparing the environment, delivering the course, engaging the participants, and closing out the course are all important components to the implementation step. This step is "where the rubber meets the road," and as soon as the participants enter the training room, they should be engaged with each other and the instructor. The instructor should be prepared to handle the unexpected and answer far-afield questions. The instructor is responsible for keeping the training program on track and the participants engaged.

Evaluation is the final step of the model; it focuses on two components: evaluating the effectiveness of the course and validating it for the future. Evaluation forms should be provided to all participants to gauge the overall response of those receiving the training. The evaluation forms should include rating areas such as instructor effectiveness and knowledge, content and material, whether the course was helpful and will be used in the scope of work, the best and least liked parts of the training, and suggestions for opportunities to improve. Additionally, an individual may be assigned to sit in during the course to evaluate the responses received from the participants. Because the instructor will be busy delivering content and focusing on the time, agenda, participant engagement, material, and other items, an assigned evaluator for the course can observe the reactions of participants and other interactions that the instructor may miss.

The assigned evaluator can then give constructive feedback on how to enhance the training. Validating a training program consists of reviewing how participants take the information and knowledge back to their work and use it. Frequent follow-ups and check-ins with those who attended training can keep the material and information fresh, helping retention. Taking this information into account is vital to validating a training program. Follow-up surveys can also assist in gaining information and insight related to how a training program is continuing to impact an employee and their work. Once data is compiled, trends can be potentially seen and reviewed to suggest recommendations for the training program.

Although the ADDIE model is an easy model to follow when creating a training program, there are a few drawbacks to consider. The steps are linear and build on each other, which may not work well in certain situations. Additionally, if there are multiple changes and continual evolution happening, this model may not work well. Repeatedly going back to previous steps due to the model's linear nature may waste time and resources or cause setbacks and delays if training is needed by a particular time. As with all techniques, there are positive and negative aspects to each, so it is important to consider each to ensure that the model or technique that is applied is the best and most appropriate method for the particular situation.

Needs Analysis

Before creating a training program, it is important to understand the organization's goals and needs. Training programs should be relevant and appropriate for both the organization and employees. A **needs analysis** can provide insight as to the training needed instead of trying to guess. The following are resources that can be used to determine training needs:

- Organization goals
- Departmental goals
- Results
- Performance measures
- Attrition
- Job descriptions
- Safety logs and performance
- Complaints
- Legal requirements and compliance needs

Additionally, interviewing or surveying employees may also provide important information. Sometimes training programs overlook speaking to and hearing from employees about the skills and training that would help them be more productive. An organization may think it knows what employees need, but unless it seeks confirmation from the employees themselves, the organization may end up providing unnecessary training. Such training can be costly, wasting time, money, resources, and energy while also undermining future training opportunities. When employees are included in the conversation about training, they are most often supportive of the training program.

Once training needs are determined, Human Resources professionals then need to decide which employees need to be trained and how often. Many training programs are necessary or even required for all employees and should be conducted on a frequent basis. Some training programs are specific to certain departments or employees at different levels of the organization.

Goals/Objectives

An important component to any training program is setting expectations and objectives. This is especially true when training adult learners. Learning objectives should be reasonable and thoughtful, and they should enable questions and feedback. Additionally, participants should be encouraged to discuss and apply the course material specific to certain situations. This enables robust discussion and can provide an opportunity for participants to learn from each other. Ground rules should also be established as a part of the expectations so that all learners feel comfortable in participating and understand what is expected of them during the class. Following along with the agenda, staying on track, staying on time, and providing periodic breaks and refreshments are also important in ensuring that the training program is accepted and respected by adult learners.

Training sessions should be as interactive as possible, encouraging conversation and engagement. Keeping participants involved and attentive can be challenging. A great way to start the session is by reviewing the course objectives. Each course should have a complete list of objectives that individuals are meant to learn by the end of the course. This is also a great opportunity to begin engaging with the participants about their own individual objectives. Questions like "why are you here?" and "what do you want to know by the end of this class?" are great ways to start a dialogue. Breaking up a training session to include various learning methods can keep a steady flow going. Incorporating quizzes, case studies and breakout discussions, role-playing and demonstrations, and debate opportunities can also keep participants engaged. Employees tend to sit near the people they know. These are the day-to-day, naturally occurring working groups. Breaking up these groups and having employees sit with unfamiliar colleagues can facilitate new conversations and ideas.

Available Training Resources

Career development and training programs can take many different formats, and Human Resources professionals are responsible for understanding which programs are best for the organization and the employees. Individuals learn in different ways, so it is important to have multiple training methods to ensure that all employees can learn and grow in a way that works for their learning style. While the variety of training methods may be limited by budget and resources, it is important that human resources regularly evaluate programs and update them by incorporating new ways of learning.

An **Individual Development Plan (IDP)** is a great way to engage employees directly in their career growth. IDPs enable employees to work with their supervisor and human resources to discuss their current position and learning opportunities to increase their knowledge and skills specific to their current role.

IDPs also enable employees to discuss future opportunities and the skills needed to achieve those opportunities and be successful. These assessments are known as skills gap assessments—they review the requirements for future positions and the skills and knowledge the employee lacks. These gaps can then be filled with training and learning opportunities, provided either in-house or outside.

Intended Audience

All employees should be trained in communication, teamwork, company policies and applicable safety, but only management employees may need training in team development and strategic planning. Knowing which employees need the training also enables insight into how the training should be developed and presented. If a software update training is being proposed for all information technology employees, understanding how these employees learn is necessary in delivering a successful training program. Allowing individuals at computer stations to practice and follow along with the instructor may ensure maximum learning for a particular group of employees. Additionally, logistics such as location, workload, schedules and coverage, work group dynamics, and cost should be taken into account when developing and delivering a training program.

As mentioned earlier, individuals learn in different ways; therefore, it is important to incorporate multiple ways of learning in each training course. Planning flexibility into the course is important because each session will be different, based on the individuals in attendance. Each participant brings unique experiences, examples, and questions that the instructor needs to integrate into that specific training session. Group dynamics also change from session to session. Experienced instructors include these exchanges in future sessions to enhance learning for all employees. A best practice is to keep a "parking lot" or list of ideas, questions, and suggestions. At the end of the program, the instructor can then compile this information and send it to all participants, so that learning can continue after the course.

Training Formats and Delivery Techniques

Learning Theories

A **learning theory** is a group of principles and concepts that explain how individuals gain, remember, and recall information. Knowledge of learning theories can help trainers better structure their training programs. Trainers can incorporate principles from these learning theories to create content, determine which tools to use, facilitate discussion, and test skills.

Many basic learning theories can be applied to a training program. Below are five standard learning theories:

- Behaviorism
- Cognitivism
- Constructivism
- Experiential
- Connectivism

Behaviorism focuses on what an individual does; the shaping, or learning, of behaviors in accordance with this theory is led by an instructor. This learning theory is centered on behaviors, reactions, and responses to situations and events. Learners in this theory are reactive in that they are responding to information, while the instructors observe new behaviors and changes. In general, a behaviorist learning theory is used to teach basic definitions, explain concepts, or perform a certain task. This theory is

43

facilitated through assessments, tests, repetition, and continued practice of the concepts. Behaviorism does not prepare the learner for problem solving, creative thinking, or critical thinking. Behaviorist learning is limited to the recall of information or the performance of a specific task. This kind of learning can be used as a building block for learning that adheres to the other theories.

Cognitivism, or cognitive information processing, focuses on how an individual processes information; learning, in accordance with this theory, is facilitated by an instructor. This learning theory centers on how new information is organized and aligned with existing knowledge. According to this theory, learners in this theory are proactive; they are reasoning and processing information at a high level. In general, a cognitivist learning theory is used to teach strategies, with an emphasis on how this information is processed. This theory is facilitated through feedback, concept mapping, use of analogies and metaphors, and providing structure. Cognitivism can build upon the knowledge learned from a behaviorist method by having participants question and discuss what they learned.

Constructivism is the learning theory that focuses on how an individual interprets new information and then applies this information to their own circumstances. Constructivism is a student-focused learning approach, with learners being very proactive, solving problems and analyzing situations critically. According to this theory, learners understand that information is constantly evolving and its applications may change frequently. In general, a constructivist approach is used to teach learners how to apply new knowledge in many contexts and perspectives. This kind of learning is facilitated through case studies, brainstorming, simulations, apprenticeships, and collaborative learning. A constructivist approach can enable participants to learn how to change their thinking and actions in response to new information. These are necessary skills when dealing with emergency situations or circumstances in which new information is constantly being provided and decisions need to be made.

Experiential learning focuses on an individual's experiences and how they learn from them. Experiential learning is instructor-led and can be a very effective learning technique when course content is lecture based or is heavy in material content. By having an individual focus on their experiences and then apply different learning techniques to each situation, individuals can then work to modify future behaviors. This learning theory assumes that individuals do, think, plan, and redo; they learn through reflecting on what they have done and what they will do. Experiential learning is facilitated through assignments that involve studying concepts, reviewing experiences, reflecting on previous actions, incorporating new ideas and concepts, and determining future opportunities.

Connectivism is a relatively new learning theory that focuses on an individual being self-directed in their learning. This learning theory is a direct response to readily available technology for individuals to access information. Connectivism is a student-focused learning approach, with learners being extremely proactive and outgoing. They are constantly looking for and educating themselves with new information. They understand the importance of sharing information and source material with others and connecting individuals together through learning. This theory is facilitated by having individuals seek out new information and knowledge in traditional and non-traditional learning settings.

Delivery Techniques

All five learning theories can yield positive learning results. Because each individual learns differently, a blended training course that taps into all these learning approaches will be a robust one. By combining various components of each theory, training programs will more accurately accommodate the ways individuals learn in everyday life. Some learning happens through simple repetition and practice, while other learning happens through brainstorming, creative thinking, and discussion.

Incorporating and applying all these learning techniques is important to ensure robust learning. Adding the following tools to a training program will increase the learning for participants and retention of the knowledge:

- Memory exercises
- Additional discussion time
- High-level critical thinking exercises
- Face-to-face interaction and conversation
- Personalized instruction to handle different paces of learning
- Various communication styles
- Virtual training including videos and simulations
- Handouts including course material and resource material for future reference

By enhancing the learning opportunities through the theories and tools above, there are multiple benefits to the participants, other employees who they will interact with, and the organization. These benefits can include the following:

- Information can be taken back to the workplace and used in the future
- Learning becomes more interesting and sought after
- Communication techniques can improve relationships and ensure clarity
- Training becomes important to employees and not just something they have to do
- Employee morale improves, resulting in positive attitudes
- Employees are presented with new ways of looking at and thinking about concepts and ideas
- Dialogue can begin or continue
- Relationships can improve, expand, or begin
- Results can improve, including efficiency, effectiveness, and profitability

Regardless of which learning theories or techniques are used in a training program, a solid program should include complete and accurate content, guidance to the participants, opportunities for the participants to practice and learn independently, and an assessment as to how each participant performed in the program. Using as much of the information regarding learning theories and techniques as possible will enhance the quality of a training program and achieve the end result of a more educated, informed, and knowledgeable workforce.

Not every training topic is exciting. Some sessions are mandatory. Some training material is difficult to grasp or even uncomfortable to listen to. Regardless, the challenge is getting individuals to participate and be engaged in the training. By incorporating various methods of learning and discussion opportunities, an instructor can usually get maximum participation. In fact, several studies show that a training session incorporating multiple learning methods is more effective, takes less time, and results in individuals retaining the information longer. Using PowerPoint slides and handouts, asking questions and involving participants, acting out situations with different outcomes, and having fun when appropriate can all support a robust and successful training program.

Teaching Styles and Retention

There are two primary teaching styles: passive and participatory. **Passive teaching** includes giving lectures, reading to an audience or having participants read materials, watching videos, and providing demonstrations. Retention rates of knowledge achieved during a passive teaching method are relatively low. The average retention rates for passive teaching methods are: lectures: 5 percent; reading: 10

learning opportunity. While some content should be taught with a passive teaching method, trainers
should also incorporate participatory teaching methods to increase the knowledge retention. A training
program may begin with a lecture on the subject matter, followed with a video, and then close with a
practice exercise that results in a group discussion. By incorporating multiple teaching methods from both
categories, participant retention can be maximized, which will result in a successful training program.

Incorporating the above methods in training programs can increase participants' retention of the
information as well as ensure a successful program. While it is important to ensure that the actual training
program is robust and incorporates multiple teaching methods, it is also important to implement
strategies after the training program. Data has shown that after participating in a training program,
individuals lose knowledge and information at a relatively quick pace unless the knowledge is immediately
applied. Some research indicates that professionals could lose up to 80% of the training material learned
within three to six months after the training is delivered. In order to maximize, enhance, and maintain
knowledge retention, it is important to implement specific strategies before, during, and after the delivery

of a training program. By having robust strategies in place, an organization can ensure that the information in maintained.

Before training is delivered, the program should be previewed to ensure that the training is complete, appropriate, and responding to a need. It is also appropriate to understand what the needs will be after the training program is delivered so that a plan can be put in place to address knowledge retention. Questions should be asked before the training is delivered to ensure that any concerns and issues can be resolved before the training is conducted. The program should then be communicated to all levels of the organization as appropriate. This communication should include the topic and subject matter, the goals and expectations of the training, and the learning objectives. This ensures buy-in at all levels of the organization, including supervisory support.

During the training, it is important that managers and leadership are visible and participating. Employees will be more likely to respect and accept training when they can see commitment from the leadership. If employees see leadership practicing principles of integrity, work ethic, honesty, and respect, they are generally more willing to exhibit these principles individually. This also is true for behaviors in the workplace. If employees see that management and leadership are not respectful of time, always arriving late to meetings or not being considerate of others' time and commitment, this will be reciprocated. Minimizing disruptions to a training is also important as it shows a clear commitment to the program and the importance of the subject matter, as well as the participation of individuals.

Virtual

Virtual training has become more prevalent in recent times within the realm of learning and development. One way to deliver virtual training is through webinars, which are convenient and cost-effective for training a large group. They are usually formatted as remote seminars involving demonstrations, presentations, and interactive elements (such as polls and Q&A sessions) to keep the group engaged. Virtual Instructor-Led Training (VILT) is defined as live training sessions in real time. Participants can interact with the instructor and their peers using video conferencing tools, text-chat elements, and breakout rooms. These functions allow VILT to combine the benefits of traditional in-person training with the flexibility of remote learning. Another form of delivery for virtual training is E-Learning Modules, which are self-paced online courses accessible at the convenience of the learner. The modules are usually a variety of video elements followed by assessments to test the learners' understanding of the material. These formats, along with others (such as Virtual Reality), give HR professionals a vast toolset to implement in training as they see fit. Utilizing one or more of these techniques while including in-person activities and training is referred to as a blended learning model.

Self-Paced

Self-paced training can be seen as a subsection of virtual training since most delivery formats require employees to access them digitally. Self-paced training is unique in that individuals may access the training at their own convenience and move through it at their own pace. Online courses are one type of self-paced training in which a structured curriculum is delivered to employees through a learning management system, or LMS. Participants may access these courses (usually comprised of modules and assessments) in their own time, progressing through the various activities at their own speed. Pre-recorded instructional videos centered around a specific skill or topic are also known as video tutorials. Tutorials usually include visual demonstrations with in-depth explanations so that learners can access them at any time and rewind, pause, or review the content until it is fully understood. Another way self-paced training can be delivered is through digital guides and manuals, often formatted as step-by-step instructions, diagrams, and real-life examples written in plain language to be referred to as needed.

Similar to online courses, interactive e-learning modules utilize multimedia, interactive exercises, and quizzes to engage learners. These modules also provide immediate feedback to reinforce the most important concepts as learners progress through them.

Instructor-Led

We have already discussed VILT, but traditional instructor-led training is certainly not limited to an online format. Classroom training, for example, occurs when learners physically attend sessions led by an instructor, such as in a traditional classroom. This type of training excels in direct interaction, engaging group discussions, the ability to immediately clarify complex concepts, and enhanced collaboration. Workshops and seminars typically involve a combination of hands-on activities, presentations, and group exercises. This specific type of training allows participants to learn from experts on the subject while also engaging in practical applications of the knowledge at hand.

On-the-Job

On-the-job training, or OTJ, is useful because learners can acquire the specific knowledge and skills needed in their position while performing their job duties. OTJ can be achieved through shadowing a current employee or general mentoring and guidance from experienced employees. This actively facilitates hands-on learning and immediate feedback during the application of theory or knowledge to real-life scenarios. On-the-job training is generally considered to be a highly effective learning technique because experiential learning involves the exact type of processes and tools the worker will be using every day.

Role Play

To simulate real-life scenarios in the workplace, HR professionals may choose to implement role-playing activities into their training sessions. During role-play, participants act out scenarios as assigned roles to practice decision-making and problem-solving skills. This allows trainees to apply the knowledge they've learned in previous training in a safe environment with immediate feedback. Role-play can assist in the development of a wide range of skills such as communication, conflict resolution, leadership, and teamwork. Engaging in realistic interactions allows participants to refine their interpersonal abilities and subsequently gain confidence in similar situations. This style of training also encourages perspective-taking and empathy by asking participants to play different characters or roles with viewpoints they may not have previously considered. Role-play exercises also promote active learning since participants must be actively engaged in the learning experience by using critical-thinking, bridging the gap between theory and practice.

Facilitation

Customizing training for adult learners is necessary to ensure a successful and effective training program. Some training is mandatory, and it may be a struggle to specifically show how the training material could affect an individual's future opportunities. It may simply be a matter of showing that the individual understands the material and applies it as appropriate. This level of honesty can be invaluable when encouraging adult learners to engage and participate in a course.

Understanding the specific needs of adult learners can assist in facilitating the learning experience. Feedback can be invaluable in this regard. Request real and honest feedback on the course, what could be done better, what they learned and will incorporate in their day-to-day work, and other suggestions for improving the course. When adult learners see their feedback solicited, they see that they are contributing to future courses, which may be a motivator for some.

In-House vs. External Training Services

Robust training combines individual skill enhancement with overall training for the entire department. Human resources can deliver such robust training opportunities by working with department managers. Human resources departments are responsible for delivering training opportunities with either internal staff or an outside third-party agency. Even if an organization employs individuals who can offer in-house training, it may be beneficial to have a third-party agency deliver certain types of training. Examples of topics that may require a third-party agency to deliver training include legal updates, compliance issues, health and safety matters, and state certifications. Examples of topics that could be provided by internal staff include written and verbal communications, developing relationships, writing emails and reports, and building effective teams.

Change Management Process

Organizational Changes

Organizational changes can come about as the result of internal forces (e.g., exit interviews revealing low job satisfaction, a rebranding initiative, or an effort to create a flatter organization by removing levels of management). Organizational changes may also be the result of findings from an environmental scan (e.g., regulatory and legal changes or discovering the need for a new service or product). **Change management** refers to an organization's ability to implement changes in a diligent and comprehensive manner. This concept of change is holistic and encompasses sweeping change of an organization.

There are many ways to initiate change management, with some processes including numerous steps and approvals; however, a basic change management process consists of the following steps:

- Step 1: Identify the need for change.
- Step 2: Define the change and prepare for it.
- Step 3: Create, implement, and manage the change.
- Step 4: Evaluate, sustain, and reinforce the change.

These four steps have specific tasks and milestones that must be accomplished before moving on to the next step. Initiating a thoughtful change management process, one that encourages employee involvement during and after the process, will most likely result in a successful change to the organization.

Change agents are individuals who are charged with implementing organizational change effectively. These individuals tend to wear many hats. For example, they:

- investigate. They need to understand the organization's dynamics as well as employees' attitudes and behaviors surrounding the change.

- advocate. They must be persistent and continually supporting the change initiative when employees have forgotten about it and are busy with their full-time jobs.

- encourage. They are skilled at listening to employees who are experiencing a wide range of emotions and may not feel comfortable taking risks or going outside of their comfort zones.

- facilitate. They design and utilize processes, tools, and forms to assist employees when going through the change.

- mediate. They manage conflict and help employees find common goals to assist them in collaborating to implement the change.

- advise. They build credibility with employees through their knowledge and ability to assist them and point them in the right direction.

- manage. They are conscientious and hold employees accountable to ensure they are on track to meet the due dates and goals for the project.

Executive sponsors, such as senior executives or the CEO, are also critical to the success of change initiatives, as they show employees they are committed to the change at their level of the organization. By being enthusiastic about the change, executive sponsors inspire employees to commit to the implementation process.

Assessing Readiness, Communication Plans, Identifying Needs, and Providing Resources and Training

During transitional periods, organizations and the employees within them must understand the importance of change management processes. Assessing readiness, creating communication plans, identifying needs, and providing resources and training are all vital components in managing change effectively.

The process of evaluating an organization's preparedness for change is referred to as assessing readiness. The organization's employee engagement, culture, and capacity for change must all be analyzed as distinct factors to fully assess readiness and identify potential barriers and resistance to change. Only once this analysis is complete can HR professionals work with the larger organization to develop strategies to mitigate risk, address resistance, and facilitate a smooth transition. Another crucial factor in change management is effective communication. To ensure that all stakeholders are well-informed about the purpose and impact of potential change, a comprehensive communication plan should be developed. A successful communication plan addresses the needs of all relevant audiences through multiple channels, including but not limited to email updates, in-person and virtual meetings, and regular team briefings. Clear and consistent communication delivered in a timely manner effectively reduces uncertainty, builds trust, and encourages employee engagement during the change process.

To ensure a smooth transition, HR professionals should identify the needs of everyone affected by change through understanding each individual's and team's specific requirements. Gaining this understanding involves assessing skill gaps, identifying training needs, and seeking out areas where additional support may be required. Conducting a needs assessment will assist the HR professional in tailoring change management initiatives to address industry- or organization-specific requirements, ensuring that all employees receive the guidance, resources, and training they require to effectively adapt to change. To support individuals and teams during the process of change, resources and training must be provided. Providing resources and training is necessary to ensure that employees have access to all of the right tools and information needed to succeed in the new environment. HR professionals may choose to implement training programs, workshops, coaching, mentoring, and readily available job aids to equip employees with the knowledge and skills needed to successfully navigate change.

Kurt Lewin's Change Model

Kurt Lewin was a social psychologist who presented a change management model back in 1947. His change process theory is a three-step organizational program that seeks to explain how entities change, the catalysts that precipitate change, and how change can be successfully accomplished. Fundamental to the theory is the notion that an entity will respond to the need for change when there is an external stimulus that compels it.

The first phase of the theory is **unfreezing**. The need for change is identified and communicated during this stage, which creates the motivation for change. During unfreezing, it is important to create a clear vision for the outcome that will follow the change while creating a sense of urgency for obtaining that new outcome. The second phase is **changing**. Communication is key during this phase as resistance to the change is managed and the organization comes into alignment with the change. Training on new processes may also take place during this phase. The final phase is **refreezing**. In this phase, the new adjustments are solidified and cemented into the functions of an entity (the change becomes the new norm). During the refreezing phase, evaluation of the outcome takes place, which may lead to some additional fine-tuning. Positive reinforcement is very important during this phase to ensure employees will not backslide into old behaviors they engaged in prior to the change.

Kurt Lewin Change Model

Unfreeze

Create the correct atmosphere for change

Change

Come into alignment with change

Refreeze

Solidify change

John Kotter's Change Model

John Kotter was a well-known change expert and professor at Harvard Business School who introduced an eight-step change model in 1955 that was built upon the previous model by Kurt Lewin. The steps in his model are described below:

- Create urgency. This step involves developing a strong business case around the need for change so employees will buy into the change.

- Form the change coalition. In this step, key stakeholders and true leaders in the organization who will be able to lead the change effort with their influence and authority are identified. The coalition should be made up of a mix of individuals from various levels and departments throughout the organization.

- Create a clear vision for the change. This step involves identifying the purpose for the change.

- Communicate the vision. Since it is important to keep the vision for the change in the forefront of employees' minds, in this step, a communication strategy is developed from the top down.

- Empower action. This step involves removing barriers to change and encouraging or rewarding employees who are thinking creatively and are willing to take risks.

- Create short-term wins. Instead of having a single, long-term goal, this step involves finding some short-term targets that can motivate employees as "wins" when they are achieved and celebrated.

- Build on the change. This step involves utilizing the short-term wins in step 6 to reinvigorate aspects of the change process that have stalled somewhat and to involve employees who have been resistant to the change effort thus far.

- Root the change. In an effort to make the change stick and replace old habits, in this step, discussions about the connections between the successes that have been experienced and the new behaviors continue.

Peter Senge

Peter Senge was the founder of the Society of Organizational Learning and continues to serve as a senior lecturer at the MIT Sloan School of Management. He is a proponent of **systems thinking**, where managers spend more time focusing on the big picture than on individual actions, since actions and consequences are all correlated with each other. In this same manner, Peter Senge believes organizations should seek out and embrace change versus waiting and responding to changes in crisis mode.

Employee Development and Training

Understanding Training Needs

Human Resources professionals are responsible for providing consultation to managers and employees on professional growth and development opportunities. In order to provide the best recommendations, it is important to have an understanding of individual, team, department, and organizational needs. Each level is vital to the overall success of an organization's holistic training program. While training programs should be provided to ensure updated information is available, new skills and techniques are learned, and certifications are renewed, it is also important to understand individual needs for employees who may be struggling to perform their job. From individual development plans to all-employee focused training programs, Human Resources professionals are responsible for delivering a robust and holistic growth and development program. Additionally, training programs should be aligned with the organization's goals and priorities to ensure that employees are working toward the same goals and priorities in their specific position.

Human Resources professionals can structure specific training programs for each position with a pre-defined career path. Another option is to enable flexibility in designing training programs and career paths for the needs expressed by employees and departments. Both are legitimate and both enable career development and growth. Training employees at an individual level as well as at a group level is also an important component to training programs. Understanding how each individual contributes to the organization's priorities and objectives is vital to overall success. Additionally, having an understanding of how each team and group can contribute to success is an important piece of the puzzle to ensure success at an individual level and an organization-wide level.

LMS

A learning management system (LMS) is software or technology that can handle all aspects of the learning process. An LMS gives employers a place to store, track, and deliver various pieces of training to employees. An LMS provides knowledge management capabilities to help instructors house content, create or deliver learning, track learner activity, and assess teaching and student performance. An LMS can house content within the software or, if web-based, digitally through cloud storage. Businesses can use an LMS to create training materials that use multiple delivery methods, including on-demand training, live instructor-led courses, or a blend of on-demand and live sessions. Depending on the LMS, trainers can either create content directly within the system or upload it once it's complete. Activity tracking is a feature of LMS that allows instructors or system administrators to monitor completion, attendance, course time, and other learner interaction metrics. Activity tracking differs from assessment activities in that it focuses on the interaction with learning, not the application. An LMS can use assessments to engage learners in applying the training concepts or so learners can rate the quality of the content, delivery methods, or other interactions within the learning experience. Businesses can track both learner activity and assessments through LMS reporting features.

Reporting

Following completion of training, it is important to study the efficiency and productivity of the program and its materials. Some questions that may be asked are: Were the primary objectives met? Were the learners' specified goals achieved? What (if any) were the most arduous aspects of the program or its materials, and how could those problems be addressed? The following list consists of tools used to assess and report on training efficiency:

- Participant surveys are a common way for employers to learn to what degree participants react favorably to the training program.

- Pre/post-testing can be a vital tool when analyzing the efficacy of a training program. A pretest assesses the knowledge of students prior to the start of a training program, and a posttest determines the knowledge students have acquired during a program.

- Performance metrics, such as an increase in sales, are utilized to determine the degree to which targeted outcomes have occurred as a result of employees completing a training program.

Balanced Scorecard

David Norton, PhD, and Robert Kaplan, PhD, developed the **balanced scorecard**. It is a tool companies can use to report on all of the elements that impact their success instead of only focusing on their financial results. The scorecard contains metrics that are financial and nonfinancial in nature that span across four perspectives: financial, customer, internal business processes, and employee learning and growth.

- The **financial perspective** addresses traditional financial measures to ensure a company is managing its bottom line in the most effective manner, such as operating margins, utilization of capital, profit and loss, and return on investment.

- The **customer perspective** looks at elements such as customer satisfaction and customer loyalty to ensure a company is meeting the expectations of its customers and can depend on receiving their repeat business in the future.

- The **internal business processes perspective** examines the processes that will need to be modified or improved to ensure a company is achieving its customers' objectives. Examples of scorecard metrics in this area are cycle time, number of hours of rework, supplier quality, number of defects, and volume shipped.

- The **employee learning and growth perspective** addresses elements such as mentoring programs, employee training and development, and succession planning to ensure a company is securing the human capital pool it will need to maintain success in the future.

A brainstorming session is typically held to determine the scorecard metrics. As the performance period progresses, the balanced scorecard metrics are labeled as red (results are below target and require immediate attention), yellow (results are within a tolerance interval below target and need to be monitored), and green (results are at or above target) and reported on in meetings. These colors alert management and HR about areas that require fast attention. Metrics in red must be addressed in a timely manner to prevent other areas from being adversely affected by poor performance. For example, a metric marked as red in the internal business processes perspective (e.g., a manufacturing bottleneck that leads to a longer cycle time), if not addressed quickly, can result in a metric turning to yellow or red in the customer perspective (e.g., lowered customer satisfaction ratings). The balanced scorecard approach serves as a powerful communication tool for all members of the company.

Post-Training Evaluation and Metrics

A training program's effectiveness can be assessed by taking metrics and measurements. The best known and most commonly used model for assessment is the Kirkpatrick Model. Developed by Donald Kirkpatrick in the late 1950s, this model evaluates a training program on four levels: reaction, learning, behavior, and results. Each level is a more progressive and broader level of evaluation than the previous one; the model moves from individual results to organizational results. Some training programs may only need to be evaluated at the lower two levels (learning and reaction), while other training programs need evaluation at all four levels.

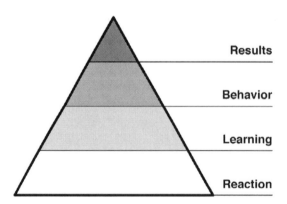

The first level of evaluation, **reaction**, measures the individual's response, determining how useful the training program was to the participants. Did participants find the training challenging? Did they find the training thoughtful and organized, with appropriately structured content? This feedback can be garnered through surveys and questionnaires, participant interviews, and formal focus groups. Gathering this feedback immediately after the training program and then at certain times afterward can help to determine whether participants believe the knowledge was useful and whether they ultimately retained it for later use. This level of evaluation is used most by training managers.

The second level of evaluation, **learning**, measures how much individuals improve their knowledge, skills, and abilities as a direct result of the training. This level determines how effective the training program is for the participants in their day-to-day work. Did participants become more efficient with their work? Did they learn a new skill that enhanced their work product? This feedback can be gained through testing or assessing participants before and after a training program, doing performance reviews and manager's reports, and making on-the-job assessments of work performed. This level of evaluation is used most by supervisors.

The third level of evaluation, **behavior**, measures how much an individual changes their behavior as a direct result of the training. This level determines how a training program affects a participant's attitude and behavior in the performance of their job duties. This level is important to assess for training programs that teach communication skills, conflict resolution, team building, and other skills specific to behavior. This feedback can be gained by having participants complete questionnaires, observing daily behaviors, and reviewing feedback provided by managers, customers, peers, and other individuals who work directly with the individual. This level of evaluation is most used by managers.

The fourth level of evaluation, **results**, evaluates how the organization as a whole benefits from the training program. This level determines how a training program impacts the organization's productivity, efficiency, effectiveness, revenues, and other high-level, organizational results. This feedback can be gained by reviewing financial reports, inspection reports, and other high-level reports that indicate the success of an organization. Reviewing this information before and after a training program is delivered, as well as after certain periods of time—immediately following the program, six months after, twelve months after—can help determine actual impacts and when they occur. This level of evaluation is most used by executives and high-ranking officers in an organization.

It is important to use accurate, valid, and time-sensitive information. Because there are costs in resources, finances, and time, it is imperative to ensure that the evaluation of a training program is effective, just like the training program itself. Using inaccurate information to evaluate a program's effectiveness is a waste of resources. If the results so obtained are used to determine training recommendations, the recommendations may not be appropriate. Once the evaluation has been conducted, it is important to ask questions to determine what can be done better for future training programs. If there was little to no impact, a decision to not conduct the training program might be made, or a program could be completely reworked to attain different results.

In addition to evaluating individual training programs, training metrics are important for determining the effectiveness of a training department and all programs being delivered. Organizations should determine what is important to measure and how readily available information is to calculate these measurements. Due to a manual process or ill-timed and potentially inaccurate data, it may not be effective to track certain pieces of data. These metrics are often referred to as **key performance indicators**, or **KPIs.**

KPIs are measurements that show the achievement of a certain goal, or in some cases, the lack of achievement. KPIs add the following value:

- Clarity by showing a clear picture of the strategy being implemented
- Focus by showing what matters and what requires attention
- Improvement by showing the progress toward the goals and objectives

Below is a list of potential KPIs to evaluate a training department:

- Average training cost per employee
- Average training hours per employee
- Budget spent on training—by department and overall
- Internal training sessions offered and attended
- External training sessions offered and attended
- Return on investment

Each KPI is a valuable metric that illustrates data used to determine the effectiveness of a training department. KPIs should be clearly defined, and any calculation required should be clearly established, including where and when data will be sourced. When put together to tell the entire story of a training department, these metrics can show where successes are occurring, where opportunities are available, and if there are deficiencies to address. The primary purpose of any metric or KPI is the behavior or change that the measurement creates. When KPIs are established, a training program can be discussed honestly and results-driven. These discussions then lead to focused training programs in areas that can actually make a difference.

Practice Quiz

1. Which of the following is used to determine if targeted outcomes have occurred as a result of employees completing a training program?
   a. Pretests
   b. Participant surveys
   c. Performance metrics
   d. Posttests

2. Individuals who are charged with implementing organizational change effectively are referred to as _____.

3. During which phase of Kurt Lewin's Change Model is the motivation for change created?
   a. Unfreezing
   b. Changing
   c. Refreezing
   d. Monitoring

4. Which of the following sections would typically be included in a company's code of ethics?
   a. Personal privacy
   b. Ownership of intellectual property
   c. The ability to run a small business at work
   d. Using your personal computer at work

5. _____ is the first formal experience that an individual has as an employee.
   a. Recruitment
   b. Onboarding
   c. New employee orientation (NEO)
   d. Completing new hire paperwork

6. Which of the following is an NEO best practice? (Select all answers that apply.)
   a. Providing program or benefit information only as needed or requested
   b. Scheduling follow-up discussions with new employees
   c. Showing employees where to access information when needed
   d. Providing a mentor or buddy
   e. Reviewing the organization, human resources information, health and safety procedures, and policies and practices

7. Which of the following allows for conversation and exchange of new ideas and solutions?
   a. Teamwork
   b. Brainstorming
   c. Leadership
   d. Collaboration

8. Norton's and Kaplan's balanced scorecard includes four perspectives to assess a company's success. Which of these perspectives considers factors such as operating margins and use of capital?
   a. Financial perspective
   b. Customer perspective
   c. Internal business processes perspective
   d. Employee learning and growth perspective

9. When preparing to create a training program, it is important to understand the organization's goals and needs. What type of study should be done that includes departmental goals, performance measures, attrition rates, and legal compliance?
   a. Workforce planning
   b. Job analysis
   c. Critical skills gap analysis
   d. Needs analysis

10. Jose needs to train some new employees. Other than his usual training sessions and professional development seminars, his co-worker suggested that he incorporate some on-the-job training as well. Jose is not sure that this is a good idea because the employees should have the skills to do their jobs when they are hired. Because of this, Jose does not want to include on-the-job training. Is Jose correct?
   a. Yes, only employees who have the necessary skills to do the job should be hired, so on-the-job training is not necessary.
   b. Yes, the training plans he has are sufficient; he does not want to overwhelm new employees.
   c. No, on-the-job training is a highly effective learning technique.
   d. No, some employees may be hired who do not have the needed skills for their specific jobs without on-the-job training opportunities.

11. Which of the following is NOT one of the KPIs for evaluating a training department?
   a. Return on investment
   b. Budget spent on training
   c. Management participation
   d. Internal and external sessions offered

See answers on the next page.

Answer Explanations

1. C: Performance metrics, such as an increase in sales, are utilized to determine the degree that targeted outcomes have occurred as a result of employees completing a training program. Participant surveys are used to find out the degree to which participants react favorably to a training program. Pretests assess the knowledge of learners prior to the start of a training program, and posttests determine the knowledge students have acquired following a training program.

2. Change agents: Individuals charged with implementing organizational change effectively are referred to as change agents.

3. A: During the unfreezing phase of Kurt Lewin's Change Model, the motivation for change is created. Communication is important during the changing phase of Kurt Lewin's Change Model, as any resistance to the change must be managed so that the organization can come into alignment with the change. During the refreezing phase of Kurt Lewin's Change Model, evaluation of the outcome takes place, which may lead to some additional fine-tuning.

4. B: The following sections are typically included in a company's code of ethics:

- Confidentiality
- Conflicts of interest
- Gifts, entertainment, and contributions
- Personal use of company assets
- Workplace privacy
- Outside employment
- Ownership of intellectual property
- Fair dealing
- Standards of business conduct
- Reporting code violations

5. C: NEO is the candidate's first formal experience as an employee. The NEO includes completing new hire paperwork and is a component of a larger onboarding process. Although recruitment is the first interaction with an organization as a future employee, the NEO is the first formal experience as an official employee.

6. B, D, & E: The NEO should incorporate best practices and standards to ensure employees have as much information as possible when joining the organization. Scheduling follow-discussions for employees to ask questions or provide additional information is a best practice to incorporate, as well as providing a mentor or buddy. Standard NEO should include reviewing the organization, human resources information, health and safety procedures, and policies and practices. It is important to provide all information as part of the NEO as well as when requested. It is also important to show employees where to access information, along with providing insight and information about the specific programs.

7. B: Brainstorming is the process in which employees converse and exchange new ideas and solutions. Choice *A*, teamwork, is important to an organization and allows employees to work together. Teamwork is important for brainstorming to be effective. Choice *C*, leadership, defines the objectives of an organization, and then brainstorming is used to come up with new ideas and solutions to achieve those objectives. Choice *D*, collaboration, is another term for teamwork, which allows for brainstorming to work effectively.

59

This content is provided exclusively for test preparation purposes and does not imply our support of any particular religious, political, or scientific point of view. Copyright © APEX Publishing. You have been licensed one copy of this document for personal use only. Any other reproduction or redistribution is strictly prohibited. All rights reserved.

8. A: The financial perspective focuses on traditional financial measures, including operating margins and use of capital. The other three perspectives focus on customer satisfaction and loyalty, Choice *B*, company processes for meeting customers' objectives, Choice *C*, and managing a company's human capital, Choice *D*.

9. D: A needs analysis includes an evaluation of organizational and departmental goals, performance measures, attrition rates, and legal compliance, as well as job descriptions, safety logs, and complaints to determine what training the company might need. Workforce planning, Choice *A*, is the process of determining an organization's current and future workforce needs. A job analysis, Choice *B*, evaluates a position within the company. Choice *C*, critical skills gap analysis, is used to define the personnel availability and needs within the organization.

10. C: On-the-job training is a highly effective experiential learning technique. While it is important to hire people who have the skills to do the job, Choice *A*, that does not automatically translate to specific knowledge of how to perform the necessary tasks. It is important not to overwhelm new employees, Choice *B*, but on-the-job training would help them get started on their jobs and would not overwhelm them the way that too many seminars and training sessions might. On-the-job training is important, but employees should not be hired who do not already possess the necessary skills to perform the job, Choice *D*.

11. C: Management participation, while important to the overall success of any training program, is not one of the KPIs used for evaluating a training department. Choices *A*, *B*, and *D*, along with average training costs and hours per employee, are all part of the KPI metrics.

Compensation and Benefits

Compensation Strategies

Total Rewards and Compensation

Total rewards refers to the entire package that an employee receives when joining an organization. This package includes compensation, benefits, work-life programs, learning and development opportunities, and performance and recognition. Each of these components is extensive, unique, and important to the entire package. **Compensation**, or pay, indicates the salary that is paid for the work being performed. Compensation also includes merit increases, bonuses, cost of living adjustments, and promotion increases.

Total rewards can impact an organization's retention in various ways. A robust total rewards package that is flexible and evolving can motivate employees to reach new goals and objectives within their position and career. Organizations should ensure that the total rewards offered to employees continue to be the most appropriate and cost effective and that they meet the needs of as many employees as possible. Individual needs change as personal circumstances change, and an organization should make an effort to ensure that various programs and benefits options are available to meet current and future needs. Additionally, it is important to continually communicate with employees to ensure they are aware of programs—both current programs and new programs being introduced.

Human Resources is instrumental in ensuring that compensation is managed appropriately and conveyed to Payroll accurately. A strong working relationship that includes direct lines of communication and understanding of the roles and expectations between these two functions will only benefit an organization and the employees. Some organizations align Payroll within the Human Resources function, while others place Payroll within the Finance function. Regardless of where these two functions lie within an organizational reporting structure, Human Resources and Payroll are integral components to each other's success.

Pay Structures

Job pricing is the process by which an organization determines the salary of positions. Job pricing utilizes information from job descriptions, job analyses, and evaluations, and any other pertinent information available to make a recommendation. Human Resources professionals will often include internal equity, external equity, and market information in the evaluation to ensure a holistic approach to setting a salary. Additional factors such as attrition and difficulty in attracting qualified candidates may also be considered when establishing a salary.

Internal equity refers to the parity of salary between positions within the same organization. Factors such as minimum qualifications, effort and responsibility, working conditions, education and training, supervisory responsibilities, scope of responsibility, and impact to the organization should be reviewed to determine similarities between positions to ensure that there is equity. It is important that employees understand how internal equity is utilized when setting a salary. If an employee believes they are not being paid a fair salary comparatively to another employee, then the organization could face scrutiny for this disparity. This could include complaints, grievances, and/or lawsuits that may result in back pay, penalties, fines, and attorney's fees. Having a robust compensation policy regarding how internal equity will be used in setting salary assists in explaining and defending salary decisions.

61

External equity and market pricing information are commonly used by organizations to establish salary for positions. This information can be found in salary surveys established either by a third-party organization or through individual survey information at the request of the organization. This information is important to review and can help to ensure that the organization is able to attract qualified candidates during the recruitment process and retain employees once hired. If a competitor is paying a much higher salary, they may easily be able to poach candidates by attracting them with the higher salary. If an organization is experiencing a high attrition rate for certain positions or difficulty in attracting qualified candidates in the recruitment process, it may be beneficial to conduct a market review to determine if competitive wages are a factor and make appropriate changes to job pricing and salary structures if necessary.

Organizations should ensure a robust compensation philosophy and strategy to attract and retain qualified candidates and employees. A common strategy is to compensate positions within five percent of the average market salary. If a position's salary falls within a range of five percent above or below the average market salary of a comparable organization's position, the salary would be accepted as appropriate, fair, and equitable. If the salary is outside of the five percent range, Human Resources professionals should assess the reasons this is occurring and make appropriate recommendations to address the disparity.

The **salary structure** is also an important component within the scope of job pricing. Salary structures generally reflect a salary range that compensates for various levels of experience. Positions have a job description that reflects minimum qualifications, specifically the experience and education required for being able to do the job. The salary range should align with these minimum qualifications in that more experienced candidates could earn more within the salary range than less experienced candidates. This type of salary structure also allows for an employee to grow within the salary structure based on their specific work with the organization.

There is flexibility for organizations to determine how broad a salary range should be. Some organizations have a practice of keeping a salary range within a ten to twenty percent range, whereas others establish salary ranges with a forty to sixty percent range. The following chart shows two sample ranges with a twenty percent and sixty percent salary range and how different these ranges can be. Note that an employee who is hired under a salary range with a larger range percentage between the minimum and maximum salary has a bigger opportunity for growth within the range.

Sample Range	Minimum Salary	Midpoint Salary	Maximum Salary	Range %
001	$50,000	$55,000	$60,000	20%
002	$50,000	$65,000	$80,000	60%

An organization can also incorporate various range percentages for different groups of positions. Entry level positions that do not require education or many years of experience may have a lower range percentage, whereas executives and professionals who do require extensive, specific experience may have ranges with a much higher percentage.

Regardless of how an organization establishes the minimum and maximum amounts of a salary range, the compensation policy should clearly establish the parameters in which new hires are offered a starting salary, when employees are eligible for increases, and how employees can be eligible for increases.

Market Analysis

In general, there are five primary methods of analyzing a job. While each may have variations, the core features of each method remain the same. The following table summarizes these five methods, their features, and the pros and cons for implementing each. In looking at this chart, it is easier to understand why using multiple methods may be beneficial for an organization.

Method	Features	Pros	Cons
Ranking Method	Ranks jobs in order based on the value in relationship to each other and to the organization	Easy to implement	Does not consider market rates or specific, individual factors of certain jobs
Classification/Grading Method	Groups jobs to reflect levels of skill at preset grade classifications	Straightforward, quick to implement	Jobs may end up being forced into a grade and not truly reflective of the work being done
Point Factor Method	Identifies factors, then adds value and weight to each with the individual factor scores, adding up to an overall score	Individual factors are considered, allows for more objectivity	Does not consider market rates and some specialized positions may not receive credit for certain factors
Factor Comparison Method	Identifies factors, then groups them, with each factor being assigned a dollar amount	Systematic and analytical process	Complex system, difficult to communicate, and can contain some subjectivity
Competitive Market Analysis Method	Reviews external data and compares jobs to like positions	Considers the organization's priorities, examines job value against market rates	Difficulty in gaining access to information and organizations may not be comparable in scope and other factors

Human Resources professionals can use various methods of evaluating a job. While there are multiple options available, methods should be selected based on the organization's needs and used consistently. Having multiple methods available can be a benefit for an organization that has widely different positions, such as administrative, construction, maintenance, executive, or engineering. One particular analysis may not work as well with all of the different positions. Having multiple tools may be necessary to ensure that jobs can be assessed properly and accurately. A position should be viewed objectively, and the selected method should fairly assess the responsibilities and ultimately, the salary. It may be prudent to hire an outside consultant to establish the process and method(s) for the organization to implement. It may also be wise to routinely have an external review conducted every few years to ensure that the organization's analysis is objective and aligned with current methods and practices.

Job Evaluation/Classifications

Another important component of compensation policy and review is the evaluation of a salary to ensure employees are being paid appropriately for their work. Work will evolve and new tasks and responsibilities may be added to an employee's workload. It is important to make sure that these new tasks are taken into account regarding compensation. Human Resources professionals should ensure the policy for requesting an evaluation is robust and clear, including forms and information for employees to complete and review. Timelines should also be included regarding the length of time it will most likely take to complete a review and how changes to salary will be handled. Supervisors and employees should have the option to submit a request to evaluate a salary and upper management should be involved in the overall process and decision making. If there is not sufficient budget to account for an increase in salary due to the added work, it may be appropriate to reassign the new work to another employee to resolve the issue or to remove other elements of work to ensure the workload is balanced.

A **market review** of an organization's compensation may also be pertinent to ensure that employees are being paid a competitive wage. A market review is an analysis of other organizations in the same or similar industry with similar demographics such as staffing levels, budget, and other components. A market review assesses how an organization aligns with other agencies in the areas of total rewards to ensure compensation and benefits are appropriate. If an organization is seeing a higher-than-normal rate of attrition, a market review might assist in determining if they are paying a wage that would encourage employees to stay with or join the organization.

Prior to conducting a market review, Human Resources professionals should work with executive management to ensure that the organization's priorities regarding compensation and total rewards are understood and align with current policies and practices. In general, market leaders set the bar; market followers do what everyone else is doing; market laggers offer less to employees. An organization's priorities regarding compensation must be clear so that the market data can be interpreted accurately and recommendations can be made that align with the priorities. If an organization is a market lagger, then recommendations that are out of the box, creative, and more than what competitors are offering will not align with the priorities set.

Pay Adjustments

Organizations should also establish the number of individual steps within a salary range to show the progression opportunities that employees are able to achieve. Below is a chart showing a sample five-step range plan that indicates how the above sample ranges could be broken down into five opportunities for increases throughout an employee's history within a specific position.

Salary Range	Step 1	Step 2	Step 3	Step 4	Step 5
001	$50,000	$52,500	$55,000	$57,500	$60,000
002	$50,000	$57,500	$65,000	$75,500	$80,000

Having multiple steps within a salary range allows an organization flexibility in hiring at different steps based on a candidate's experience and qualifications. Having multiple steps also allows an organization to provide additional compensation for outstanding performance attached to a stellar year of performance. These are items that should be clearly written as policy and practiced within the organization to ensure that all individuals are treated fairly and provided with the same opportunities for advancement.

An example of this would be a policy that dictates all new employees will be hired at Step 1 except in the circumstance that they provide salary information indicating that this would be a lesser compensation amount than they are currently earning. The policy can also dictate when to offer a higher step based on the experience the candidate is bringing to the organization. Additionally, the policy can provide direction for requesting additional steps due to performance and the process to initiate this action. Many

64

organizations tie salary increases within a salary range to the employee's service date, on an annual basis, and to their annual performance review. Compensation policies should not only discuss movement within a range, but also movement between ranges and how the appropriate step should be selected.

Incentive Programs

Incentives such as pay for performance, bonus pay, and special monetary awards due to performing work that has substantial impact to the organization, such as cost savings, should be considered in alignment with the base compensation for a position. In the context of special incentive programs, all information available for each position being considered should be reviewed consistently.

Performance and recognition programs include service awards, contribution awards, and formal or informal recognition of achievements. Each of these components lends to the overall total rewards package that is offered to new employees. HR professionals should be fully aware of each of the elements and ensure that new employees have this information when offered a position.

Health Benefit and Insurance Programs

Benefit Options

Human Resources professionals are responsible for understanding the needs of the organization and its employees. This includes having a robust knowledge of the best options in the areas of health insurance, retirement programs, employee assistance programs, life insurance, disability insurance, workers' compensation programs, flexible spending accounts, and voluntary insurance programs such as short-term and long-term disability programs.

It might be beneficial to conduct surveys with other agencies that provide similar services to ensure that an organization's offerings are appropriate for the employee population. It could also be beneficial to survey the current employees to determine which elements of the benefit package are meeting their needs and which elements should be reviewed or added.

Frequent review of costs and services should also be conducted to ensure that the return on investment of these programs is appropriate. It may be time to conduct an analysis to determine if another program or vendor would be suitable to provide better services at a lower cost.

Employee assistance programs usually offer services related to a wide array of personal and professional counseling, including legal, financial, change management, stress management, marriage, divorce, parental counseling, and many other topics that individuals deal with in their personal and professional lives.

Communication of these plans is extremely important so that employees understand their options and have the information to make informed choices. Often, organizations conduct a health fair or benefits exposition with vendors from all their benefit providers to allow employees direct access.

Many organizations also allow a **cafeteria style plan**, which is a type of benefit plan dictated by Section 125 of the Internal Revenue Code. This type of plan allows employees to choose from two or more benefits consisting of cash or a qualified benefit plan. A Section 125 plan would identify a certain dollar amount that an employee is eligible for to assist them in paying for their benefits. If there are dollars remaining after their selections have been made, the employee can opt to take those dollars in another way. Employees could also "opt out" and receive the dollars provided as compensation.

Usually, in order to assist with paying for benefits, an organization will structure their Section 125 plan to where the "opt out" amount is substantially less than the total amount given. This has become a huge matter in the State of California with a recent settled lawsuit *Flores v. City of San Gabriel*, in which the dollars received from the insurance "opt out" should have been considered when calculating overtime and other premium pay. As a general reminder, it is important for Human Resources professionals to know as much as possible regarding federal and state laws—as well as current case law—as they might change the way an organization needs to implement benefit programs.

HR professionals must ensure that all programs, practices, policies, and initiatives comply with federal and state laws and regulations. The only exception to this is if the organization wants to increase the benefits afforded to employees and provide a more lucrative program than what is required under the law. An example of this would be regarding the Family Medical Leave Act (FMLA) and maternity leave. While FMLA leave is unpaid, an organization could provide a paid maternity leave benefit, which would be considered an additional benefit while also remaining in compliance with the requirement of the law. HR professionals should regularly audit the policies and procedures to ensure compliance with both current and new laws and regulations. Not doing so can put the organization at risk. In some states, individual employees can also be held personally responsible for not adhering to the laws, even if they were following policy at the time.

Eligibility Requirements

As with all programs offered by an organization, having a robust and clear policy is vital to ensure that employees understand their rights and entitlements as well as their responsibilities. Benefits programs can be complex, and it is in the best interest of both the organization and the employees to provide as much information as possible. It is common for organizations to provide an overview of the total rewards package during the hiring and recruitment process to attract candidates. Additional information should be provided to candidates during the offer process to ensure that a complete view is available to make a decision in joining an organization. Once an employee is hired, a thorough new hire orientation should be offered to review each benefit—from insurance programs available, vacation leave time accruals, employee assistance programs, and other noncash rewards. During the new hire orientation, employees should be afforded the opportunity to complete necessary paperwork or to take the paperwork with them to review options if they are not prepared to make benefit selections at that time.

Benefits programs policies should be inclusive of details such as how premiums are paid and when, whether opt out options are provided or participation is mandatory, eligibility terms and waiting periods, and contact information for the specific service providers. Employees should also understand enrollment periods, how changes to a benefit can be made outside of an enrollment period, and any other pertinent information that is helpful to understand how benefits work.

Human Resources professionals are responsible for ensuring that employees understand how to make benefit selections and coverage changes and how to sign up for a new program. An important component with benefits is having an understanding of timeframes. New employees should understand how long they are required to wait before they are eligible for coverage. Some organizations may have a waiting period of thirty days with coverage starting the first of the month following that timeframe. Some organizations may offer immediate eligibility for coverage. Regardless of when benefits eligibility starts, employees must understand this important piece of information so that they can make informed

66

decisions. Generally, employees are provided with a yearly open enrollment period during which they may make changes to their benefits for the next calendar year.

Enrollment Periods

Employees may only change their medical benefit selections on an annual basis during a defined period of time, usually in September and/or October. It is important to ensure employees understand this, as **open enrollment** is the only time employees can make changes to their selections unless they experience a qualifying event during the year. Qualifying events are marriage, divorce, birth or adoption of a child, and the loss or gain of a spouse's job.

The policy should clearly outline and define **qualifying events** as well as the timeframe required for employees to complete paperwork to change their coverage if one of the events occurs outside of open enrollment. Employees have a window of time to make changes and if an employee does not abide by the timeframe, they will not be allowed to make a change until the open enrollment period for the following year. An example of this would be providing employees a window of thirty days after the birth of a child to provide paperwork and supporting documentation to add the new child to the medical insurance. If the paperwork is submitted outside of this window, the employee will need to wait until the next open enrollment period to add the child for the next year.

An additional element that should be detailed in a benefits policy regarding medical insurance coverage is when this coverage ends upon an employee leaving the organization. Some organizations will end coverage effective immediately, on an employee's last day with the organization. Other organizations will provide coverage through the end of the month that the employee leaves. Regardless of when coverage ends, it is important to ensure that employees understand this component, as it will assist them in making decisions about retirement or changing employers.

Benefits policies should also be put in place regarding leave programs. Vacation and sick leave should be fully explained, and terms such as accrual rates, caps for maximum balances, usage and how to request leave, requesting leave donations, and payout information should be covered. Many organizations are changing over to a Paid time Off (PTO) program, which allows employees to accrue PTO to cover any types of absence regardless of the reason. PTO would cover vacation requests, sick leave, and any other kind of leave request. The same terms should be explained regarding PTO just as if the leave is broken down into separate balances. Many organizations with a PTO program find it easier to implement and manage for employees.

High Deductible Plans

A **high-deductible health plan (HDHP)** is a health plan that has low monthly premiums but a high deductible for healthcare costs. A deductible is the portion of a bill the insured party must pay out-of-pocket before their policy will cover the service. A monthly premium is the cost the insured must pay monthly to maintain coverage. The deductible threshold for a plan to be considered an HDHP changes from year to year. Currently, the IRS defines an individual deductible of $1,400 for individuals or $2,800 for families. An HDHP is often paired with a Health Savings Account (HSA), which provides tax-advantaged savings for medical services and is a benefit exclusive to HDHPs.

Health Savings and Flexible Spending Accounts

Health Savings Accounts (HSA) and Flexible Spending Accounts (FSA) are tax-advantaged accounts used to pay for medical expenses. Both accounts use pretax contributions or tax-deductible contributions, meaning the insured party can save on medical costs due to tax benefits. Insured parties may have either an HSA or an FSA, not both. **HSA accounts** are only available for individuals enrolled in a high-deductible health plan. **FSA accounts** are only offered by employers. The IRS determines contribution limits for HSA and FSA funds, but HSA funds can roll over yearly, whereas FSA funds are available on a use-it-or-lose-it basis.

Preferred Provider Organizations

Organizations can offer multiple choices to employees for health insurance coverage, including both preferred provider organization (PPO) and health maintenance organization (HMO) options as well as many choices of each type of plan to ensure that the needs of employees can be met. Dental insurance, vision insurance, and prescription coverage are also options that employers offer to employees to ensure employees protect their health on all levels.

Short or Long-Term Disability

Short-term disability (STD) and long-term disability (LTD) are types of voluntary insurance coverage that help maintain an employee's income if they have a temporary disability. STD covers the insured party's income for an immediate disability. In contrast, LTD maintains income when a disability keeps the employee from working for an extended period. The percentage of coverage offered by an STD or LTD is specific to the plan but will either cover a portion or all of the employee's lost income while they are unable to work. The length of coverage for STDs and LTDs also depends on the plan coverage, but typically, STDs cover up to a maximum of twelve months and LTDs can cover multiple years.

Supplemental Wellness and Fringe Benefit Programs

As with all programs, it is necessary for Human Resources to fully communicate to employees the benefits available. While most employees are very aware of medical insurance benefits due to having to complete annual enrollment forms and getting insurance cards, many employees can be unaware of other programs available. Communicating clearly and frequently is vital to the success of any program.

Noncash Compensation

Noncash compensation can be a powerful incentive and motivator for employees. Organizations have seen a shift in the importance of these programs relative to the recruitment and retention of employees. Previously, the base salary was the primary factor in accepting a position or staying with an organization. In the last several years, this has shifted to an overall review of all compensation variables, including base salary and noncash compensation. Employees are looking for options, flexibility, and programs that allow for self-care, family time, community involvement, recognition, development, and overall flexibility.

EAPs

Employee counseling refers to the process used when a performance problem cannot be addressed with training or coaching methods. Employee counseling is vital to uncovering the reasons for poor performance and focuses on performance-related behaviors to ensure a positive outcome. Ensuring the

68

employee understands and accepts the problem is the first goal of employee counseling. Once this has occurred, solutions can be explored to manage the expectations and resolve the issue. Sometimes, the root cause of a performance concern is a personal issue that the employee is dealing with. In these circumstances, once this has been discovered, Human Resources professionals can direct the employee to resources available to assist. **Employee Assistance Programs (EAPs)** are excellent programs to have available to employees to help them work through personal issues so that the employees can focus on work at work.

Many organizations have a third-party administrator deliver certain programs such as voluntary insurance programs or employee assistance programs. An EAP is a non-financial reward that provides confidential services at no cost to employees, helping them to deal with challenges of everyday life. EAPs can assist with family counseling, legal discussions, reducing stress and conflict, and many other challenges. Having representatives from these companies offer to meet with employees in person is also a great way to ensure employees are informed and understand the benefits offered.

Gym Membership and Online Therapy

Gym memberships and online therapy are wellness benefits employers can offer to help maintain or improve employees' health. Although wellness benefits are perks that businesses are not required to provide to their employees, wellness benefits can enhance other health coverage. Employers can cover the total cost of gym memberships or offer employees a discounted rate. Alternatively, businesses might have a fitness facility available for employee use. Online therapy is a wellness benefit that allows employees to talk to a mental health practitioner online. HIPAA covers any online therapy provided by employers, which ensures employees can maintain confidentiality while seeking out mental health resources.

Housing or Relocation Assistance and Travel/Transportation Stipends

Housing or relocation assistance and travel/transportation stipends are fringe benefits that employers offer in order to help with employment-related expenses. **Relocation assistance** helps cover expenses for employees who are moving to a different location because of a job requirement. Relocation benefits can be offered to new or existing employees to lessen the financial impact of relocation. **Travel/transportation stipends** are funds allocated by an employer to help pay for personal travel expenses. The amount of money allocated for relocation assistance and travel/transportation stipends depends on the employer but is intended to ease the cost of moving or traveling.

Employee Retirement Plans

Defined Benefit and Defined Contribution Plans

Eligibility in retirement plans is determined based on the specific plan type. Based on current IRS regulations, employees over 21 with one year of service behind them are typically eligible to enroll in retirement plans. Currently, there are two types of employer-provided retirement plans: defined benefit plans and defined contribution plans. **Defined benefit plans** are pensions paid by the company in a lump sum and depend on factors like tenure, age, and earnings history. **Defined contribution plans** are based on an individual's contribution to their retirement funds, and an employer may match the contributions of the individual up to a certain predetermined percentage. Different types of organizations offer different defined contribution plans. 401(k) plans are typically for private sector employees, 403(b)s are typically for public education employees, and 457(b)s are typically for nonprofit employees. Once an employee is enrolled in a retirement plan, there is typically a vesting period for their funds. Vesting refers to ownership of the funds. Most retirement plans with an employer match have an eligibility period of up to three to five years before the employer contribution is completely vested and employees can receive the full match.

401(k) and 457(b)

401(k) and 457(b) are elective, tax-advantaged defined benefit plans that allow employees to save for retirement on a pretax basis. The IRS monitors 401(k) and 457(b) plans, determining the maximum fund contributions allowed by individuals each year and when contributions can be withdrawn. 401(k) and 457(b) plans both allow for early withdrawals before age 59 ½, with a 10 percent penalty on the funds being withdrawn. 401(k) plans are typically offered by private or for-profit businesses, while public employers or nonprofits offer 457(b) accounts. Many 401(k) and 457(b) plans offer Roth contributions, allowing individuals to pay taxes on their income at the current rate; traditional contributions are not taxed until the employee withdraws from the account.

Catch-Up Contributions and Hardship Withdrawals

Catch-up contributions are offered to individuals over fifty to contribute additional income to their retirement accounts over the normal contribution limits. Catch-up contributions help those closer to retirement take advantage of extra savings to compensate for any years that participants didn't contribute. As with traditional retirement fund contributions, the IRS determines the catch-up contribution limit. Hardship withdrawals are withdrawals from an individual's elective deferral account due to a significant financial need. Unlike with early withdrawals, the IRS does not penalize hardship withdrawals. The IRS determines the criteria for a hardship withdrawal; eligible circumstances include, but are not limited to, medical care, tuition, and funeral expenses. However, the money used is taxed and is not paid back to the account.

Wage Statements and Payroll Processing

Just as it is important for department managers to understand personnel costs in the budgeting process, it is equally important for employees to understand their paychecks and how they are paid. Beginning with new hire orientation, Human Resources professionals should strive to ensure that employees understand their paychecks. Determining an hourly rate is only one component. In addition to communicating to employees how often they will be paid, employers should also explain how that pay will be distributed. Some organizations allow their employees to be paid with a paper check, a direct deposit, or even a transfer to a debit card. While some organizations allow this flexibility in how to receive the pay, other organizations streamline their payroll by requiring employees to adhere to their pay policy with only one form of payment. The most common form of payment is direct deposit, which can be requested by employees with the submission of a voided check.

Each organization prepares paychecks differently; therefore, it is important to communicate to employees the layout of the paychecks so there is understanding of each line item. Salary, including overtime, payouts, differentials, and other forms of payment should be clearly itemized. Deductions such as federal and state taxes, social security, disability, and workers' compensation insurance should each have their own line item and be clearly identified. Contributions to pensions and medical premiums, additional compensation such as car or phone allowances, and any other special premium pay should be clearly communicated on employees' paychecks.

It is important for each type of compensation, deduction, and contribution to be specifically identified for many reasons: employees may need to separate out certain pay for tax purposes, wage garnishments may need to be made based on base pay only, pension contributions need to be calculated based on certain types of pay, and it is easier to identify certain types of compensation or benefits when auditing. An additional item that many organizations include on paychecks is the leave balance status including vacation, sick, personal, short-term disability, holiday, or other types of leave. This ensures that employees are receiving this information on a regular basis so that they can manage their time appropriately.

Every employee must complete the appropriate paperwork when beginning their employment with an organization. This includes paperwork to set up their employee profile in the system. Employees should expect to complete several forms specific to just their pay. W-4 forms for federal and state tax withholdings, direct deposit forms, benefit enrollment forms, deferred compensation forms, and retirement forms are some of the most common forms that new employees can expect to complete. After new hire orientation, it is important for Human Resources to communicate to all employees where they can find these forms to update their information in the future. Tax withholdings may need to change due to a divorce or marriage, banking information may change, benefits may need to be updated due to the birth of a child, or employees may want to increase their voluntary contribution to their deferred compensation account. Employees will have different needs at different times, and it is important to ensure that they know where to find the forms and information needed when they need it.

There may be times when an error is made on a paycheck, so that there is an overpayment or an underpayment. There could be multiple reasons for an error, but it is important for Human Resources and Payroll to work together in a consistent practice to correct the mistake for the employees as well as to conduct an audit to ensure the mistake did not occur in other cases. If the mistake was a one-time event, the issue can be resolved quickly; however, if it is discovered during the audit that the mistake was ongoing and occurred on multiple occasions, potentially with multiple employees, it would be prudent to review policy and practice to ensure that the mistake is fully understood and corrected so that it does not occur again in the future.

Taxation

Taxes that are withheld from employees' wages (for example, federal and state income tax, Social Security, and Medicare) must be included in wage statements provided to employees. These are referred to as withholdings and are based on the employee's tax filing status, applicable tax rates, and exemptions. In addition to withholdings, deductions should also be listed on employees' wage statements. Pre-tax deductions for employee benefits can include factors like retirement contributions and health insurance premiums, as applicable. Withholdings and deductions must be accurately calculated and documented to maintain compliance with tax regulations.

The filing of tax forms in a timely manner is another crucial aspect of payroll processing. Form 1099 for independent contractors and Form W-2 for employees are two of the most common tax forms. HR professionals must understand how to properly generate and distribute these forms to employees in addition to filing them with the appropriate tax authorities. Payroll processing and wage statements must comply with local, state, and federal tax laws and regulations. To ensure compliance, HR professionals should always be up to date on tax law changes, reporting requirements, and thresholds to maintain accurate tax calculations and compliance with tax obligations. Detailed payroll records that include wage statements, tax forms, and supporting documentation are essential for taxation purposes, potential audits, inquiries, and reporting obligations.

Differentials

Pay differentials are essentially extra wages given to an employee for a variety of reasons, most of which relate to providing an incentive for employees to work additional or unusual hours and shifts. HR professionals should ensure that wage statements clearly reflect any differentials earned by employees, most often accomplished by giving each one their own line item. All differentials must be calculated and documented accurately to guarantee fair compensation for employees who have worked non-standard shifts.

One type of differential is a shift differential, which is extra compensation given to employees for working any shift that might be outside of their normal work schedule. These shifts can include weekends, evenings, nights, or mornings depending on the employee's regular schedule. Weekend differentials are a type of shift differential given specifically to employees for working during the weekend, often used as an incentive for employees to work when there may be higher demand or staffing requirements. Another form of differential is overtime, provided to employees who either work beyond their regular hours or exceed the predetermined weekly thresholds for overtime. Overtime differentials are regulated by the U.S. Department of Labor (DOL). As such, employers are required to provide employees covered by the Fair Labor Standards Act with overtime pay that is no less than one and a half times their hourly rate.

Differentials can also be provided due to the conditions or location where work is taking place. One such example is a hazard pay differential. Hazard pay is granted to employees working in hazardous or risky conditions, possibly with dangerous substances, in extreme temperatures, or in otherwise high-risk environments that lead to physical hardship. Additionally, geographic differentials are provided to employees who work in states or areas with a significantly greater cost of living. Compensation can also be adjusted for employees who work in locations where there is a lower concentration of their specific talents. The decision to offer geographic pay differentials has been made more complicated in recent years due to the increase in remote work and fully remote positions. While some organizations may decide to offer a fixed salary for the given role and allow employees to choose where they reside, others may offer a flexible salary dependent on the employee's permanent location.

The final type of differential is an on-call differential. On-call differentials are granted when employees are required to be available, or on-call, to return to work outside of their regularly scheduled hours or shifts. The purpose of these differentials, as with all others, is to ensure that employees are fairly and accurately compensated for their readiness and availability to work. Some organizations may also offer differentials specific to their industry or surrounding circumstances. These include working in healthcare or emergency services, employees who speak multiple languages receiving language differentials, and an increase in pay for employees with long tenures (referred to as experience-based differentials), among others.

Garnishments

A garnishment can be defined as a court-ordered deduction from an employee's earned wages. Garnishments are used to repay outstanding debts such as student loans, tax debts, child support, and many others. HR professionals should possess a solid understanding of the laws and regulations that concern garnishments, such as the Consumer Credit Protection Act. It is the responsibility of HR professionals to notify employees when they receive a garnishment order. Specific details about the order must be included in the notification, such as the type or source of the debt, the amount being deducted, options for seeking legal counsel to dispute the garnishment, and any other relevant legal information.

As previously stated, there are a variety of different garnishments to be aware of. Some of the most common are child support or alimony, creditor garnishments, student loan garnishments, and tax levies. With each type, there are slightly different rules and regulations that must be followed. To avoid legal consequences and remain in compliance with court orders, HR professionals must be sure to calculate the amount being deducted accurately based on the garnishment order. When processing wage statements, the correct amount must be deducted from each paycheck and reflected clearly in the employee's statement.

Even though any garnishment order is likely to fall within legal limits and regulations, HR professionals need to be aware of federal and state guidelines. The federal limit on wage garnishments is no more than 25 percent (or a quarter) of an employee's disposable income, unless the garnishment is categorized as spousal or child support. Regardless, living expenses will always be taken into account so that the garnishment does not affect an employee's ability to meet basic needs.

HR professionals should also protect the employee's personal and financial information related to the garnishment to maintain confidentiality. Documentation of the court order, a calculation of the deductions, and payments allocated to the proper entities should all be kept on file as records of the garnishment. When necessary, HR professionals must also provide reports to the court, government agencies, or creditors as required by law. Effective communication alongside proper support and guidance is a crucial part of the garnishment process. HR professionals can offer information on financial counseling and assistance programs to assist employees with managing their financial situations.

Leave Reporting

Policies should communicate when employees will receive their paycheck and the options they have regarding how to receive their paycheck. Options such as a paper check or direct deposit should be communicated along with how to request and set up each. Overtime policies should dictate how and when overtime is earned, how it is paid based on a time-and-a-half rate, and if compensatory time can be selected as an option. Compensatory time, commonly known as "comp time," is an option that employees can select instead of receiving overtime pay. In lieu of receiving the overtime pay, employees receive the time-and-a-half, or one and a half hours, of leave instead of pay. Compensation policies should also address holiday pay with a defined list of approved holidays. Vacation leave policies should be communicated to employees and include accrual rates, maximum accrual balance, carryover year to year, and cash out options.

Employees should clearly understand what they will earn in vacation leave and when they will earn it. An organization can determine when it will provide employees with their vacation leave. Two options would be to provide the vacation leave annually in January, based on service from the previous year, or to have employees earn their leave on a bi-weekly or monthly basis. While employees should be held responsible for managing their own leave appropriately, it is the responsibility of Human Resources to ensure that employees understand their rights and options regarding vacation leave.

Final Pay

Regardless of the type of termination, all employees should receive exit paperwork that documents information such as the following:

- Final paycheck details, including if a special check will be issued and when
- Leave balance payouts
- Insurance information including when coverage will end
- COBRA and insurance extension information
- Contact information for Human Resources
- Unemployment information

Human Resources professionals should be familiar with state requirements regarding when final paychecks are to be processed. For instance, in the state of California, all private organizations must issue the final paycheck, including all leave balance payouts and any compensation owed, within specific timeframes. If the employer has terminated the employee involuntarily, the final paycheck must be processed and provided to the employee at the time of termination. If an employee resigns and provides no notice, the employer must process the paycheck and provide it to the former employee within three working days. And if an employee resigns with a period of notice, the final paycheck must be processed and provided to the employee on their last working day. It is vital to understand these legal requirements as the organization can face penalties and fines if they are not followed accurately.

Total Reward Statements

It is important for Human Resources professionals to continuously review and analyze benefits programs and their corresponding policies. Programs should be reviewed to ensure they are appropriate and provide employees with the necessary benefits for their health and well-being. Policy reviews should also include a look into costs and effectiveness. New programs are being created frequently in the competitive market, and incorporating new and fresh programs to a total rewards package can be invigorating to employees. Even if programs are not replaced, the corresponding policy should be reviewed on a regular basis to provide updates that may be implemented by either the vendor providing the service or the organization.

When analyzing a benefits program, many different variables should be looked at to ensure a robust analysis. Items to be examined should include a review of costs for both the employer and employee, deductible and out-of-pocket maximum amount changes, network reviews, covered services, copays, prescription drug coverage and costs, and other items specific to coverages such as maternity, mental health, substance abuse, and other commonly used services through insurance plans. Benchmarking these benefit terms with other available options, like benchmarking salary discussed earlier, will allow Human Resources professionals to understand how their benefits align with those of competitors. This analysis can then be used to support recommendations made for changes to benefits.

Total rewards should be reviewed often to ensure employees are provided with a package inclusive of compensation and benefits that is competitive, fair, equitable, and appropriate for the work that will be done. Whether this is performed annually, every five years, or just as needed based on changes to the workforce (such as attrition), these assessments should be thorough and done with updated information.

There are numerous components to total rewards, each ranging in various levels of complexity. Additionally, because each employee values programs differently, it is important to be clear, concise, and thorough when communicating. Incorporating various methods of communication ensures that all employees receive the same information in a manner that is specific to their style and needs. From in-person meetings; print communications such as brochures, emails and memos; online portals; social media; and training sessions, human resources can incorporate multiple modes of communication as necessary.

Practice Quiz

1. _____ are excellent services that can provide various resources to help employees manage change.
   a. Employee assistance programs
   b. Employee referral programs
   c. Communications plans
   d. Onboarding programs

2. Human Resources professionals interact frequently with the _____ department regarding compensation practices.
   a. Legal
   b. Information Technology
   c. Payroll
   d. None of the above

3. Which of the following programs are considered noncash rewards? (Select all that apply.)
   a. Alternative work schedules
   b. Recognition programs
   c. Overtime
   d. Professional development
   e. On-site facilities

4. Why is communication with employees regarding benefits extremely important? (Select all that apply.)
   a. So that employees understand their options
   b. So that employees can train new employees
   c. So that employees have information to make informed choices
   d. So that employees realize the costs and obligations of the organization

5. A _____ is an analysis of other organizations in the same or similar industry with similar demographics.
   a. Policy review
   b. Process audit
   c. Market review
   d. Classification audit

6. Which of the following is NOT included in an organization's compensation policy?
   a. How employees can be eligible for increased compensation
   b. When current employees are eligible for raises
   c. The parameters for starting salaries offered to new hires
   d. The number of employees currently earning the minimum and maximum salaries

7. What was the core issue in the *Flores v. City of San Gabriel* court case in the state of California?
   a.   The dollars received from the opt-out choice in a Section 125 plan were not disclosed when calculating overtime and other benefit pay.
   b.   Employers were able to require employees to agree to arbitration and waive their rights to file class-action lawsuits.
   c.   The case addressed the issue of delayed reporting with regard to sexual harassment cases.
   d.   An employer was accused of age discrimination, with the employee claiming that the employer favored younger employees for promotions and training opportunities.

8. An employee has come to Lynne to update her records because she got married a couple of weeks ago. Lynne has updated the employee's information in the system, but she knows that there is a form the employee needs to complete to update tax information as well. Which form does she need?
   a.   W-4
   b.   W-2
   c.   1099
   d.   I-9

9. An employee has been terminated from Organization A, located in California. When does HR have to issue the employee's final paycheck?
   a.   Within one week of termination
   b.   On the next scheduled pay day
   c.   At the time of termination
   d.   Within thirty days of termination

10. Victor agreed to work an eight-hour shift on Saturday, even though he has already worked a full forty-hour week. He has also chosen to receive comp time rather than overtime pay. How many hours of comp time is the company required to give Victor for working the extra shift?
   a.   Sixteen hours
   b.   Ten hours
   c.   Eight hours
   d.   Twelve hours

11. How often should a total rewards review assessment be conducted?
   a.   Annually
   b.   As needed
   c.   Every five years
   d.   Every two years

See answers on the next page.

Answer Explanations

1. A: Employee assistance programs (EAPs) can be an excellent resource for employees who are managing change within the organization, the department, or the position. These programs can also offer resources for personal matters as well. Employee referral programs are the programs that support recommending individuals to an organization for employment consideration. Communications plans are the complete plans for communicating a particular message, which could be the details for the employee assistance program and how employees can access these services. Onboarding refers to the process to bring a new employee into the organization, which could include details for the employee assistance program.

2. C: Human Resources professionals frequently interact with Payroll in numerous ways, and working together is integral to an organization and the compensation practices and policies. Human Resources will work closely with Legal and Information Technology related to many matters but not on a daily basis regarding compensation practices.

3. A, B, D, & E: Alternative work schedules, recognition programs, professional development, and on-site facilities are all noncash rewards that an organization can offer to employees. Overtime is a cash payment for hours worked over forty hours per week or eight hours per day based on the organization's policy.

4. A & C: Communication regarding benefits is vital between employers and employees so there is an understanding of all benefits and options when making decisions. This allows employees to have information to make informed choices. It is not the responsibility of employees to train new employees in benefits, but rather the responsibility of Human Resources. While it is beneficial for employees to understand costs and how the organization operates, it is not a requirement that employees realize the costs and obligations of the organization regarding benefits.

5. C: A market review is the analysis of competitor's compensation and benefits to ensure an organization is paying employees a competitive salary. Choices *A, B,* and *D* are incorrect as a policy review is an in-depth review of current policies and practices to determine updates and changes, a process audit is a look into a particular procedure, and a classification audit is a review of a particular job and its corresponding job description.

6. D: The number of employees earning the minimum and maximum salaries is not relevant to establishing an organization's compensation policy. Choices *A, B,* and *C,* however, should be included in the policy.

7. A: Generally, the opt-out amount in a Section 125 plan is substantially less than the amount given to assist with paying for benefits, which led to the court case involving the calculation of overtime and other premium pay amounts. Choice *B* refers to the *Epic Systems v. Lewis* case. Choice *C* is the *Minarsky v. Susquehanna County* case, and Choice *D* is the case of *Paine v. IKEA Holding US, Inc.*

8. A: A W-4 form is used not only when an employee is a new hire but also when an employee has a change in their tax circumstances, such as getting married, getting divorced, or changing their name. A W-2 form, Choice *B,* is the tax reporting form provided to employees at the end of the year. A 1099, Choice *C,* is a tax reporting form for nonemployees, such as independent contractors, and the I-9 form, Choice *D,* is completed at the time of hire. It is not necessary to redo that form once an employee's identification has been established upon hire.

9. C: In the event of a termination in the state of California, the employee must be provided their final paycheck at the time of termination. Choices *A*, *B*, and *D* are all violations of California state law. HR personnel are expected to know and adhere to the laws in their specific states.

10. D: Like overtime, comp time is paid at a rate of time and a half, meaning that for every hour of comp time worked, the employee is to be compensated an hour and a half. Thus, an eight-hour shift is paid at a comp time rate of twelve hours (eight hours plus an additional four). Choice *A* represents a double time calculation, Choice *B* is time and a quarter, and Choice *C* does not include any extra pay for the overage period.

11. B: Companies typically establish a total rewards review schedule based on their specific needs. Some companies do this every year, Choice *A*; every two years, Choice *D*, every five years, Choice *C*, or any other time frame that works for their organization. However, there is no law nor specific rule that dictates when these assessments should be done.

Employee Relations

Employee relations is defined as the intended strategy of an organization about what needs to be changed relative to the relationships with employees and, if applicable, their representative unions. Additionally, employee relations is a study of the rules, policies, procedures, and agreements that employees are managed against as individuals and as departments. Employee relations management is about ensuring that any organizational changes recommended are accepted and successfully implemented. To establish a best-class employee relations program, Human Resources professionals should understand the individual components within employee relations and work to align these components with the overall strategy and vision of the employee relations program. Employee relations includes the following components, which lend to establishing a strong employee relations program:

- Employee involvement
- Employee communication
- Employee counseling
- Employee discipline
- Employee rights

These components build the organizational culture that employees work within. The ultimate goal of the organizational culture and employee relations strategy is to create an environment in which employees feel they are being treated fairly. Positive and successful employee relations can have significant impacts to the organization such as improving productivity, ensuring implementation of key initiatives, reducing employee costs, and helping employees to grow and develop. Employees are more likely to have a willingness to perform their job well, maintain a positive attitude, stay motivated and motivate others, and have a high level of satisfaction and commitment to the organization. Additionally, employees are more likely to understand their roles and goals within the organization, with their concerns and needs being addressed quickly and efficiently. Finally, employees have the ability to align their personal goals with the department and organizational goals, which can improve morale, loyalty, and productivity.

Mission, Vision, and Value Statements

After a scan of a company's external and internal environments has taken place, the executive team can turn their focus to developing the vision, mission, and value statements to guide the company over the long term.

Mission Statements

A company creates a **mission statement** to detail how it will work toward obtaining its vision. A mission statement tells employees what the company does, where the company is going in the mid to long term, and how the company is different from other organizations. A company's mission statement should stay constant throughout a company's life cycle.

Items that may be addressed in a company's mission statement include:

- Where does the company compete geographically?
- What are the company's top products or services?
- Who are the company's customers?
- What is the company's competitive advantage?

80

- How responsive is the company to environmental concerns?
- Does the company consider its employees to be a valuable asset?
- Is the company committed to financial stability?

Vision Statements

A **vision statement** can be best described as a concise statement that reflects organizational confidence and long-term aspirations regarding how a company will achieve more than economic success (it is forward-thinking). Some questions that can be addressed in a vision statement are: How does this company fit into the world? How would it positively change the world? Institutionally, how does the company plan to deliver its product or service less expensively and more efficiently than its competitors? Ultimately, vision statements serve the purpose of boosting trust and confidence and creating an image that the company is engaging in a task larger than itself.

Value Statements

A company's value statement communicates to employees the standards by which they are expected to adhere to while conducting business, such as integrity, open-mindedness, respect, safety, and teamwork. Values are the things that are most important to a company, which is why they should be deeply ingrained in the corporate culture and demonstrated in employees' daily business interactions with stakeholders and customers. HR can play an important role in reinforcing a company's values by leading by example and communicating them to employees.

Organizational Culture

Organizational culture is defined as the shared beliefs, values, philosophies, and assumptions within an organization. There can be various cultures within an organization—division, department, workgroup, and teams—but in general, all separate cultures should align with the higher-level cultures.

Four Primary Culture Types

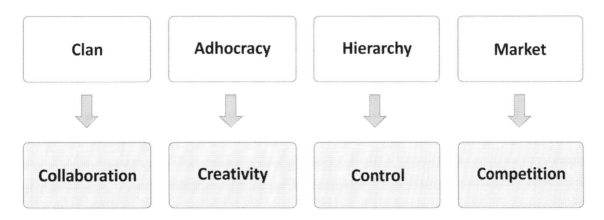

There are four primary culture types: clan, adhocracy, hierarchy, and market. Each culture has different benefits to an organization relative to flexibility, stability, control, focus, and strategy. The **clan culture** focuses on collaboration with leaders that are facilitators, mentors, and team builders. The clan culture is

81

built on a foundation of employee development and participation at all levels of the organization. The **adhocracy culture** focuses on creativity with leaders who are innovators, entrepreneurs, and visionaries. The adhocracy culture is built on a foundation of innovation, vision, and new resources. The **hierarchy culture** focuses on control and process with leaders that are organizers, coordinators, and monitors. The hierarchy culture is built on a foundation of control and efficiency through the use of stable and consistent processes. The **market culture** focuses on competition with leaders that are hard driven, competitors, and producers. The market culture is built on a foundation of aggressive competitiveness and customer focus.

When Human Resources professionals identify, or are made aware of, concerns and issues within an organization's culture, it is important to fully understand the issues and provide recommendations to leadership that fully address these issues. It may be a good idea to incorporate elements from different organizational cultures into an organization's holistic philosophy. Each organization, department, and team will naturally create and maintain a culture within the individual work groups. It is important to ensure that the overall culture and philosophies flow downward and upward to each level, allowing smaller groups to nurture a culture that aligns within the overall organizational culture. To change or strengthen the culture of an organization, Human Resources professionals should follow a standard process to ensure effective and productive results.

First, it is important to understand the values and personalities of leadership. Transformational leadership can reshape and change a culture but must take ownership and be held accountable for initiating change at the highest levels of the organization. Once the leadership style is understood, it is important to align the facts and information to determine the changes needed to initiate a cultural change at each level of the organization. Once the recommendations have been proposed and accepted for implementation, it is important to align these recommendations with rewards and incentives that support the changes. Employees who understand how and when their behavior will be rewarded and incentivized will be more likely to embrace and support the changes being implemented.

Strengthening organizational culture will occur when leadership supports workforce stability and communicates to employees regularly and frequently. Communication is key to any initiative and communication plans can determine success or failure of a program. Finally, Human Resources professionals should incorporate the culture and cultural initiatives into the recruitment process. Newly hired employees should understand the organization and the culture prior to accepting an offer of employment. Ensuring that there is a cultural fit for both the organization and employee is vital to the employment experience and retaining the most qualified individuals.

Organizational Goals and Objectives

HR Policies, Procedures, and Operations

Policies and procedures are significant, as they communicate the values and expectations of an organization. They ensure accountability, implement best practices, and facilitate decision making. **Policies** are the standards or guides to the organizational philosophy, mission, and values. **Procedures** are targeted and specific action plans to achieve the organization's goals. Most organizations implement various procedures to ensure consistency, equity, and fairness, including standard operating procedures, employee handbooks, and time/attendance rules.

Functions of HRIS

Human resources information systems (HRIS) are unique to each organization and HR department. As each agency has its own specific needs when it comes to reporting and the information to be tracked, HRIS platforms can be uniquely tailored to meet these needs. HRIS reports and data should be used to address issues and solve problems when appropriate. HR should use the data available to review trends, analyze performance evaluation information, and assess recruitment effectiveness. Using this data can provide insights, which can then be used to modify the departmental objectives. It is important to understand that the reports are only as good as the data entered. If incorrect data is entered into the system, then the reports created from the system will not provide accurate details. Trends and resolutions that are created from inaccurate information will lead to bigger issues instead of resolving the issues that the data was intended to fix. A robust HRIS has multiple benefits for the organization, including faster processing and time savings, improved planning and organization, recruitment status and details, and a more accurate level of performance.

Organizational Structures

Organizational structure is used to help companies achieve their goals by defining the hierarchy of employees and allocating resources through decisions surrounding the following factors:

- **Chain of command**: This clarifies who employees report to. It is the continuous line of authority from senior-level managers to employees at the lowest levels of the company.

- **Centralization**: A company where lower-level employees carry out the decisions made by senior-level managers is highly centralized. The opposite of this is decentralization or employee empowerment.

- **Span of control**: This refers to the number of employees a manager can effectively supervise. This can be affected by such things as a manager's skills, the physical proximity of the employees, the employees' characteristics, and the complexity of the work being performed.

- **Formalization**: An organization with jobs that are standardized, allowing for little discretion over what is to be done because the work is guided by rules, has a high degree of formalization. The opposite of this is low formalization, where employees have more freedom to decide how they can complete their tasks.

- **Work specialization**: This is also known as **division of labor** and refers to the degree to which a company divides tasks into separate jobs that are completed by different employees. This allows employees to become very proficient in a specialized area, such as painting or framing.

- **Departmentalization**: This comes into play when a company divides up its work by the specialization of its departments. Companies are known to departmentalize by function, product, geography, or division.

Functional Structure

This is the most common type of organizational structure where jobs are based on function, such as finance, IT, sales, purchasing, and HR. Efficiencies are gained from grouping together individuals with common knowledge and skills. This type of organizational structure is good for a company that has one product line that can benefit from specialization. However, employees can have a limited view of the company's goals, and there can be poor communication across the various functional areas.

Product Structure

This is a type of organizational structure where jobs are grouped by product line. For example, a product organizational structure for a transportation company might be grouped by rail products, mass transit products, and recreational and utility vehicle products. Organizing by product allows managers to become experts in their industry and for specialization in certain products and services. However, employees can have a limited view of the company's goals, and there is a duplication of functions within each product line.

Geographic Structure

This is a type of organizational structure where jobs are grouped according to geographic location. For example, a company's sales directors for various regions (Eastern, Western, Midwestern, and Southern) may each be responsible for the business functions in their areas and report to the company's vice president of sales. This type of structure is the best way to serve the unique needs and issues that may arise in different geographic markets. Since most decisions are made at the location level, decision making is decentralized. However, employees may feel isolated from other organizational areas, and there is a duplication of functions within each geographic region.

Division Structure

This is a type of organizational structure where jobs are grouped by industry or market. A divisional organizational structure also experiences decentralized decision making and is similar in nature to the geographic structure.

Matrix Structure

Employees report to two managers in this type of organizational structure. Typically, one manager has functional responsibility and the other manager has product line responsibility. Employees have a primary manager they report to and a second manager they also work for on specified projects. In order for a matrix structure to be successful, there must be a high degree of trust and communication among the employees involved. This type of structure is a good way to share resources across functions.

Preparing HR-Related Documents

Standard operating procedures (SOPs) ensure that processes are completed accurately and efficiently every time. SOPs are documents that describe specific details of a task or operation to ensure the quality of work completed. They provide a set of instructions, steps, and guidelines for individuals to follow to ensure safety, compliance, and accuracy each time the process is completed. Additionally, SOPs maximize efficiency and productivity by minimizing errors and rework while maximizing resources and continuous improvement. SOPs can also protect the organization and employees when questions of legality or compliance arise.

Employee handbooks are structured manuals that communicate expectations regarding the employment experience. Provided with a handbook, employees can take ownership of locating answers to commonly asked questions or understanding a specific program. Employee handbooks should strive to achieve the following:

- Introduce employees to the organizational culture, including the mission, values, and goals

- Communicate expectations for employees and management

- Ensure key policies are clearly understood

- Showcase the benefits offered to employees, such as wellness programs, employee assistance programs, discounts, recognition programs, training opportunities, and more

- Ensure compliance with federal and state laws

- Provide employees with their rights, responsibilities, and where to go for help

- Defend against employment claims

Employee handbooks should also define the standard work schedule, the performance evaluation process, the dress code, and emergency procedures. Employee handbooks serve many purposes, specifically being a reference guide, a communication tool, and an enforcement of company policies. A common best practice that protects the organization from frivolous claims pertaining to not knowing about a particular program or policy is to require all new employees to read the handbook and return a notification that the handbook has been read and understood.

Basic Communication Flows and Methods

Communication Strategy

A successful communication strategy incorporates opportunities for management to share information with employees using a top-down approach while still affording staff an opportunity to express their concerns via bottom-up communication methods. Top-down and bottom-up communication are both considered **vertical communication**.

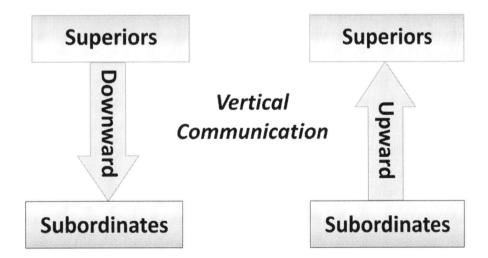

Top-Down Communication

In a **top-down communication** channel, communication takes place in a downward direction. This tends to be the traditional view of communication where information is transmitted from individuals in positions of higher authority (leaders and managers) to individuals in positions of lower levels of authority (employees). This type of communication tends to be unidirectional in nature and does not require a response from the recipient. Examples of top-down communication include an upper-management presentation to staff on the company's mission and vision and managers receiving an email from the board of directors on a new objective they will be required to meet. Occasionally, differences in status, knowledge, and levels of authority can lead to misinterpretations or misunderstandings in top-down communication. Since a company's success relies on effective top-down communication, individuals delivering these types of messages must make an effort to use clear and concise wording with a respectful tone and ensure that employees understand the information.

Bottom-Up Communication

In a **bottom-up communication** channel, communication takes place in an upward direction. In this type of communication, information is transmitted from individuals in positions of lower levels of authority (employees) to individuals in positions of higher authority (leaders and managers). An example of bottom-up communication is a brown bag lunch program, which is a type of informal meeting held between employees and management to discuss company problems. The lunch setting and company-provided meal can help create a relaxed setting for exchanging ideas. Staff meetings, which are more formal gatherings of employees and management from a given team, typically take place on a set day and time allow everyone involved to meet to talk about project updates and offer each other support and suggestions. In addition, all-hands meetings, which are formal gatherings for the entire company, tend to focus on sharing information that concerns the overall organization.

An open-door policy is used to establish a relationship where employees feel comfortable speaking directly with management about problems and suggestions. In essence, an open-door policy allows a supervisor or manager to be a "human suggestion box." In certain situations, it can be difficult to create an environment where employees feel comfortable discussing problems in person with management. In addition, depending on the problem reported, it may not be possible to maintain confidentiality. However, in the right situation, an open-door policy can help companies identify problems quickly, almost in real time, without having to wait for a formal meeting to address an ongoing issue.

Horizontal Communication

In a **horizontal communication** channel, communication takes place in a horizontal direction. In this type of communication, information is transmitted between individuals who are working on the same level of a company. Examples of horizontal communication include two managers who are working together on a project rollout and two employees on the same team who are working together to try to solve a customer's issue. Horizontal communication is great for collaborating, sharing information, and solving problems between employees who work together in the same environment. However, sometimes differences in personalities, territoriality, and rivalry between employees can negatively affect this form of communication.

Communication Methods

It is important to answer the following questions before deciding on an appropriate communication method to use:

- Who is the intended audience for the communication?
- What is the objective of the communication?
- Who is providing the information for the communication?
- Is the information contained within the communication time sensitive in nature?
- What information is going to be provided in the communication?

There are multiple means a company can use to communicate with its employees. Each method has its own potential advantages and drawbacks.

Email makes it easy to get information to a lot of people very quickly. However, this communication method can result in employees suffering from "information overload" from too many emails, making it more likely that important information is overlooked. Also, there is a danger that confidential information may be accidentally communicated to the wrong people.

The **intranet** (internal website and computer network) has the benefit of no risk of important information being accessed by someone outside the organization. Intranets can be very effective at communicating important ongoing information about the company, such as policies and procedures. In addition, companies often store necessary workplace documentation such as HR-related forms on an intranet, allowing employees to access that information when they need it. However, if outside parties need information on the intranet, they cannot access it. In addition, intranet communication is often "top-down" and does not allow for feedback from employees. It is also important to note that some intranet systems are not user-friendly so employees can be discouraged from using them.

Newsletters can provide a variety of information and have the potential to do so in an engaging, welcoming manner. However, newsletters can be labor intensive. Since they are relatively infrequent (compared to the ease of sending an email), newsletters are not always useful for communicating urgent or immediate information. In addition, newsletters do not allow for formal two-way communication from employees (although this can be remedied by involving employees in the creation of the newsletter).

Word of mouth can quickly spread information throughout a group of people. However, as in the children's game, Telephone, information can become muddled, misinterpreted, and downright unrecognizable as it is passed from person to person. A manager or supervisor has no control over misinterpretations and misunderstandings that can result from word-of-mouth communication.

Finally, taking into consideration an organization's culture, generational differences that may be present within a company, and gender differences can also help with selecting an appropriate method to ensure improved communication.

Strategic Planning

A company's strategic planning process comprises the following four steps:

- Strategy Formulation: During this first step of the strategic planning process, a company focuses on the business it is in and develops its vision, mission, and value statements accordingly. Plans are also made for how best to communicate the company's mission and when it may be necessary to change the company's mission or adjust its strategy. This first step can be summed up by identifying where a company currently is and defining where it wants to be in the future and how it can arrive at that place.

- Strategy Development: Environmental scanning and a SWOT (Strengths, Weaknesses, Opportunities, Threats) analysis are performed during this step of the strategic planning process. Additionally, long-range plans are established that will set the company's direction for the next three to five years. This second step can be summed up by collecting information that is both internal and external to the company, along with developing alternative strategies.

- Strategy Implementation: During this step of the strategic planning process, short-range plans are created that will set the company's direction for the next six to twelve months. Additionally, there is a focus on motivating employees by developing action plans and allocating the necessary resources in order to achieve objectives (e.g., human, financial, and technological). This step can be summed up by implementing a plan for the strategy that is chosen.

- Strategy Evaluation: During this last step of the strategic planning process, a company agrees to continue reviewing an implemented strategy at specific intervals by performing a SWOT analysis and taking note of any changes. In the event of changes, corrective action may be necessary. This step can be summed up by evaluating the success of the implemented strategy while continuing to monitor it and make any necessary tweaks.

Strategic planning is dependent on the knowledge and awareness of the goals and objectives for both the organization and the HR department. Ensuring alignment between the organization and HR is vital to being successful at every level within an organization. Strategic alignment of goals and objectives sets up success for individual employees, teams, departments, and the organization. This strategy also allows for better decision making for the business, which includes policy changes, practice updates, and possible reevaluation and redesign of the current state. Business decisions that are strategically implemented using this information will have a higher likelihood of being successful.

Environmental Scanning and SWOT Analysis

An environmental scan is used to collect the necessary information from a company's internal and external environments to develop its strategic plan. A SWOT analysis is a tool used during the environmental scan as a company examines its internal strengths and weaknesses along with any external opportunities and threats it may be facing.

Identified, internal strengths are hard to copy and give a company a competitive advantage, which improves its position in the marketplace. A company's internal strengths also create value for its customers. Examples of strengths are brand recognition, strong employee skill sets, a high level of innovation, and solid financing.

Any internal weaknesses can potentially reduce a company's ability to reach its objectives and place it at a competitive disadvantage. Outdated equipment, unreliable suppliers, ineffective leadership, and insufficient marketing campaigns are examples of weaknesses.

It is important to note, when assessing a company's strengths and weaknesses, it is much easier to analyze its physical and financial assets than to assess examples of its intangible assets mentioned above.

A possible way for a company to identify opportunities is to analyze the weaknesses of its competitors. Opportunities are identified, external factors that enable a company to become increasingly profitable and grow. Examples of opportunities are advances in technology, depth in supplier relationships, consumer trends, and potential new markets.

A possible way for a company to identify threats is to analyze the strengths of its competitors. Threats are identified, external factors that a company must strive to overcome. Regulatory constraints, a labor shortage, a declining economy, and a changing political climate are examples of threats.

Engaging Employees and Improving Employee Satisfaction

Engaging Employees

The combination of employees' knowledge, skills, and abilities makes up a company's human capital, which can lead to creativity and a competitive advantage. Since employees are a company's most valuable asset, it is important to keep them engaged. **Employee engagement** is the willingness of employees to remain with a company, "go the extra mile" when completing their work, and speak highly of the company when outside of its doors. Employees tend to be more engaged when they understand how their daily responsibilities affect how the company reaches its goals. The following elements are important for employee engagement to occur as well:

- **Leadership**: It is important for employees to work for managers who support the company's goals and follow through on their commitments to them. It is also important for managers to clearly communicate employee expectations in regard to a company's goals.

- **Professional development**: It is important for employees to feel they are being invested in and groomed for higher-level positions.

- **Employee recognition**: It is important for employees to receive monetary and nonmonetary rewards in exchange for performing above expectations.

Employee Satisfaction

In recent years, a large focus has been directed toward noncash rewards and benefits that an organization offers to employees. It is becoming more important for organizations to focus on offering a wide array of these types of benefits to attract and retain top talent. While in previous years, the salary and take-home pay were the primary components of accepting a position with a company, times have changed. Employees want programs that allow for a more holistic approach to their lives versus just focusing on an hourly salary. Organizations have responded with programs that allow for more work/life balance, community-focused programs, and recognition. Employees now have options available to them such as:

- telecommuting for a portion, or all, of their workweek.
- adhering to an alternative work schedule such as a 9X80 or 4X10 schedule.
- being paid for volunteering their time to a charity organization.
- on-site daycare and exercise facilities.
- fresh, healthy, and affordable meal options.
- tuition reimbursement and furthering education goals.
- formal and informal employee recognition programs.

Each of the above noncash rewards is an option for an organization to consider. Some may be viable options, but others, based on the business model, organizational structure, customer needs, and staffing levels, may not be options that can be offered. It is important to assess each program individually to determine if it will have an impact for employees, both current and future. While some programs may offer a larger return on investment than others, each employee will value one or more at different levels. For a single mother with a young child, an on-site daycare facility may be the noncash reward that holds the largest, most significant impact. For a seasoned professional with over two decades of work experience, being offered the opportunity to be paid while working with Habitat for Humanity might hold a special value for this individual.

Understanding an organization's employees and their needs allows for a proper assessment of which programs would be the best to offer for the biggest impact. It may be appropriate to survey current employees to discover what options would be most valued or to gather more creative and flexible ideas directly from them. Exit interviews are also an excellent tool for discovering from employees leaving the organization what impacted their decision to leave and if their new organization offers a specific noncash reward that attracted them.

In addition to creating and implementing these programs and options for employees, it is even more important to ensure that Human Resources communicates the programs with employees. A very common response from employees when asked if they knew about certain programs is "I had no idea we had that!" It is the responsibility of Human Resources to communicate frequently and regularly about such programs to make sure that employees are aware of them. Employees also appreciate the opportunity to regularly submit feedback on current programs as well as ideas for new programs. Having an online suggestion box or even soliciting random feedback from employees regarding new ideas is a fantastic way to engage employees so that they are part of the process.

Employee Recognition Programs

Recognition programs, both formal and informal, should be a common and frequent practice that organizations engage. Recognizing employees informally at department meetings, issuing a monthly write up in a newsletter to highlight a job well done, or scheduling a formal annual event to recognize service and special contributions to the organization are all important aspects to recognizing employees and the work they do on a daily, weekly, monthly, and annual basis. Special awards such as "Employee of the Year" are important to employees and should not be minimized. Organizations can align special awards with their corporate values and engage their employees by encouraging everyone, regardless of their title and level, to nominate those who display specific traits in their work or went above and beyond for customers or the team.

Stay Interviews

Stay interviews are conversations with existing employees to understand why they have stayed with the organization, what would make them leave, and how the organization can continue to improve. Stay interviews help ensure that employees maintain high levels of engagement in the organization. Unlike exit interviews, which identify factors that made an employee leave, stay interviews aim to retain valued talent and ensure high levels of employee engagement. Typically, stay interviews take place between an employee and their manager in a casual environment. This helps establish trust in the relationship and ensures managers can continue to give employees opportunities they find exciting and enriching.

Work/Life Balance Initiatives

Human Resources professionals are responsible for researching, implementing, and managing noncash compensation programs. These programs can be extensive and require heavy involvement, or they can be simple and easily facilitated. Regardless of the complexity of noncash programs, overall, employees appreciate options that allow for a more balanced and healthier lifestyle. These programs can include on-site facilities such as daycare or exercise facilities, tuition reimbursement, professional development, and community involvement programs.

More organizations are offering employees on-site facilities such as daycare, exercise facilities, and meal service. Rising daycare costs are a huge issue that parents face in addition to allocating time in the day for drop off and pick up. While there are many things to consider with having a daycare facility on-site, including liability, insurance, proper facilities, and trained staff, it is an option that more organizations are considering, as it can increase employee morale and performance as well as retention for the organization.

Exercise facilities are also being incorporated into the facility plans to allow employees an opportunity to exercise on breaks and lunch or before and after work. Having this convenient option available is one that many employees appreciate as it can help maximize the time during the day and help enforce a healthy lifestyle. In the same vein of healthy living, having convenient, affordable, and healthy meal options available to employees is another noncash program that can have a dramatic impact with employees, both future and current. If the facility is unable to have a cafeteria and healthy, fresh food available, organizations can work with local restaurants and grocery stores to provide discounts or incentives to employees.

Tuition reimbursement and professional development are more common programs that have been in place for some time with some organizations. Encouraging education by supporting employees with reimbursement for tuition costs is an excellent way for an organization to support and motivate their employees. This further education can positively impact the organization by having a more educated workforce that is well trained, knowledgeable, and more proactive and productive in their work. Policies should be developed that provide an understanding of the expectations of employees and the organization, including terms to pay back the reimbursement if an employee leaves the organization within a certain time period.

Professional development—through training programs offered by the organization as well as through outside agencies and professional organizations—is an excellent opportunity for employees to continue progressing on their professional career path. When an organization shows their employees that education, knowledge, training, and development are important, employees will generally be energized, motivated, and passionate about what they do.

Community involvement programs are an excellent way to engage employees in their passions and show support. Some organizations will provide employees with additional leave time that is to be used specifically for community involvement. Whether working at a local food bank or building homes with Habitat for Humanity, employees have the flexibility and ability to use a certain amount of time—without having to use their personal vacation leave time—to give back to their communities.

Alternative Work Arrangements

Many organizations have begun to implement a flexible and alternative work schedule. These work schedules deviate from the standard weekly work schedule of 9:00 a.m. to 5:00 p.m., Monday through Friday. Depending on the customer service needs and standard business operating hours, organizations are implementing different work schedules such a 4X10 or 9X80 schedule. On a 4X10 work schedule, employees work four days a week for ten hours each day. Some organizations may be able to close for the fifth workday, so all employees are off work, or allow employees to select their day off each week. On a 9X80 work schedule, in a two-week period, employees work a full eighty hours in only nine days. For eight of these days, employees work nine hours, and for one day, employees work eight hours. These types of flexible work schedules can allow employees to have a more balanced work and home life. The table below provides some examples of flexible work schedules:

Work Schedule	Monday	Tuesday	Wednesday	Thursday	Friday
5X8	8 hours	8 hours	8 hours	8 hours	8 hours
4X10	10 hours	10 hours	10 hours	10 hours	OFF
9X80 week 1	9 hours	9 hours	9 hours	9 hours	8 hours
9X80 week 2	9 hours	9 hours	9 hours	9 hours	OFF

Collecting Feedback

Employee suggestion programs are great ways to receive feedback from employees regarding current programs and new, future programs. Having employees involved in the review of current programs and outlining new programs is an excellent way to engage and involve employees. Engaged employees are generally more involved in these programs and can engage other employees by communicating the information during everyday interactions.

An important aspect of noncash compensation is creativity. While policies are necessary for the administration of each program, it is important to understand what employees want and what they value. What may seem like a great idea on paper may not be an incentive that employees actually appreciate or need. Engaging employees in the process of creating these programs is essential to ensuring their success.

Engagement Surveys
Gathering employee engagement data through a survey is an excellent best practice to implement within an organization; however, it is just as important to ensure that the results are communicated and action is taken. Without communication and action, positive changes will not be seen from the survey alone.

Employee surveys are an efficient and effective method to measure employee attitudes, opinions, and overall satisfaction. Surveys can provide perspectives at various levels of the organization, including the satisfaction of individuals with their specific position, supervisor, executive leadership, and the entire organization and company culture. Surveys allow an organization to monitor trends in specific areas, assess impacts of policy changes, compare employee satisfaction with other organizations and competitors, and provide insight on the areas of improvement that are important to employees. Additionally, surveys can offer the opportunity to review employee perspectives regarding compensation, benefits, time off, recognition, training opportunities, communication, culture, leadership, and any other area that may need to be assessed. The survey results can then be used to determine and support necessary actions to implement for improvement.

The first step to initiate an employee engagement survey is to plan the survey. Planning the survey involves determining the data that should be collected, how the data will be collected, setting up the method to analyze the information gathered, writing the questions, and setting up the survey. Once the survey is initiated, it cannot be changed. It is important to ensure the survey is appropriate during the planning phase and will yield the information needed.

The second step is to establish a communications plan. The communications plan should include who will be responsible for each message, what will be communicated, timeframes, and directions. The communications should be written for the employees who will be taking the survey. Ensuring that all messages are clear, concise, and specific is vital for all communications and will lead to better participation rates and responses. Additionally, employees should fully understand how the survey was planned and prepared, how the data will be analyzed and used, and that all responses will be kept confidential. While it may be necessary for employees to identify the department and area they work in, employees should be confident that their responses will not be used inappropriately.

The third step is to run the survey and allow employees adequate time to complete and turn in the survey. Employees should know how and where to ask for assistance, when and where surveys are to be submitted, and how to complete the survey. Surveys may be available online or in paper format, and employees should understand how to complete either format based on their comfort level with each. While the survey is being conducted, it is important to continue communications with employees by sending reminders and requests to complete the survey.

Once the survey has been completed, the fourth step is to analyze the results. Computing a response rate is one of the first measurements that should be calculated, as this will show how effective the survey was in receiving feedback from employees. The response rate may even be a standard benchmark metric for the department to use to track success in the future. After calculating and analyzing the results, recommendations should be proposed to address key areas of improvement. Additionally, it is also important to recognize areas that are successful. Focusing on the areas that are done well is just as important as focusing on the areas that need improvement.

Once the recommendations have been approved for implementation, it is vitally important to communicate the results and the action plans to employees. Employees need to know how the information will be used and what they can expect in the future. If there is ultimately no action or change implemented, employees will be less engaged in the future to participate and provide feedback. Conducting surveys frequently is a great way to determine if employees are responding to new programs. If an organization is taking proactive steps to communicate, implement change, and keep employees engaged and motivated, momentum and innovation will continue to grow and become part of the culture of the overall organization.

Workforce Management

Performance Management

Performance management is the continuous process of planning, coaching, evaluating, and rewarding the performance of individual employees, workgroups or teams, and departments with the goal of aligning performance and achievements with the overall strategic goals and mission of the organization.

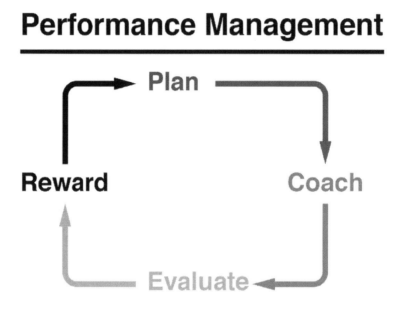

A typical performance management process begins with executive leadership planning and finalizing overall organizational goals for a given year. These goals are then translated to specific objectives and achievements for departments and management and then further defined to align with programs and performance targets for individual employees. Once the goals and objectives have been planned at all levels of the organization, supervisors can then begin to coach employees on the best way to be successful in achieving the goals within the context of the job.

Utilizing a formal performance review process that includes performance appraisals and development plans is an excellent resource to engage employees in discussions about performance, achievements, training, resources, and development. Informal reviews are also a helpful tool to provide employees insight as to their progress in achieving the goals outlined for the year. Providing status updates throughout the year ensures that employees are on track to reach their goals and also provides an opportunity to reassess the objectives or the position, if needed.

If the position needs to be reviewed to ensure the job description and responsibilities are an accurate representation of the work being done, tools such as a job analysis can be used. It is important to conduct these conversations within the performance management process, but not at the end during the evaluation process. This could lead to unsatisfactory performance evaluations that are not technically warranted and have other further reaching consequences such as poor employee morale, higher turnover, decreased productivity, and negative customer satisfaction. Evaluations should be fair, clear, accurate, and succinct. They should present a picture of the work that the employee has completed throughout the

94

year, showing how the achieved objectives assist in the organization achieving its overall goals and objectives.

Finally, employees should be rewarded as appropriate and available. Recognition should be given for a job well done, and if budgetary resources are available, merit increases, bonus awards, or other pay for performance programs should be enacted. If budgetary resources are not available for a monetary award, other awards should be considered to continue to incentivize employees to exceed their goals and objectives. Top performers can be recognized in employee newsletters with specific examples of the accomplishments achieved. Recognition programs that acknowledge employee accomplishments quarterly and annually—even resulting in a highly coveted "Employee of the Year" award—can be implemented to continue to recognize employees' achievements.

A vitally important tool to utilize throughout the entire performance management process is communication and feedback in both directions—up and down. It is a common occurrence for communication to only flow down: leadership to management to supervision to individual employees. Employees should be encouraged to speak with peers, supervisors, management, and leadership as appropriate regarding concerns, questions, or needs such as resources or training. Ensuring this flow of communication promotes engagement throughout the process, increasing the success of the overall process and ultimately meeting the achievements at all levels.

Offboarding

Employees who are involuntarily terminated should be provided with due process based on the reasoning for the separation. If an employee is being terminated for poor performance or failure of probation, the manager should work with Human Resources prior to the termination to ensure that the employee is aware of this issue and allowed to have an appropriate amount of time to correct the issues. If sufficient progress is not made within a specified period of time, Human Resources should then work through the appropriate process to terminate employment. In the case of terminating an employee due to inappropriate conduct or policy violations, again, due process should be afforded. Conducting a proper investigation and determining the appropriate level of discipline should be standard procedure. Depending on the violation, immediate termination may be appropriate; however, if progressive discipline is appropriate, the employee will need to progress through the levels of disciplinary action prior to being terminated.

When an employee is terminated in these circumstances, Human Resources should ensure that a safe and secure environment is provided to deliver the message. A common practice is to terminate an employee at the end of their scheduled shift and/or at the end of the workweek. Efforts should be taken to ensure the safety of all employees and may include having a security guard or a police officer on-site and available in the case of emergencies. Employees being terminated should be afforded the opportunity to collect their belongings; however, in some circumstances, it may be more appropriate to mail personal belongings to the individual to expedite leaving the premises. The information technology department should be notified to immediately disable all access to systems, change passwords, and set up out-of-office messages and auto-forwarding of emails.

In the event that an employee is being laid off, Human Resources should ensure that the employee is provided with as much notice as possible and any resources are made available to the employee. On-site counselors may be appropriate to ensure employees receive the message in a safe environment with readily available resources. When an employee is laid off, it is important to remember that each individual will handle this news differently. Reactions from crying or yelling to no reaction at all are normal. Human Resources professionals should be trained and prepared to handle any situation.

95

When an employee voluntarily resigns, a common practice is to provide a two-week notice to the employer to make arrangements and transition the employee out of the organization. An exit interview is a best practice that many organizations utilize to provide the employee an opportunity to communicate what the organization does well and what the organization could do better. Additionally, questions regarding compensation, benefits, programs, training, opportunities, supervision, and other topics are appropriate to ask in order to learn more about the impact these items may have had in the decision to leave. Some organizations use this opportunity to ask questions about policy violations, harassment, discrimination, or other inappropriate behaviors that the employee may have witnessed or been subjected to during their employment. This information allows the organization to respond accordingly and take corrective action if necessary. Understanding the reasons why employees voluntarily exit an organization can help determine ways to retain current and future employees and address the gaps and needs to increase retention.

Turnover/Retention

Attrition is the rate at which employees are leaving an organization. Knowing the turnover rate is important, but knowing why employees are leaving the organization is even more important. If the turnover rate is low, it is important to know why employees are choosing to stay; simultaneously, if the turnover rate is high, it is important to know why employees are leaving. Retention can be encouraged through recognition and acknowledgement as well as ensuring appropriate and necessary compensation and benefits.

Employee Behavior Issues

Progressive Discipline

Employee discipline refers to the tool used by management to improve poor performance and enforce appropriate behavior to ensure a productive and safe workplace. It is vital to ensure that employee discipline is fair and equitable and that employees clearly understand the rules and regulations being enforced, the process to raise concerns and issues, the investigation process, and the penalties involved. If progressive discipline is utilized, employees should understand the intention and when it is appropriate to be used.

Progressive discipline is a discipline system that imposes progressively greater disciplinary measures based on the conduct of an employee. An example of this would be an employee receiving a written warning for attendance issues. If the attendance issues do not change after a stipulated period of time, the employee would receive a day of discipline imposed. Additional future incidents may then be given increased discipline time off until either the behavior is changed permanently or other corrective action is needed.

Similarly, it is important that employees understand some behavior may not warrant progressive discipline and the corrective action may be immediate termination. An example of this would be engaging in a physical altercation with or sexually harassing a fellow employee. Both of these examples would be appropriate to progress to discipline beyond a written warning after the first offense, including immediate termination after conducting a full investigation. Employees should have clearly defined expectations regarding their behavior and performance as well as what will occur if there are issues with either.

Absenteeism

Time and attendance procedures establish the requirements and expectations of employees regarding reliability and punctuality. Ensuring employees are available, on time, and at work maintains a productive and fair work environment for all employees. These procedures should communicate the process for requesting and scheduling time off from work, including vacation and illness leave, as appropriate. Procedures for requesting medical leave, such as the Family Medical Leave Act (FMLA), should also be detailed in the time and attendance procedures.

Employees should have a clear understanding of their responsibilities when it comes to not being at work. Excessive absenteeism and tardiness create a burden on the company and other employees. **Absenteeism** calculates how many employees are absent from work. Whether on vacation or sick leave, when employees are absent from work, there is a cost. Knowing this cost can be beneficial for staffing and workforce budgeting. When an employee will be late or absent at the last minute, it is important to have an established procedure in which they can call in to report being late or absent due to an emergency or unforeseen circumstance. Time and attendance procedures should also stipulate the consequences for failing to adhere to the expectations of being on time and at work. These consequences could include disciplinary action—up to and including termination—depending on the severity and frequency of the absences and tardiness.

Termination/Separation

Employees can be terminated from an organization for many reasons. **Involuntary terminations** are the separation of employees that are warranted due to poor performance, failure of probation, disciplinary actions due to inappropriate conduct or policy violations, or layoffs. **Voluntary terminations** are the separations of employees due to a decision made solely by the employee. Generally, voluntary terminations are resignations due to taking a position with another organization, retirement, or leaving the workforce due to personal reasons such as relocation, choosing to have a family and stay home with the children, or health concerns.

Organizations that have no choice but to end the employment relationship often work to create an affordable severance package for employees. Offering severance in the form of compensation, benefit extension, career transition services, employee assistance programs, and other services is an excellent option that can help employees transition out of the organization smoothly.

Employee Complaints, Investigations, and Conflict Resolution

Complaints and Conflict Resolution

Managing complaints or concerns should always be addressed in a fair and consistent manner regardless of the subject of the complaint. While specific complaints may require different processes due to complexity or legal issues, it is important to have standardized processes and practices. It is also important to understand when to inform leadership of issues and concerns. It may be appropriate to communicate a synopsis, including resolutions, at the end of a process for informational purposes only; however, based on the issue, severity, risks, and impacts, it may be necessary to communicate to leadership immediately after the complaint is received. Leadership may need to be involved in the investigation and process, including the recommendations and action plan to resolve the concerns. It is important to understand the level of communication needed based on the issue.

Handling complaints, either informal or formal, should follow a structured process. Employees should have a full understanding of how and to whom a complaint can be submitted as well as an understanding of how the process will unfold and an estimate of time needed. Seeking to understand as much as possible about the issue should be at the core of the process. This is accomplished by asking questions, researching practices, analyzing data, and following up on additional pieces of information gained throughout the process. Being respectful, responsive, attentive, empathetic, and available will assist in ensuring an effective complaint handling process.

The goal of handling any complaint is to resolve the issue at the lowest level possible. To be successful, employees, especially supervisors, should be trained in conflict resolution methods. **Conflict resolution** involves the following:

- Identifying the problem that is causing the issue

- Identifying the feelings, perceptions, and opinions regarding the issue

- Identifying the potential impacts of the issue as well as the impacts of any resolution implemented

- Identifying the recommendation and actions to implement to resolve the issue

- Working toward resolution of the issue

- Communicating the resolution with all parties as appropriate

If conflict resolution methods do not resolve the issue, then more formal approaches should be taken to escalate the issue. Ensuring that the issue is resolved in the most effective and efficient way possible is the goal of any process. Filing a grievance, submitting a formal complaint, or reaching out to other oversight organizations that investigate matters such as safety issues (Occupational Safety and Health Administration) or employment practices (Equal Employment Opportunity Commission) may be appropriate as a next step. However, it is important to note that depending on the issue, it may be appropriate to begin the complaint handling process at a more formal level. Examples of these issues would be sexual harassment, workplace violence, discriminatory practices regarding promotions, unsafe working conditions, or other concerns that deserve an escalated response. In each of these examples, leadership should be notified immediately to ensure that the issues are addressed promptly and appropriately. Once a case has been resolved, it may be appropriate to review applicable policies and procedures to ensure that necessary changes are made so that future incidents may be avoided.

Investigations

Internal investigations are conducted when issues arise or complaints are submitted. Regardless of how an issue comes to the attention of Human Resources, an investigation should be conducted to ensure that any concerns or potential policy violations are corrected and that appropriate responses and actions are delivered. Employees should understand how to submit a complaint regardless of who it is against or what the subject matter is. Internal investigations can be both informal and formal, but both should be conducted with good-faith efforts that result in a rational and supported conclusion. Informal investigations could result in a formal investigation to ensure the issues are fully reviewed and understood. Additionally, a formal investigation could result in an external third-party investigation to ensure impartiality and a full vetting of the issues from an outside perspective. While it is a best practice to attempt to resolve issues and concerns at the lowest level possible, there will always be a need to investigate claims and concerns. Human Resources professionals should be properly and formally trained to investigate complaints.

Internal investigations should always include interviews with the employee making the complaint, the employee who the complaint is against (if any), all witnesses to the incident, and any other party that may have firsthand information and knowledge of the incident. While it is a good practice to have prepared questions for all interviews, it is also appropriate to ask additional questions if new information is presented during the interview to ensure that a full understanding of the incident is gathered. It may be necessary to schedule follow-up interviews based on the information that is gathered or new evidence that is gained. At the conclusion of gathering all of the information, interviewing all of the appropriate parties, and assessing the credibility of the investigation, Human Resources professionals should prepare a conclusion and recommendation to resolve the initial complaint.

Investigation conclusions should be rational, specific, legally defensible, and based solely on the information gathered during the investigation. Resolution could be conflict resolution between two employees, changing policy or procedure to address a workplace issue, creating training programs for employees to work better together in a team dynamic, and/or discipline if appropriate. Multiple resolutions may be necessary to ensure that the issue is fully addressed and potential future occurrences are eliminated.

When conducting an internal investigation, there are various best practices to incorporate into the process to ensure a thorough and fair investigation. First, it is important to be proactive and not reactive. Investigators should take a proactive approach when gathering information from employees and researching data and details. Being proactive allows the organization to gather the most recent and current information available. Witnesses are more likely to remember details and specifics of an incident that is fresh and recent. It is harder to recount information regarding incidents that happened longer ago. Being proactive also includes being broad and open to identifying new resources that would have information pertinent to the case rather than relying on one individual's account of an incident. A common quote used to describe this is to "follow the leads." If an investigator follows the leads and goes where the evidence leads, the investigation is more likely to yield an accurate assessment and conclusion of the incident.

Second, it is important to agree to the purpose and specific issue being investigated. When employees understand what the investigation is attempting to define or discover, they are more likely to be able to provide specifics to the incidents being claimed. During the investigation, information may arise that is outside of the original scope, and it is important to ensure that either the initial investigation is expanded or a secondary investigation is conducted to review the new information.

Third, investigations should always be independent and impartial. Investigations should be conducted by individuals who can review the evidence, conduct interviews that are not biased, and are not looking for only one perspective. Depending on the professional relationship between the employee complaining and the Human Resources professional conducting the investigation, it may be appropriate to bring in an external investigator who can maintain impartiality. Not only does this allow for a fair and accurate investigation, conclusion, and proposed recommendation, but it also avoids allegations or the perception of conflicts of interest.

Fourth, completed investigations and recommendations should align with the organization's policies, procedures, and goals. If there is no alignment, based on the behavior of employees, the investigation may prompt a review and evaluation of the policies, procedures, and goals of the organization. Regularly reviewing these items against the behaviors of employees allows the organization to implement programs that can affect cultural change and promote appropriate and respectful behavior.

Finally, investigations should always consider the consequences and repercussions of the issues being brought forward and the effects of not handling and resolving the issues quickly and completely. Many states have laws that hold supervisors responsible for their behavior, as well as the organization, if appropriate actions are not taken to correct behavior or hold employees responsible. Society today is holding individuals to a higher standard regarding sexual harassment, and many federal statutes are being passed to ensure accountability, transparency, understanding, and consequences. In addition to this, many states are mandating frequent training and requirements regarding training for specific levels of employees. Supervisors may be required to frequently attend expanded training sessions to ensure a thorough knowledge and understanding of the responsibilities when supervising others. However, organizations are responsible for ensuring that training requirements are met and that actions are taken to address issues. By conducting fair, impartial, thorough, and proactive investigations, Human Resources professionals can protect employees and the organization.

Employee Rights

Employee rights refers to the rights that all employees have, including fair and equitable treatment, representation, privacy, grievances, and appeals processes. Employees have the right to know that any investigation conducted was fair and thorough, with sufficient opportunities provided to convey all sides of the situation. Employees should be afforded the right to representation, if applicable. If employees are represented by a union, representation should be offered, especially during disciplinary procedures and investigations. If an employee is not afforded this right, it could interfere with the integrity of the investigation and subsequent discipline. Employees should be afforded the right of privacy. Any disciplinary action, corrective counseling, investigation information, or other details specific to an employee should be held with an appropriate level of confidentiality. Additionally, employees should understand the rights associated with filing a grievance or appeal to resolve an issue or argue a decision such as a disciplinary action.

Retaliation and Documentation

Retaliation refers to an employer creating a negative consequence for an employee for engaging in a protected activity. Protected activities for retaliation include engaging with a union, filing a harassment complaint, or any other concern the employee may raise about a violation in the workplace. The typical consequences an employer may impose include suspension, demotion, firing, or any other event with adverse effects. Multiple laws prohibit employers from retaliating against an employee. Whistleblower protections are laws that protect employees from retaliation for revealing workplace violations committed by private or public employers. HR can help prevent retaliation concerns by ensuring proper documentation. Documentation refers to a record of a specific instance or occurrence within the workplace that provides evidence for a report on employment events. Proper documentation helps to provide information necessary to comply with regulations and show how the employer has addressed workplace concerns. Employees should also document events if they are concerned about retaliation. Documentation can be either written or electronic but should not be verbal so it can be referenced for later use.

Diversity and Inclusion Initiatives

Diversity is defined as the similarities, differences, and opportunities inherent in the individual and organizational characteristics that form the workplace. Diversity includes differences in gender, race, ethnicity, religion, age, generation, marital status, physical abilities, education, geographic background,

100

national origin, and experience. Understanding how each of these elements of diversity can enhance the workforce is a key function of HR professionals.

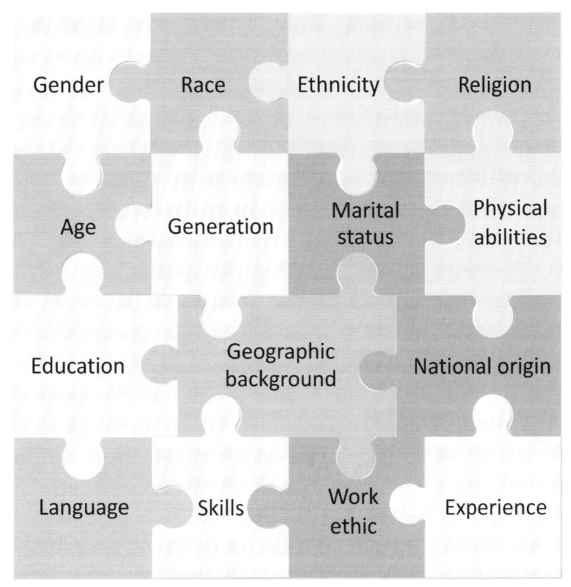

Inclusion is defined as respecting and valuing diversity. A simple and extremely accurate definition provided by Andres Tapia states that, "Diversity is the mix. Inclusion is making the mix work." Verna Myers provided the description "Diversity is being invited to the party; inclusion is being asked to dance." Both of these specific definitions provide the basis of how diversity is integral to inclusion, but inclusion is the actual end result and goal. Inclusion is not simply about being in the same location/office or working for the same company. Inclusion is intentionally engaging all employees in the achievement of objectives that are aligned with the overall success of an organization.

The impacts of a strong diversity and inclusion strategy are far reaching, beyond the internal employees and organization. The culture and core values of the organization are the foundation for the framework of an organization's mission and align with achieving the overall objectives. There are four main areas that an organization's diversity and inclusion strategy will impact:

- Workplace
- Workforce
- Marketplace
- Community

Diversity and inclusion within the workplace foster an inclusive environment in which different backgrounds, perspectives, behaviors, and experiences are valued and respected. Diversity and inclusion within the workforce build a diverse talent pipeline and provide high impact engagement, innovation, involvement, and development programs. Diversity and inclusion within the marketplace serve the diverse needs of customers, shareholders, and executive leadership through the products and services provided. Additionally, diversity within and among suppliers and vendors, as well as marketing efforts, is recognized with preference given to the brand and organization. Diversity and inclusion within the community shows the organization as a good corporate citizen with demonstrated social responsibility through community leadership, involvement, philanthropy, and volunteering. Overall, the organization is able to build and sustain a culture and environment where all employees are embraced and valued for who they are. This allows each employee to reach their full potential and enables the organization to meet and exceed the goals and achievements identified.

Historically, diversity initiatives were incorporated into organizations based on a moral imperative to have the workforce reflect the external labor market and community population. Recruitment programs and methods were incorporated to attract and hire individuals from various backgrounds. The issue that has become apparent over the years, however, is that simply hiring more diverse individuals is not enough and should not be the ending point for establishing a diverse working environment. Currently, organizations are focusing on inclusion and establishing an inclusive working environment for all employees. Organizations establish inclusion by:

- utilizing diverse perspectives and opinions to broaden problem solving, innovation, and creativity.
- encouraging collaboration and learning from differences, flexibility, and fairness.
- embedding inclusive values in organizational structures, policies, and practices.

Each individual has a distinct and unique set of skills, values, goals, and motivations for both their professional and personal life. For an organization to attract a diverse, talented, and best-in-class workforce, an inclusive environment and culture must be present.

To establish an inclusive workplace, four pillars must be created, supported, and functional: awareness, mobilization, action, and alignment.

Awareness is the pillar that raises the understanding and mindfulness of the organization and employees toward the diversity and inclusion initiatives. Awareness prepares employees for the acceptance of the culture and the willingness to accept changes that increase inclusion. Activities that encourage awareness include education, bias training, cultural immersion, and job training.

Mobilization is the pillar that sets up the policies, processes, procedures, and systems that allow for accountability for all employees at all levels.

Action is the pillar that implements the strategies through specific efforts and tactics. Activities within the action pillar include working with diverse suppliers and vendors, actively engaging employees to build an inclusive workplace, and structuring programs that align with inclusion.

Alignment is the pillar that is essential to ensuring a successful implementation of all diversity and inclusion strategies. Alignment focuses on analyzing, reviewing, and revising strategies, policies, and ways of conducting business to meet employee and customer expectations. Additionally, alignment strengthens innovation, engagement, and loyalty from both employees and customers.

For diversity and inclusion strategies to be successful, organizations must have leaders who understand and value a diverse workforce, as well as recognize the learning and challenges that different perspectives can provide. The organizational culture must create a high standard of performance for all employees at all levels and the culture must encourage openness, honesty, and transparency. The culture must stimulate personal development, make employees feel valued, and be clear in the commitment to employees. Finally, the organization must have a clear vision and define success related to diversity and inclusion.

Organizations that have a culture that values and is committed to diversity and inclusion see real and high-impact benefits. Diverse thinking and bringing in different opinions and perspectives leads to an almost seventy percent increase in innovation. Inclusive leadership and management increase the likelihood of new customers and employees, leading to an almost fifty percent increase in the likelihood to grow market share and market presence. Motivated teams lead to employees being twice as engaged and motivated to provide input and affect change. Overall, performance at all levels within the organization is stronger when diverse leadership and different experiences are available.

Social Responsibility Initiatives

Corporate social responsibility (CSR) is a sustainable, operational strategy that should be incorporated into policies, processes, and practices to ensure that the business operates in a socially acceptable manner to employees, leadership, stakeholders, and the public. CSR principles address social issues that are important to the workplace, marketplace, environment, and community beyond the concept of being a philanthropic organization. Many organizations have implemented environmental programs that limit printing to save paper or provide additional leave time for employees to perform charitable work; however, CSR goes beyond these concepts by working to incorporate these same types of principles throughout the organization at a deeper level. CSR incorporates the initiatives of values, commitment, integrity, honesty, collaboration, sensitivity, partnership, charity, and environmental focus at every level within the organization. In doing so, the organization will see numerous benefits such as increased employment engagement, lower turnover rates, higher productivity, stronger profitability, increased customer satisfaction, and more.

Companies must decide where they will fall on the spectrum of **corporate social responsibility** (CSR). For example, some companies only have a **social obligation**, which means they do nothing in addition to meeting their legal and economic responsibilities. Other companies experience a **social responsiveness** and choose to respond to some popular social needs by engaging in social actions. Some companies bear a **social responsibility**, which is a set intention to act in ways that are good for society and to do the right things.

Companies that practice CSR do not just view themselves as independent entities that are solely responsible to stockholders. Rather, these companies feel they have a moral responsibility to society at large and that it is necessary to become involved in legal, political, and social issues. Some arguments companies have for social responsibility include the following:

- CSR can be profitable and a good way for companies to attract top talent and build good public relations.

- Companies practicing CSR may help prevent new government regulations.

- Companies' stock prices will increase in the long run.

- Companies have the resources available to help solve problems found in society, such as pollution.

Cultural Sensitivity and Acceptance

It is important to understand cultural differences to ensure that HR initiatives align with the standards relevant to various cultures. For example, an informal birthday party is thrown for an employee. In some cultures, this may not be seen as a positive event and could create an awkward or tense dynamic with a team. Additionally, an employee may be offended if a cultural practice is not adhered to. HR should ensure that any HR practice, either formal or informal, aligns with cultural norms and standard behaviors. When employees see an organization's commitment to being culturally sensitive in its initiatives and programs, employees are more likely to be engaged, motivated, and satisfied.

When an organization has a presence in more than one country, it is important to understand how this global context affects the HR strategic plan. Incorporating global elements into HR plans helps to support the organization's overall initiatives and provide opportunities for employees. Providing training to employees that develops multicultural learning and awareness as well as relationship building provides for a more well-rounded workforce that can approach situations that are uniquely tailored to the specific country and culture. Being aware of and understanding the cultural differences, language barriers, acceptable norms, and appropriate practices is only one component of working in a global context. Having an awareness of the political, economic, societal, technological, legal, and environmental aspects

104

are also important, as they will have an impact on the organization and its business model. Ensuring that the employees are trained in these areas will allow for a more effective and productive workforce in these different countries.

Unconscious Bias and Stereotypes

HR professionals are responsible for ensuring that appropriate training and development opportunities are available to all employees. While some training opportunities are specific to an employee's position or level in an organization, many training opportunities should be made available to all employees, regardless of the function or scope of their role. Examples of training that should be available to everyone are communication, computer skills, leadership, time management, and diversity and inclusion. Many diversity and inclusion training programs incorporate sessions related to **biases**—both conscious and unconscious—so that employees can work to become self-aware of their own beliefs and opinions while working to address them. Becoming self-aware of an issue or belief and then working to address these issues or beliefs is a vital component to personal growth and development.

HR professionals should never take action against an employee based on personal bias, whether conscious or unconscious. If this is something that an HR professional cannot avoid, then they should consider another line of work. Ensuring fair and ethical treatment of all employees is the foundation of ethical human resources practices. Adverse actions based on personal biases could include discipline, demotion, or any other action that would have a negative impact on an employee and their employment situation. HR professionals should consider the facts, context, and detailed information gained through insightful and thorough investigation while adhering to legal and regulatory standards. Only when this is done should an HR professional move forward with actions to address inappropriate behavior.

The key to creating a diverse and inclusive culture is cultivating a workplace environment in which everyone feels wanted, respected, and supported. In doing so, the HR professional advocates for representation of candidates regardless of race, gender, sexual orientation, ethnicity, religious beliefs, country of origin, education, and abilities. In addition to advocating for a diverse workplace community, the HR professional is also responsible for confronting evidences of bias, stereotyping, harassment, microaggressions, and any form of exclusion that might be present within an organization.

Practice Quiz

1. During which step of the strategic planning process does environmental scanning take place?
   a. Strategy Formulation
   b. Strategy Development
   c. Strategy Implementation
   d. Strategy Evaluation

2. Which of the following is an example of a weakness that may be uncovered during a SWOT analysis that can affect an organization's ability to reach its objectives?
   a. Outdated equipment
   b. Consumer trends
   c. A labor shortage
   d. A changing political climate

3. Which of the following statements is used by a company to explain what it does differently from other companies?
   a. Code of conduct
   b. Mission statement
   c. Corporate values
   d. Vision statement

4. Teamwork, respect, safety, and integrity are examples of a company's _____.

5. An organization where employees have the freedom to make decisions on how they complete their tasks has a low degree of _____.

6. Match the key term with the appropriate description.
   a. Employee relations
   b. Employee involvement
   c. Employee communication
   d. Employee counseling
   e. Employee discipline
   f. Employee rights

   1. Process used to address a performance problem when training or coaching methods do not resolve the issue
   2. Study of the rules, policies, procedures, and agreements that employees are held accountable to
   3. Vertical and horizontal lines of messages
   4. Tools used by management to improve poor performance and enforce appropriate behavior
   5. Environment that values employees and seeks out input
   6. Privileges that all employees are afforded, including fair and equitable treatment

7. Drop and drag the types of message that align with each style of communication:
    a. Suggestion boxes
    b. Formal   Vertical
    c. Coordination
    d. Problem solving   Horizontal
    e. Informal
    f. Department meetings
    g. Peer-to-peer

8. What term is defined as the organization's commitment to foster a positive working relationship with its employees?
    a. Labor relations
    b. Workforce planning
    c. Employee relations
    d. Mission statement

9. What is the appropriate alignment, or order, of the four responsibilities of corporate social responsibility?
    a. Economic, legal, ethical, and philanthropic
    b. Legal, economic, philanthropic, and ethical
    c. Philanthropic, legal, economic, and ethical
    d. Ethical, philanthropic, legal, and economic

10. Which of the following is NOT one of the pillars of corporate social responsibility (CSR)?
    a. Economic
    b. Social
    c. Environmental
    d. Political

11. Which of the following hiring practices does NOT help employers ensure their hiring process is unbiased?
    a. Limit the number of people on the hiring team.
    b. Blindly review resumes.
    c. Use objective evaluation criteria.
    d. Use job experience, in lieu of education, when evaluating job candidates.

See answers on the next page.

Answer Explanations

1. B: Environmental scanning and a SWOT analysis are performed during the Strategy Development step of the strategic planning process. During this step, long-range plans are also established that will set the company's direction for the next three to five years.

2. A: Outdated equipment, unreliable suppliers, ineffective leadership, and insufficient marketing campaigns are examples of weaknesses that can be uncovered during a SWOT analysis. Internal weaknesses can potentially reduce a company's ability to reach its objectives and place it at a competitive disadvantage. Consumer trends are an example of an opportunity. A labor shortage and a changing political climate are examples of threats.

3. B: A mission statement tells employees what the company does, where the company is going in the mid to long term, and how the company is different and unique from other organizations. A code of conduct is a set of principles a company is committed to follow. Corporate values, such as integrity, open-mindedness, respect, safety, and teamwork, communicate to employees the standards by which they are expected to adhere to while conducting business. A vision statement is a concise statement that reflects organizational confidence and long-term aspirations regarding how a company will achieve more than economic success.

4. Values: Teamwork, respect, safety, and integrity are examples of a company's values.

5. Formalization: An organization that has jobs that are standardized, allowing for little discretion over what is to be done because the work is guided by rules, has a high degree of formalization. The opposite of this is low formalization, where employees have more freedom on how they can complete their tasks.

6. A – 2, B – 5, C – 3, D – 1, E – 4, & F – 6: Employee relations is the study of the rules, policies, procedures, and agreements that employees are managed against. Employee involvement is creating an environment that values employees and seeks out input directly from every individual. Employee communication refers to the messaging that occurs within an organization, both vertical and horizontal. Employee counseling is the process used to address a performance problem when training or coaching methods do not resolve the issue. Employee discipline refers to the tools used by management to improve poor performance and enforce appropriate behavior. Employee rights are the privileges that all employees are afforded, which include fair and equitable treatment.

7. Vertical – A, B, & F; Horizontal – C, D, E, & G: Vertical communications include suggestion boxes, department meetings, and are formal by nature. Horizontal communications include coordination, problem solving, peer-to-peer, and are informal by nature.

8. C: Employee relations is defined as the organization's commitment to foster a positive working relationship with its employees. Choice *A* is incorrect because labor relations refers to the actual relationship between an organization's leadership and the employees, often through a bargaining union. Choice *B* is incorrect because workforce planning is the process used to align an organization's needs and priorities with the available workforce and skills. Choice *D* is incorrect because the mission statement is the short statement that describes the fundamentals and goals of the organization.

9. A: The appropriate alignment, or order, of the four responsibilities of corporate social responsibility are economic, legal, ethical, and philanthropic. The foundation of economics must be solid to then allow the CSR to expand to the next level of legal, then ethical, and finally philanthropic. Choices *B, C,* and *D* are

108

incorrect because they are not representative of the appropriate alignment of the CSR responsibilities. Without a solid economic foundation, the organization will not be able to continue to build further into the other responsibilities.

10. D: Political is not one of the pillars of CSR. Environmental responsibility in CSR means employers should be as environmentally friendly as possible. Economic responsibility refers to making financial decisions that work in the best interest of the people, the environment, and society, not just the business. Social responsibility refers to creating a work environment that protects human rights.

11. A: Companies should ensure that the hiring team comprises individuals of diverse backgrounds and experiences to create more diverse and inclusive hiring practices. Limiting the hiring team to only a few individuals may also limit the diversity of the hiring team and can create biased candidate evaluations.

Compliance and Risk Management

Records Management

Effective records and information management is extremely important. Human Resources professionals should familiarize themselves with all federal and state regulations regarding recordkeeping. Different pieces of information have different retention periods to maintain compliance. Ensuring compliance is extremely important because if an organization is outside of compliance, the ramifications, such as paying hefty fines or losing data critical for lawsuits, could be far reaching and expensive. Ensuring a robust recordkeeping process should be a high priority to limit exposure and liability for an organization.

Personnel files are one of the most important and fundamental recordkeeping functions within Human Resources. When an employee is hired, a file should be created that is the primary storage location for all matters relating to the individual employees. The personnel file should include, but is not limited to:

- Recruitment flyer for position hired into

- Application

- Offer letter and acceptance

- New hire checklist

- New hire documents, including the employee's employment eligibility form (I-9), federal and state tax forms, direct deposit form, benefits enrollment paperwork, and copies of all corresponding documentation such driver's license, passport, social security card, marriage license, birth certificate, and voided check(s)

As an employee continues employment with the organization, new forms and documents should be added to the personnel file. This could include promotional offers of employment, benefits change forms, performance evaluations, medical leave requests and documentation, disciplinary records, training records, and letters of resignation or termination. It is important to understand the retention rules regarding the personnel file as well as the items contained within the personnel file when applying the organization's policies to files. As with any other policy, it is necessary to review recordkeeping policies and practices frequently. If updates are needed, they should be vetted and fully understood before implementation. As retention schedules are changed, organizations should see that updates to the policies are implemented swiftly to ensure compliance with the new required timeframe.

An organization may choose to standardize a filing system in which all records for an employee are maintained within the personnel file; a common best practice is to separate specific documents and maintain a separate filing system. This type of filing practice can be easier to use in cases of audits or file destruction. Reviewing all employee files could be cumbersome and time-consuming; however, if an organization must review all of the I-9 forms to ensure those that require destruction per the retention period are completed, it would be much easier to have a specified binder or file with all employee I-9 documents available. Similarly, training documents would also be another file to maintain separately to ensure easier access when reviewing statistics and ensuring compliance for mandatory training.

When establishing methods for recordkeeping, organizations should ensure that records are maintained to meet the internal needs of the business as well as the department that is managing them. Records should be maintained in such a way that can assist in defending actions and providing justifications and history. Organizations must remain in compliance regarding records and are also responsible for ensuring that resources are available and used in the most efficient and effective manner possible.

All records should be kept in a manner that ensures privacy and confidentiality. From locking cabinets to establishing a locking mechanism on the doors to rooms that house personnel files, Human Resources should make every attempt and effort to safeguard employee personnel files. Information contained within these files is sensitive and includes everything from social security numbers, dates of birth, and other information for the employee as well as for their spouse and children. If a data breach does occur, organizations should do everything to ensure that their employees and families are protected in the case of identity theft.

In addition to employee personnel files, organizations are also required to keep thorough and detailed records specific to areas within the organization. Each department is responsible for maintaining compliance regarding records specific to their areas of expertise.

Many organizations have shifted to electronic platforms to manage employee records, documents, and information; however, efforts still must be taken to ensure confidentiality and privacy to protect the data. Cybersecurity has escalated with the increase of hacking, phishing, and malware, and it provides a different level of protection.

Laws Related to Employee/Employer Rights and Responsibilities

The United States has many federal and state laws and regulations regarding the rights of employees and the responsibilities of employers. These laws are in the primary areas of discrimination, pay, employee privacy, and workplace safety. Each of these areas have specific government agencies working to enforce the laws—the Equal Employment Opportunity Commission (EEOC) enforces the laws regarding discrimination, the Department of Labor (DOL) enforces the laws regarding compensation, the Department of Justice (DOJ) enforces the laws regarding employee privacy, and the Occupational Safety and Health Administration (OSHA) enforces the laws regarding workplace safety. As an HR professional, it is vital to have an awareness and full understanding of these laws and regulations at both the federal and state levels. Many state laws have elements that are more expansive and inclusive than the federal laws. In these cases, the law that provides the higher level of benefit to the employee should be followed.

A general rule of thumb is that the federal law is the minimum level of benefit afforded to an employee. If state legislation creates a more comprehensive law that provides additional benefits, those standards should be followed. Additionally, HR professionals should know how these laws and regulations are applied to an organization's policies, practices, and procedures. While there are some businesses that may be exempt from particular laws due to the size of the organization or other factors, most organizations must adhere to all components of these areas that are dictated in the law. If an organization does not comply with these laws and regulations, the penalties could be severe.

Laws and Regulations Related to Talent Acquisition

Hiring programs must comply with all federal hiring laws; these include Title VII of the Civil Rights Act of 1964 (Title VII), the Americans with Disabilities Act (ADA), the Age Discrimination in Employment Act (ADEA), and the Fair Labor Standards Act (FLSA). These laws ensure that all individuals—regardless of their gender, race, ethnicity, religious affiliation, physical ability, or age—are afforded the same rights for a fair hiring opportunity. Additionally, some states have their own hiring laws to comply with. Sometimes the state law differs from the federal law; in these situations, the law that is the most generous to the individual is the law that should be followed. Human Resources professionals must ensure that recruitment and hiring methods comply with the most generous level of protection.

Disparate impact is an important hiring practice concept. **Disparate impact** means policies or practices disproportionately impact a specific group of individuals. Artificial recruitment barriers can increase the likelihood of disparate impact. An **artificial recruitment barrier** is a qualification that is not truly necessary for a particular position but that could cause applicants to be disqualified from consideration. If an audit shows that a particular protected class now has been screened out from consideration due to this barrier, a disparate impact has occurred. Organizations should strive to regularly audit their hiring and selection processes to ensure that all qualifications are appropriate and screening processes are fair and equitable.

An organization's policies should ensure that all candidates are provided with a fair and equitable opportunity to be considered for employment. Policies should clearly communicate rights as well as responsibilities of the employer and the candidate. These policies are especially important when making decisions to disqualify or remove a candidate from consideration. One such reason for disqualification is nepotism. **Nepotism** is defined as favoritism based on a personal or familial relationship such as friendship, marriage, or family connection. If a candidate has a familial or personal relationship with a hiring manager or supervisor, it may present a conflict of interest. In circumstances such as this, it is important to have a policy that identifies which relationships—both personal and professional –disqualify a potential candidate from consideration.

A nepotism policy should clearly define which exclusions and exceptions will be made. Although a husband may not be able to report directly to his wife as a manager, he may be able to be employed in a different department where he has no direct reporting relationship or connection to his spouse. Some organizations may stipulate that spouses simply cannot work for the organization, in an effort to mitigate any potential conflicts of interest. Nepotism policies should clearly outline any and all exceptions so that there is no confusion. Candidates should be asked about nepotism early in the application process. Many organizations have a standard question in the initial application, such as "Do any of your relatives work for this organization? If yes, who?" These questions enable an immediate review of the nepotism policy in relation to each specific circumstance. Any decision to disqualify an applicant from consideration should be connected to and supported by a specific written policy.

EEOC, Title VII, and the ADA

Title VII was passed in 1964 and originally prohibited discrimination in employment based on race, color, sex, religion, or national origin. After multiple amendments, the following protected classes were added: disability, pregnancy, and genetic information. Title VII was amended in 1972 to add educational institutions and again in 1991 to provide remedies for individuals who have been discriminated against. The **Equal Employment Opportunity Commission (EEOC)** is responsible for investigating complaints of Title VII violations and making determinations to file a lawsuit in federal or state court. Additionally, individuals who believe they are the victims of discrimination can also file a lawsuit directly. It is important to understand that harassment is a form of discrimination and Title VII therefore prohibits harassment on the basis of race, color, sex, religion, national origin, age, disability, pregnancy, or genetic information.

The **ADEA** was passed in 1967 and prohibits discrimination on the basis of age. The ADEA stipulates that an employer may not fail or refuse to hire an individual based on age. An employer may not terminate an individual based on age. An employer may not fail to provide or offer employment opportunities such as

112

promotions or transfers based on age. An employer may not reduce an individual's wage based on age. No employment action may be taken simply due to an individual's age. Originally, this law protected individuals from ages 40 to 65. In 1986, the upper age limit was removed completely.

The **ADA** is a civil rights law that was passed in 1990 and prohibits employment discrimination on the basis of disability. A disabled individual can request reasonable accommodations to allow them to perform the essential functions of their job. Employers are required to provide these reasonable accommodations as requested; however, the accommodations must be reasonable. If the accommodations create an undue hardship or change the job substantially, the employer may have the right to decline the accommodations.

The **Pregnancy Discrimination Act (PDA)** was passed in 1978 as an amendment to Title VII and bans employment discrimination against women who are pregnant. The PDA requires employers to treat pregnancy just like any other medical condition. In doing so, pregnancy is, therefore, covered under the ADA and afforded the same protections. An employer may not refuse to hire a woman or terminate a current employee because she is pregnant. Additionally, employers may not force a pregnant employee to take pregnancy leave prior to the birth of her child if she is able to work. During the recruitment process, the PDA prohibits an employer from asking questions about family plans or other personal details such as marital status and number of children.

The **Genetic Information Nondiscrimination Act (GINA)** was passed in 2009 and prohibits discrimination in employment based on genetic information. Employers may not ask an applicant or employee to provide genetic information, submit to a genetic test, or discuss family genetics. An employer may never use genetic information to make an employment decision as this information is not relevant to an individual's ability to do the work. This law has been especially important relative to health insurance coverage because a genetic condition may be considered a pre-existing condition so some insurance companies may deny coverage. Between GINA and the Affordable Care Act (ACA), individuals are now protected from being discriminated against from both angles of being employed and being provided with insurance coverage.

DOL

The **Department of Labor (DOL)** administers and enforces over 180 federal laws, many of which govern the areas of Wages and Hours, Workplace Safety and Health, Workers' Compensation, Employee Benefit Safety, Unions and Their Members, and Garnishment of Wages. While all federal laws and regulations are important and must be incorporated into an organization's policies and practices, the focus of this section is on the following: the **Family and Medical Leave Act (FMLA)**.

The Family and Medical Leave Act (FMLA) of 1993 requires covered employers to provide employees with job protection and unpaid leave for qualifying medical and family reasons.

FMLA entitles eligible employees to take up to twelve weeks of unpaid, job-protected leave each year for the following reasons:

- The birth or care of a child
- The placement of a child for adoption or foster care
- The care of a child, spouse, or parent with a serious health condition
- The employee's own serious health condition

Additionally, covered servicemembers with a serious injury or illness may take up to twenty-six weeks of FMLA leave. Organizations must be covered under the FMLA law to be able to offer their employees FMLA—this requires employing more than fifty employees for at least 20 weeks of the calendar year. Employees must have been employed with this employer at least twelve months and have worked a minimum of 1,250 hours within that time period to be eligible for FMLA.

While FMLA is unpaid, employees can take their accrued leave to cover this time and ensure they remain in a paid status while on FMLA. Depending on the organization's policies, employees usually can take sick leave, vacation leave, personal leave, and other forms of leave to receive a paycheck during the time being on FMLA. Many states such as California have programs such as disability insurance and paid family leave for which employees can apply to assist with compensation while out on FMLA. Organizations can then coordinate benefits with these state programs so that employees receive the maximum amount of benefits while on FMLA. Human Resources and Payroll will work with the employee and the state agencies to provide accurate compensation and leave information to coordinate benefits and determine how to best assist the employee during their leave. In many cases, depending on the salary, leave balances, and state benefits, an employee may be able to collect one hundred percent of their salary between all the available benefits during their FMLA leave.

It is also important to understand that certain states may have their own regulations allowing additional unpaid leave relating to specific qualifying events. For example, in the state of California, the California Family Rights Act (CFRA) allows for eligible employees to take additional unpaid time off for qualified leave requests. These additional state laws require a robust partnership between Human Resources and Payroll to ensure that employees receive the maximum benefits allowable under federal and state laws. Understanding how each regulation works and how they interconnect or differ from each other is vital to ensuring that policies are written to reflect all benefits afforded to employees. These policies should be reviewed periodically to ensure that they comply with the current regulations. As lawmakers frequently pass new bills to add, change, or update benefits, it is vital to ensure that the organization complies with managing an employee's FMLA and other leave benefits. And as previously mentioned, if there are differences between the federal and state laws, the law that is the most generous to the employee is the law that should be followed.

I-9 Form Completion

Employment Eligibility Verification, Form I-9, is a document used by employers to verify the identity and employment authorization of candidates chosen for employment in the United States. Form I-9's main purpose is to ensure employer compliance with the Immigration Reform and Control Act (IRCA) passed in 1986. The IRCA ultimately prohibits any individual who is not legally authorized to work in the US from gaining employment. HR professionals must provide employees with the I-9 and assist them in completing the form in an accurate and timely manner. HR professionals should provide training and education throughout the process of I-9 completion whenever questions or issues arise from the employee. Training should cover the proper form completion practices, identification of acceptable documents provided in section two of the form, and the importance of avoiding discrimination. Additionally, the standard procedures for handling reverifications, rehires, and any other updates to the form—such as a change in address or legal name—should also be covered in Form I-9 completion training.

There are three distinct sections included in the I-9. Section one of the form is completed by employees on their first scheduled day or any time after formally accepting the job offer. Section one asks the employee for his or her legal name, date of birth, current address, and citizenship status among other

114

identifying information, if applicable. Section two of the form must be completed by the employer within three days of the employee's start date. The purpose of section two is for the employer to review any identifying documents provided by the candidate—such as a driver's license, birth certificate, or passport—and make note of the legitimacy of those documents, the dates of when they are being reviewed, and the employee's start date. Employers are required by law to examine the original documents provided by employees and verify that they appear to be related to the employee and are genuine. Once section two has been completed, HR professionals should retain the completed form for the required period of time, which is the later of either three years after the employee's date of hire or one year after the employee leaves the organization. Section three is only completed if the employee requires employment reauthorization, the employment authorization has expired, or they undergo a legal name change.

Laws and regulations surrounding Form I-9 completion must be adhered to, and HR professionals must be aware of and understand them. Violating the laws and regulations contained in the IRCA can lead to severe penalties such as loss of government contracts, fines, and criminal charges. Employers can be subjected to investigations and audits by the US Immigrations and Customs Enforcement (ICE) to establish compliance with Form I-9 requirements. There are three distinct categories or factors that can trigger an I-9 audit from the Department of Homeland Security (DHS) in conjunction with ICE. The three categories are complaints from individuals (usually current or former employees), data analysis, and government resources through information provided by other federal agencies, like the IRS. HR professionals should establish stringent processes internally for maintaining accurate records and self-audits, subsequently correcting any deficiencies or errors. HR professionals can effectively minimize organizational risk by cooperating with government agencies during audits and investigations.

Employment-at-Will

At-will employment means an employer can terminate an employee for any reason, at any time. An employee can also leave an organization at any time without notice or consequences under employment-at-will. At-will employment does not excuse an employer from wrongful termination, and the organization is still responsible for following legal guidelines. Any violation of employee acts or protected classes could result in a wrongful termination lawsuit. Exceptions to employment-at-will include express or implied contracts, where the organization makes a written or verbal agreement with the employee regarding terms of employment.

Immigration Reform and Control Act

The Immigration Reform and Control Act of 1986 (IRCA) prohibits employers from knowingly hiring or referring employees who are unauthorized to work. The act also makes it unlawful for an employer to continue to employ an alien, knowing their unauthorized work status. The Immigration and Naturalization Service enforces the IRCA. Employers who do not comply could be subject to civil and criminal liability. The IRCA also requires employers to verify and attest to the worker's employment eligibility. To ensure compliance, employers must document an I-9 form that identifies the employee's citizenship status and employment eligibility.

Title 17 (Copyright Law)

The **Copyright Act of 1976** is the foundational law in the United States regarding property ownership of literary and pictorial works, radio, film, musical and dramatic works, and architectural structures. The statute supersedes all local and state copyright laws.

In order to lawfully reproduce, disseminate, modify, publicly display, or perform copyrighted material, one must hold a copyright over such material—published or unpublished. Stipulated by the Copyright Act of 1976, a copyright lasts for the duration of the author's life, plus an additional 70 years after their death.

However, the law incorporates a policy of "fair use." Fair use enumerates some instances in which a person may use copyrighted material and is determined by the following:

- The intended purpose of the work (e.g., commercial gain or nonprofit education)
- The nature or type of work in question
- The amount or proportion of the copyrighted work being used
- The potential variation in market value

Educational purposes, research, scholarship, teaching, or news reporting are the categories that would determine the applicability of fair use.

When employees create original works in the course of their employment at a company, they are unable to claim ownership of copyrights. Since their employer paid them to complete the work, the employer owns any associated copyrights. Additionally, in some instances, an employer hires freelance employees to complete work on behalf of a company (i.e., freelance marketers). In this case, the employer also owns any associated copyrights for the end work products because the employer commissioned the work to be completed. This is known as a **work-for-hire exception**. HR personnel can assist management with any confusion that may occur surrounding intellectual property ownership.

Laws Related to Employment in Union Environments

WARN Act

The **Worker Adjustment and Retraining Notification Act of 1988 (WARN)** requires employers with over one hundred employees to provide sixty days advanced notice to affected employees before closing a plant or enacting a mass layoff. The WARN Act protects employees by ensuring that employees and their families can transition and plan for a potential loss of employment by seeking alternative employment or taking advantage of workforce training programs. In cases of an unexpected event resulting in a business closure, employers must provide the Department of Labor with the circumstances and information of the closure to determine whether or not they are exempt from WARN.

NLRA

The **National Labor Relations Act (NLRA)** is the basic law governing relations between labor unions and employees, giving employees the right to organize and bargain collectively. The NLRA is also known as the **Wagner Act** and was passed in 1935. The NLRA prohibits both employers and unions from violating the basic rights of employees, which include the following:

- The right to self-organize a union to negotiate with the employer
- The right to form, join, or assist labor organizations
- The right to bargain collectively about wages, working conditions, and other subjects
- The right to discuss employment terms and conditions of employment
- The right to choose representatives to bargain
- The right to take action to improve working conditions by raising work-related complaints
- The right to strike and picket, as appropriate

116

- The right to engage in protected activities
- The right to refrain from any of the above

Additionally, the NLRA stipulates that employers cannot prohibit employees from soliciting for a union during nonwork time or from distributing union literature or communications during nonwork time. The NLRA also prohibits the union from threatening employees with termination or other unjust actions unless union support is given. Finally, the NLRA established the **National Labor Relations Board (NLRB).** The NLRB certifies organized labor unions, supervises elections, and has the power to act against unfair business practices.

The NLRA establishes that both parties must negotiate and bargain in "good faith." **Good faith bargaining** refers to the honest attempt made by both the employer and union to reach an agreement. Good faith bargaining does not obligate either the employer or union to specific concessions or proposals. The basic requirements for bargaining in good faith include approaching negotiations with sincere resolve to reach an agreement, meeting regularly and at reasonable times, putting agreements in writing if requested, and having authorized representatives available and present at the scheduled times. The NLRA also establishes that mandatory subjects of bargaining must be negotiated between labor and management. **Mandatory subjects of bargaining** include wages, benefits, time off, hours, seniority, safety conditions, working conditions, employee testing protocols, disciplinary procedures, and recruitment issues such as promotion and demotion.

In 1947, the **Taft-Hartley Act**, or the **Labor-Management Relations Act,** was passed to amend the NLRA and limit employee labor rights. The Taft-Hartley Act provided that employers also have the right to go to the NLRB and allows for protections to the employers. This act prohibited unions from engaging in the following behavior:

- Forcing employees to support and join the union
- Refusing to bargain in good faith with employers
- Carrying out certain kinds of strikes
- Charging excessive union fees
- Going on strike during certain periods of time

It also provides for a cooling-off period in negotiation. Additionally, this act allowed states to pass "right-to-work laws," banned union contributions to political campaigns, required that union leaders swear they were not communists, and allowed for government intervention in certain circumstances. Finally, the Taft-Hartley Act established the **Federal Mediation and Conciliation Service (FMCS)** to help resolve negotiating disputes.

In 1959, the **Landrum-Griffin Act,** or the **Labor-Management Reporting and Disclosure Act,** was passed to again amend the NLRA. The Landrum-Griffin Act increased reporting requirements, regulated union affairs, and protected union members from improper union leadership to safeguard union member rights and prevent inappropriate practices by employers and union officers. This act is a bill of rights for union members, providing election procedures, accounting practices, and leadership oversight. This act was intended to protect the interests of the individual union members. This act provides union members the right to:

- Identify and propose candidates for office
- Vote in elections to select a board of representatives
- Attend and participate in union meetings

- Vote on union business
- Review and audit union accounts and records for transparency and accountability
- File grievances against union officers as appropriate to protect the integrity of the union

The history of unions in the United States goes back to ensuring a fair wage for a fair day's work, with employers providing a safe workplace. Employees should leave work in the same physical condition that they arrived. While there are various federal laws enacted to protect worker's rights as discussed above, as well as laws that protect wages, working conditions, safety and wellness, and other areas of concern, some individuals still want unions to represent their interest with employers.

While there are many misperceptions about why employees might consider and want a union, the following are the most common reasons for unionizing a workforce:

- Poor communications
- Poor leadership and management
- Supervisor and employee treatment
- Stagnate wages and benefits
- Healthcare and retirement plans
- Safety and working conditions
- Workload and stress
- Job security
- Employee morale
- Lack of employee recognition and appreciation

There is usually not one specific reason that a group of employees may look to unionize, but rather a culmination of multiple factors that lead to a disengaged, unmotivated, and dissatisfied group of employees.

Collective Bargaining

The first major labor statute passed in the United States was the Norris-LaGuardia Act of 1932. The **Norris-LaGuardia Act** endorsed collective bargaining as public policy and established government recognition that the job to a worker is more important than a worker to a corporation. Establishing this relationship was vital in showing that the only real power an employee has is in impacting employers through concerted activity. While this act did not create new rights, it curbed the power of courts to intervene in labor disputes and declared that unions could operate free from corporate control and interference.

Collective bargaining refers to the process of negotiation between management and union representatives regarding issues such as compensation, benefits, working hours, disciplinary processes, layoffs and terminations, grievance and arbitration processes, union activities, and employee rights. Furthermore, collective bargaining is the continued relationship between management and union representatives that involves the exchange of commitments to resolve conflicts and issues. While collective bargaining is required by law for both parties to negotiate in good faith, success is only achieved when both parties are willing to listen, understand, and compromise. **Good faith bargaining** refers to the duty of both parties to demonstrate a sincere and honest intent to reach agreement, be reasonable, communicate honestly, and negotiate in the best interest of the employees. It is important to note that collective bargaining is a group action that many refer to as an art form. Collective bargaining should not be a competitive process, but rather a continuous and logical process that involves strategy and understanding.

Collective bargaining is the formal process to negotiate contracts and agreements between an employer and union representative. There are various objectives that collective bargaining seeks to achieve:

- Settle disputes or conflicts regarding wages, benefits, working conditions, or safety concerns

- Protect employees' interests

- Resolve differences over difficult and stressful issues

- Negotiate voluntarily and as needed, without the influence or interference of an outside third party who is not as familiar with the organization and employees

- Agree to amicable terms and conditions through a give-and-take strategy

- Co-exist and work together peacefully for the mutual benefit and morale of all employees

- Maintain employee and employer relationships

A best practice that many negotiators utilize at the bargaining table is to establish ground rules at the beginning of the process. **Ground rules** refer to a set of items agreed upon by both parties to assist the negotiations process. Ground rules establish respect for both parties, the time and efforts each puts forth, and other specific areas that may arise during negotiations. Ground rules should establish the following:

- Who speaks for the parties and the individuals representing each party

- When subject matter experts will be called in and the specific purpose

- Where, when, and how long the parties will meet

- A cut-off date for submitting new proposals

- How formal proposals and responses will be made

- Communications plans regarding media or external communications

- What form of agreement will be acceptable: full and complete document or an itemized list of changes agreed to

- Any other specific details pertinent to the negotiations

There are five basic steps to the collective bargaining process: prepare, discuss, propose, bargain, and settlement. While this process is shown below as a linear process, there can be multiple twists and turns when bargaining in real life. Negotiators should be prepared for surprises and unexpected events that could derail negotiations.

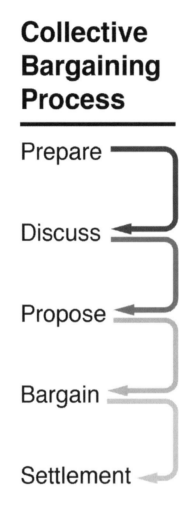

Collective Bargaining Process

Prepare

Discuss

Propose

Bargain

Settlement

Prior to beginning the negotiation process, it is vital for both sides to begin preparation and determining what needs to be changed, added, updated, deleted, or remain status quo. Each side should come to the negotiation table well prepared and ready to begin discussions. During discussions, new ideas may be presented from the opposing side that require additional preparation before they can be conducted. This should be discussed, and a plan to engage in further discussions should be made.

Proposals should be given that are thoughtful and based on the needs of the party. They should be clear, concise, and fully communicate the intent of the suggestion as well as provide an understanding of the effects of the change. The employer usually bears the responsibility of costing out a contract and determining the expenses related to new proposals. As each new proposal is discussed, the open dialogue should include transparency regarding the costs associated with each. If an organization only has authorization to spend a certain amount of money to settle a contract, there will need to be negotiations conducted about how to spend that money. If every proposal has a cost attached, each side may have to agree to the proposals that will meet the cost allocation provided and have the most positive impact to the organization and employees.

An example of this is proposing a five percent increase in wages and additional time off that would equate to an additional two percent increase in cost. If the organization is only approved to negotiate an increase of four percent, the parties may want to negotiate a smaller increase to both wages and time off so that both areas are receiving an increase while the overall cost is within the approved cost threshold. When situations like this arise, it is vital to understand the needs and wants of the employees so that the best decision can be made. When all of the proposals have been discussed and bargaining has occurred for each, the parties can agree to the terms and conditions through a formal settlement.

Each side should have the opportunity to review the final documents before signing. Once the official settlement has occurred, the union representatives must then begin the education and communication process with the membership for ratification of the proposal. **Ratification** is the process in which represented employees vote to approve or deny the proposed settlement. If the settlement is ratified, then the organization will move forward to receiving final approval through a board or executive authority and then finally implementing the terms of the settlement.

Once a final settlement is achieved and ready for implementation, it is important to roll out a communication plan so that employees will understand what will happen and when. Employees should clearly understand what changed, what stayed the same, and, if appropriate, why.

ADR Methods

Alternative dispute resolution (ADR) refers to many different processes and techniques that assist two parties in resolving their issues without filing a lawsuit or going to court. ADR processes include informal and voluntary processes such as negotiation and mediation as well as formal and mandatory processes such as conciliation and arbitration. The more informal the process, the more control each party has regarding recommendations to the resolution. The two parties are generally negotiating between themselves without intervention. As the process becomes more formal, there is less control by either party as an arbitrator, judge, or jury determines the resolution. The goals of ADR are to expedite the exchange of information and decision making, while lowering costs and achieving resolution quickly and confidentially.

The techniques used in ADR are flexible and can be customized to the parties involved and the specific issue that requires resolution. **Negotiation** is a voluntary agreement that works out a solution directly between the two parties involved. **Mediation** is a facilitated negotiation that works out a solution between the two parties through a neutral third party or mediator. **Conciliation** is a non-binding formal process in which a conciliator explains the law and provides the parties with non-binding recommendations to resolve the issue. **Arbitration** is a formal process in which an arbitrator considers evidence presented by each party and determines a solution that is binding and final. It is a common practice to work through the four ADR processes respectively, as described above. Progressing through the four ADR processes above prior to filing a lawsuit or claim is an appropriate path to follow if the matter cannot be resolved. Human Resources is an important resource for each of these steps as HR professionals can provide insights and information that can assist with negotiating an agreement at any of these levels.

Laws Related to Compensation and Benefits

Regardless of the programs offered concerning total rewards, each program must be federally compliant with all laws. It is important to remember that some states have their own individual laws and versions of compliance. In some cases, the state law does not align with the federal law. In these situations, it is important to remember that, in general, the law that is the most generous to the employee is the law that should be followed. From the Fair Labor Standards Act (FLSA), the Family and Medical Leave Act (FMLA), Americans with Disabilities Act (ADA), Affordable Care Act (ACA), and other state leave programs providing benefits such as paid family leave, additional leave rights, disability, and workers' compensation, Human Resources professionals must ensure that every benefit and program aligns with the most generous level of benefit provided.

An organization's policies should ensure that employees receive compensation and benefits in alignment with these federal laws. Policies should clearly communicate to employees their rights as well as the responsibilities of the employer and employee. While an employer may offer FMLA because the company employs more than fifty employees, it should be clearly communicated that employees must be employed for twelve months and have worked at least 1,250 hours in that twelve-month time period to be eligible under the FMLA law. The policy should also clearly communicate the procedure for applying for this benefit, what the benefit is (including how compensation is handled), and what is expected of both parties throughout the process. In the same manner, employees should know the process for working with their employer if they have a disability under the ADA. This process should be clearly outlined in the policy and include the rights and responsibilities of the employer and employee, the complete process, including how to request reasonable accommodations and work restrictions, and how independent medical evaluations will be handled.

Additionally, it is important to understand the **Equal Pay Act (EPA)** of 1963. Gender equality in pay is a major topic of discussion today, and organizations must ensure that their practices regarding compensation and benefits are compliant with these laws. The EPA amended the FLSA law relative to gender inequality to ensure that men and women are paid the same wage for the same work. The Equal Pay Act of 2010 was passed to help correct the disparity that many women faced regarding their pay when doing similar jobs that their male counterparts were doing. This law helped to ensure that a woman's contract terms for a position were the same as a man's contract terms. Continued legislation has been seen to correct these disparities as well. Recently, the state of California passed a law stating that an organization cannot request historical salary information from a candidate to use in preparing an offer of employment. The reasoning for this is that if a woman has experienced discrimination in her job history relative to pay and that information is used to determine her new salary, the disparity of pay will most likely continue and never be corrected.

Monetary and Non-Monetary Entitlement

Monetary entitlements refer to all of an employee's financial compensation included in their financial compensation package. Bonuses, commissions, incentives, and base salary, as well as any other form of direct financial payments in return for work, are included in monetary entitlements. HR professionals should be aware of the laws surrounding monetary entitlements, for example, minimum wage and overtime regulations. Non-monetary entitlements encompass any benefits or rewards given to employees that are non-financial in nature. The most common facets of non-monetary entitlements are health insurance, training and development programs, paid time off, and retirement plans. Often, an employee will be required to accrue a predefined number of hours or wages to qualify for non-monetary benefits such as PTO. Legal requirements included in the Employee Retirement Income Security Act and the Affordable Care Act (among others that affect the provision of these benefits) are important for HR professionals to be aware of.

As previously stated, HR professionals need to ensure that any benefits, monetary or non-monetary, are provided in accordance with employment laws. The Family and Medical Leave Act, the Fair Labor Standards Act, and the Equal Pay Act are a few noteworthy examples, though there are many others. Maintaining a thorough understanding of these laws is crucial in avoiding legal risks and ensuring fair and equitable employees. All employees should be provided with clear and transparent information regarding all applicable types of compensation and benefits and any possible restrictions on them. In addition to communication with employees, HR professionals should maintain accurate documentation of all entitlements to stay within legal compliance and in the case of any dispute so that it may be accurately resolved.

ERISA

The Employee Retirement Income Security Act of 1974 (ERISA) is a law that establishes the minimum criteria an organization must provide their employees for their retirement and health plans. The Department of Labor enforces ERISA and requires private-sector business to provide plan participants with information about the plan features and funding. Governmental agencies, churches, and benefit plans required to comply with laws on workers' rights are not covered under ERISA. ERISA sets minimum standards for plan areas like reporting, protection, plan participation, fiduciary standards, and information disclosures. To comply with ERISA, employers must provide specific plan information to all participants and act in the participants' best interest. ERISA covers defined benefit plans, such as 401(k)s, and pension plans. ERISA ensures employers cannot remove retirement or pension benefits without legal repercussions.

COBRA

The Consolidated Omnibus Budget Reconciliation Act of 1985 (COBRA) gives workers and their dependents who lose health care coverage from their group health plan the ability to maintain their coverage for an extended period. The Department of Labor enforces COBRA and provides a temporary extension of coverage. Employees who have changed their employment due to voluntary/involuntary job loss, reduced work hours, job transition, or any other qualifying life event are eligible to continue their coverage under COBRA. Employers must provide notice to qualifying employees about COBRA rights within ninety days of coverage beginning. Employees have sixty days from a qualifying event to elect to continue coverage. The length of coverage allowed by COBRA is eighteen to thirty-six months from the date of the qualifying event.

FLSA

The **FLSA** federal statute was passed to ensure that workers are protected from abuses related to compensation. The FLSA ensures that workers are paid a living wage and mandates how workers are paid for overtime work. Often referred to as the "wage and hour law," the FLSA controls minimum wage, overtime, equal pay, recordkeeping, and child labor. Private sector and public sector employers are subject to following the FLSA and understanding which guidelines apply. In addition to the above list of compensation-related items, government agencies must also be familiar with other labor laws such as the Davis-Bacon Act, which requires the agency to pay a prevailing wage rate and fringe benefits to certain contractors for certain work.

The overtime rule under the FLSA requires that employees be paid an annual salary of $23,660 or more in order to qualify as an exempt employee. This salary threshold is in addition to a duties test that would qualify a position as exempt or nonexempt. In general, executive, administrative, professional, outside sales, and certain computer-related employees are exempt from the FLSA. There are other exemptions; therefore, each position should be evaluated to determine its specific FLSA status based on the most recent law and current duties of the position.

An **exempt employee** is not subject to the FLSA requirements, and as such is not eligible for overtime. Exempt employees are paid a fixed salary regardless of the total number of hours they work. They are paid for a body of work regardless of how long it takes to complete the work. Per the FLSA, there is no limit on the number of hours an exempt employee may work. A **nonexempt employee** is an employee who is subject to the FLSA requirements and is eligible for overtime. Nonexempt employees are considered hourly employees and are to be paid at least the minimum wage of the state as well as all overtime due. Overtime must be paid at time-and-a-half for all hours worked over forty hours in any one week. Some agencies have practices put in place to pay daily overtime for all hours worked over eight hours in any one day. However, it is up to the Human Resources and Payroll professionals to ensure that all criteria are met based on the state requirements for paying overtime and the policies, procedures, and practices that align.

USERRA

The Uniformed Services Employment and Reemployment Rights Act of 1994 (USERRA) is a federal law that protects service members from discrimination as they return to the civilian workforce. USERRA covers current service members and veterans. Enforced by the Department of Labor, USERRA is intended to guarantee that service members are not disadvantaged in their civilian careers due to their military service and ensures that they do not face discrimination because of their military service. Under USERRA, former service members can return to their former job or a comparable position with the same benefits.

PPACA

The federal government, as well as many state governments, mandate that certain benefits are made available to employees. The **Patient Protection and Affordable Care Act (PPACA)** requires that health care coverage be provided and defines eligibility and program requirements. While the insurance plan or plans made available can be determined by the organization, the government-mandated requirements must be met with the plans offered.

Tax Treatment

Tax treatment refers to the way employers tax an employee's earnings for payroll. Employers are responsible for withholding an employee's taxes from any form of income provided by the employer to the employee unless otherwise noted by the Internal Revenue Code. Income from employers to employees that is subject to taxes includes, but is not limited to, regular wages, overtime pay, gifts, and any other form of payment to the employee that impacts the employee's income. Taxes that the employer withholds from the employee's income include Social Security, Medicare, and any other state or local tax.

Laws Related to Workplace Health, Safety, Security, and Privacy

Workplace Safety and Security Risks

Workplace security is defined as managing all personnel, equipment, and facilities in order to protect each and is concerned with mitigating and managing risks such as violence, bomb threats, natural or manmade disasters, cyberthreats, or data breaches. To have a safe workplace, risk assessments should be conducted frequently to determine and evaluate potential weaknesses. Employers are required to identify hazards and remove them, evaluate risks, reduce or control risks, and record the issues discovered in the assessment. Employees are required to cooperate with the employer regarding health and safety matters, inform supervisors about potential safety matters, and adhere to all work and safety policies and procedures. A safer workplace for everyone should always be the goal.

A safe working environment is one of the biggest concerns for employers and employees. Organizations can instigate the following practices regarding workplace safety:

- Each employee is responsible for their own safety AND the safety of their fellow employees
- All accidents are preventable
- Follow all organizational rules, regulations, policies, and procedures
- Assess any risk by stopping and thinking BEFORE acting
- Be proactive about safety
- Obey all safety signs
- Use the right tool for the job
- Wear all protective equipment
- Avoid any unnecessary hazards
- Do not engage in activities if not properly trained
- Manage lifting appropriately and safely
- Do not take shortcuts or skip steps in a process
- Incorporate good housekeeping by maintaining a clean and orderly work area
- Always be prepared

By incorporating these rules and encouraging employees to consistently follow and practice each, an organization can inspire a safety-focused culture that is employee driven. It is not enough to have great policies on paper. Safety must be practiced in every action by employees and supported by a committed leadership.

In addition to following the above rules, employees should also be engaged regarding maintaining a safe workspace. Employees should be informed, trained, and regularly updated regarding evacuation routes and appropriate responses to fire, tornadoes, floods, tsunamis, and other natural disasters. Depending on the location of the facility, employees should know proper procedures to deal with the applicable natural disasters. Additionally, employees should also be trained in the appropriate responses to active shooter situations, bomb threats, or suspicious mail and packages. Employees need to know where to find the fire extinguisher, AED, and first aid kit, as well as know the protocol regarding communication plans and contact information. It is far better to have the knowledge and not need it than to need the knowledge and not have it. Being prepared is a far better situation to be in than not being prepared.

A common catchphrase used recently is "if you see something, say something." While cliché, it is also incredibly accurate and appropriate in the workplace regarding safety and security. Employees should be encouraged and supported to report concerns and issues, even if it seems unimportant or insignificant. While one employee may not see significance in an event, there may be a history they are unaware of. Additionally, another employee may have a different perspective that offers insight and potentially changes a course of action for the better. If someone feels that something is not quite right, it is better to report the issue for further review by experts and trained professionals than to remain silent and have something happen.

Ultimately, safety and security are the responsibility of all employees. Regardless of the specific situation, a technique that can be applied to any circumstance is the STAR technique:

S Stop

T Think

A Act

R Review

By following each of these steps when faced with a safety or security concern, employees can protect themselves and others by making the best decisions and taking the appropriate actions. By providing information on as many safety issues and concerns as possible, an organization can help facilitate learning with employees. A best practice is to have regular safety meetings that provide tips and techniques that can be used on a daily basis. Office safety basics can include how to select, wear, and clean safety glasses; lift boxes safely; effectively use a fire extinguisher; climb and use a ladder; walk in winter climates; clean and organize a workspace; and wear and clean appropriate work attire such as personal protection equipment.

A final topic in workplace safety is ergonomics. **Ergonomics** is defined as fitting an employee's workplace conditions to the job demands and the specific needs of the individual. Ergonomics can include a proper chair with specific back support. Ergonomics needs can be addressed with simple or complex solutions depending on the physical need. The goals are to ensure employee safety and minimize injuries in the workplace. Carpal tunnel syndrome is a real and costly issue that many employees face. Identifying different keyboard options to minimize discomfort and resolve the physical issue for employees is a great example of how ergonomics can be applied. From standing desks to monitor arms for computer screens, there are numerous options that can resolve physical issues as well as ensure safety and well-being for employees.

OSHA

The **Occupational Safety and Health Act (OSHA)** is a federal regulation that requires training in various safety and health areas. Organizations are required to ensure that all employees are trained in the emergency plan. Each facility should have a specific plan that is regularly communicated and delivered to employees via a training plan. Providing practice drills along with classroom training enables employees to not only read the emergency plan's materials and maps but to physically familiarize themselves with such details as escape routes, meeting points, and signage. Many organizations require this training on an annual basis for all employees and provide additional opportunities throughout the year for newly hired and transferred employees. While all facilities should have plans for fires and other events, they should also have plans for location-specific natural disasters. Depending on the location, possible natural disasters include earthquakes, tsunamis, floods, hurricanes, and tornadoes. Employees should never have to guess about safety protocol in the case of an emergency.

OSHA also requires employees to be fully trained in all areas related to safety for their specific job. Every employee should be made aware of all safety procedures and protocols before beginning their work. Specific training related to safety procedures include, but are not limited to, machinery and equipment, fire hazards, chemicals and other hazards, hearing protection, personal protective equipment (PPE), and Automated External Defibrillator (AED) equipment. **PPE** is the required gear provided to an employee to perform their job safely and effectively; it includes clothing, footwear, tools, and vehicles. PPE can range from safety glasses or steel-toed boots to coveralls or Kevlar gloves. PPE can also include specific tools or items necessary to perform the job. Employees should be fully trained on every piece of equipment they use to do their job. Each position should have a specific training schedule depending on the equipment being used. Organizations may even provide a separate training program for PPE alone. Some positions require multiple pieces of PPE, and training should include not only how to use the PPE in the scope of the work being performed, but also how to clean, prepare, and request new PPE. From the use coveralls and safety glasses to Kevlar vests and handguns, organizations are responsible for delivering the training programs that ensure that employees are completely aware of and understand how to accurately use the PPE.

Many organizations require that an employee complete and sign a written notification that training has been provided and that the employee understands all aspects of performing their job safely. This document can be important if an employee refuses to abide by the protocols and needs to be disciplined. Additionally, refresher training should be provided to ensure that employees are aware of updates to regulations and procedures. The goal should be to ensure that employees leave work at the end of the day in the same physical condition in which they arrived. Providing consistent, frequent, and thorough safety training will decrease on-the-job injuries and accidents. Many organizations reward employees for adhering to safety practices and procedures. Another common practice is to communicate how many days have elapsed without a safety incident or accident.

Drug-Free Workplace Act

The Drug-Free Workplace Act of 1988 requires some federal contractors and all federal grantees to agree to maintain a drug-free workplace in order to receive a tax or grant from a federal agency. Under the Drug-Free Workplace Act, employers must adopt a drug-free workplace policy and establish a drug-free awareness program. Policy statements should notify employees that the organization prohibits unlawful drug use and state the actions the employer will take should an employee violate the policy. Drug-free awareness programs should cover the dangers of substance abuse, policy information, available services and resources related to substance use, and disclosure of penalties for policy violations.

ADA

The **Americans with Disabilities Act (ADA)** requires that employers make reasonable accommodations to support an employee in the workplace, as long as the request does not cause an undue hardship to the organization. An undue hardship could be excessive cost or substantially changing the core functions of the job. Most requested accommodations are either implemented fully or partially to address the main concern of the employee. Typical accommodations can include:

- Increasing accessibility to the workspace
- Modifying work schedules
- Reassigning the employee to another position
- Modifying or acquiring new equipment or devices
- Providing interpretation services

Workplace accommodations can be informal or formal, and they can be based on ergonomic, religious, or medical needs. Typically, a workplace accommodation begins with an employee making a request to the HR department. Depending on the request, further documentation may be required from a medical provider or religious leader. Some common examples of workplace accommodations are:

- Purchasing a new ergonomic chair that provides lumbar support
- Allowing for additional breaks and a secure, private area to allow for nursing mothers to lactate
- Modifying the work schedule to allow for regular physical or mental therapy appointments
- Installing a sit/stand ergonomic desk to allow for wheelchair access
- Approving a telecommuting arrangement to work from home due to an injury

There are numerous types of workplace accommodations, and HR should evaluate each based on the needs of the employee and the specific circumstances. While a specific request may not be feasible, HR can work with the individual to determine other options that can be provided to meet their needs.

HIPAA

The Heath Insurance Portability and Accountability Act of 1996 (HIPAA) is a federal law that prohibits protected health information (PHI) from being disclosed without the patient's knowledge or consent. HIPAA's privacy rule requires covered entities to control how PHI is used. PHI includes any identifiable health information, past or present. Covered entities under HIPAA include healthcare providers, health plans, healthcare clearinghouses, and business associates. Compliance with HIPAA requires covered entities to ensure the confidentiality of all PHI, create protections against anticipated threats to PHI security, protect and prevent misuse of PHI, and ensure workplace compliance with HIPAA guidelines.

Sarbanes-Oxley Act

The **Sarbanes-Oxley Act**, or SOX, is federal legislation passed in 2002 designed to establish higher levels of accountability and standards for a company's senior executives. The act was passed in reaction to the global corporate and accounting scandals of WorldCom and Enron. A particular section contained within SOX (806) provides protection for employees who have knowledge of, or have been a witness to, actions that are in direct violation of federal securities laws or Securities and Exchange Commission (SEC) regulations and wish to report their concerns. Examples of such actions include fraudulent financial reporting and billing for goods that were not delivered. OSHA is charged with enforcing the whistle-blower protections.

Employers cannot retaliate against employees who serve in the capacity of whistle-blowers. This means that, as a result of providing information, whistle-blowers cannot be disciplined, have their work hours or pay reduced, be laid off or terminated, or be blackmailed. This also applies if an employee is assisting other employees with providing information or if an employee is assisting with a SOX investigation. In addition, employees' identities must remain confidential whenever possible.

HR personnel must ensure there is a system in place to handle the following components to guarantee whistle-blower protection:

- Employee training on recognizing unethical or unlawful activities
- Policy on the procedure to follow when there is a need to report unethical or unlawful activities
- Manager training on maintaining employee confidentiality and preventing retaliation
- Tracking system for complaints, investigation records, and complaint resolutions
- Procedure to follow for investigations, including the associated disciplinary actions

Sexual Harassment

The Supreme Court has ruled that organizations can be held liable for sexual harassment if there is not reasonable effort made to prevent and correct inappropriate workplace behavior. Even if the organization is unaware of the behavior, it may still be liable for an employee's inappropriate behavior. Therefore, organizations must take every action necessary to provide training about sexual harassment. This training should include definitions and examples of sexual harassment, appropriate examples of lawsuits and case law, legal standards, the workplace policy, and the process for reporting sexual harassment. Additionally, training should include prevention techniques, employee responsibilities, and how sexual harassment investigations are conducted.

Sexual harassment training should occur frequently to ensure that employees understand the organization's policies and procedures as well as the legal ramifications for individuals and for the organization. Some states have passed legislation mandating sexual harassment training, and they conduct audits to ensure compliance. For example, in the state of California, Assembly Bill 1825 requires that all employers with 50 or more employees have their supervisors attend a two-hour class on sexual harassment at least once every two years. Additionally, all new supervisory employees must attend this training within six months of their hire or promotion to the supervisory role. Organizations must keep accurate records of when these trainings are offered, employees in attendance, and the content delivered.

Some organizations may choose to include diversity training in the scope of sexual harassment training. This inclusion can ensure that employees understand that, although these are separate topics, they intertwine with each other on many levels. Diversity training enables employees to be exposed to information regarding individuals with differences working together, providing different perspectives and allowing for a more robust dialogue. Employees should understand an organization's policies regarding diversity and how each individual plays a part in creating the culture of the organization. Valuing each other's differences and treating each other with respect is vital to the success of the team, department, and organization.

Risk Assessment and Mitigation Techniques

Proactive Risk Management Steps

Organizations face countless **internal risks** (e.g., workplace violence, employee substance abuse, and ill or injured employees) and **external risks** (e.g., cyber vulnerability, changes in market conditions, and natural disasters) on a daily basis. In order for organizations to be prepared, they must proactively manage their risk using the following four-step process:

1. Identify assets that may be subject to risks. This can include failing to have a succession plan in place and a candidate identified to move into the vice president of sales position when the current individual in that role steps down. This can also include liability issues the company can be sued over, such as a disabled employee who feels she was discriminated against and overlooked in a hiring decision.

2. Assess possible risks. This involves utilizing a formula to determine the probability of a risk occurring and the associated consequences to the company (risks = probability x consequences). For example, if a company does not train its managers on proper interviewing techniques, it is at risk of lawsuits due to failing to comply with employment law. However, the probability of that risk would be much lower if the company provided its managers with a training course on interviewing skills.

3. Manage risks. Once the risks are recognized and prioritized, they can be managed in one of the following ways:

   o Elimination: An example would be moving a piece of equipment that has cords laying across the floor where employees have to walk every day. Moving the equipment to a new location where the cords are out of sight eliminates the risk of employees tripping and falling.

   o Mitigation: Introducing the use of personal protective equipment when working with a dangerous chemical is an example of mitigation. This measure reduces employees' exposure to a known hazard.

   o Transfer: An example of a company transferring risk is outsourcing a specific type of work to a vendor. For example, a company knows it needs to provide employees with a training class on sexual harassment. However, management does not have the expertise surrounding laws about sexual harassment in all of the locations in which it conducts business. Therefore, outsourcing the creation of this class to a training vendor transfers the risk of providing employees with inaccurate information.

   o Acceptance: Deciding to purchase a new, innovative piece of equipment whose long-term performance and maintenance needs are not yet known is an example of acceptance. This is when a company knows the risk and decides to live with it as a cost of conducting business. Although this means there are no controls in place to manage this particular risk, the benefit is that it will allow a company to allocate more resources to focus on more serious risks.

4. Review and monitor. It is important for organizations to continuously monitor their risk management decisions in order to identify and handle any new risks as well as to check to see that the current strategies are still working effectively.

Risk Management

As with nearly all aspects of business, there are risks that an HR department may face and should preemptively work to minimize and manage. At its very core, the HR management department is focused on hiring and training the right people for the right jobs, ensuring they have the skills, attitudes, and knowledge needed to advance the organization and not hamper its future. To accomplish this, the HR department must ensure that their hiring, training, and support programs and policies are robust and aligned with the organization's mission, values, and needs. It is critical for the HR management professionals to have their fingers on the pulse of the company so they can anticipate any change in needs for workforce staffing and planning.

For example, if the company has an aging workforce, comprised primarily of those on the brink of retiring, strategic workforce planning might involve succession planning and hiring new employees who will have ample time to train with the seasoned employees before they retire. Similarly, high turnover is another pertinent risk for HR risk management. In addition to the critical role of hiring the right people committed to the job, the company can take strides to reduce turnover rate by offering competitive salaries and benefits, rewarding hard-working employees, building the company culture, offering flexibility with schedules, etc.

In addition to the risks inherent in staffing, HR management professionals will be integral in managing other risks for the company. For example, worker-related injuries and Occupational Health and Safety violations must be prevented in order to avoid legal and financial obligations as well as long-term health problems and lost productivity of workers. Proper safety procedures must be in place and checked routinely and staff must have proper training and equipment. Other risks include financial abuse, property risks, embezzlement and theft, reputation risks, environmental risks, etc. When considering the risks a company faces, both general risks (applicable to all or nearly all organizations) and company-specific risks need to be identified.

After a comprehensive list of risks is compiled, the next step is to evaluate the likelihood of occurrence of each risk and assess the severity of the consequences should that risk come to fruition. Then, for each identified risk, strategies must be assigned to manage the risk. Usually, one of the following four categories of strategies is most appropriate:

- Avoiding: A service or activity deemed too risky is ceased or no longer offered.

- Accepting: While still deemed risky, the activity or service is still offered or provided because it is key to the organization.

- Modifying: To reduce the likelihood that an adverse event or risk will occur, and/or to reduce the severity of the consequences if it does, the activity is changed in some way, typically via modifying policies and procedures.

- Transferring/Sharing: Risks are shared or transferred to other companies by buying insurance or signing contractual agreements with other companies.

Selecting the most appropriate risk management strategy for each risk also involves considering the costs (financial and otherwise) of changing the policies and procedures in place and/or taking on the risk. Once the strategies have been determined, a concrete plan naming the specific individuals responsible for each element in the plan should be created, communicated, rehearsed, and assessed/evaluated.

Emergency Evacuation Procedures

Emergency response, disaster management, emergency management, and emergency planning are all forms of the same principle: organizations must be prepared in the case of an emergency, with all employees understanding the plan and the individual roles played within the plan. **Emergency action plans** should be developed and implemented to ensure the safe evacuation of employees. These plans should address the circumstances in which specific actions should be deployed, covering as many situations as possible. They should also address the methods and resources available to protect employees, as well as the responsibilities of all employees, including champions or team leaders.

Emergency management focuses on four key areas: preparedness, response, recovery, and mitigation. Each of these four areas is vital to the overall success of handling an emergency.

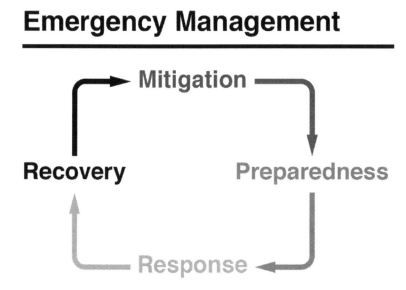

Preparedness focuses on any and all activities that an organization engages in prior to a disaster occurring. Drafting plans and action items, initiating evacuation drills, training employees, and providing opportunities to assess the effectiveness of the plan are all key initiatives to address when preparing for emergencies and the responses necessary.

Response focuses on any and all activities that occur during a disaster. Issuing public warnings, engaging emergency operations and centers of operations, evacuating facilities, and communicating to employees are vital to managing a disaster effectively and efficiently. Additionally, working in real time and with live data and information can assist in redirecting resources to meet new and changing needs during the disaster.

Recovery focuses on any and all activities following a disaster. Establishing temporary workspaces, initiating and processing injury reports and claims, providing counseling services, and approving time off are essential to ensuring the work operations return to business as usual as quickly as possible. Many organizations have a special policy regarding additional paid time off to attend to personal business as a result of an emergency or disaster. Depending on the circumstances and requests, organizations may approve additional time from vacation or sick leave time for employees to attend to personal needs.

Mitigation focuses on any and all activities that reduce the effects of a disaster. At the conclusion of a disaster, reviewing the response and corresponding outcomes can provide additional insight as to what went right and what went wrong. This analysis allows an organization to effectively update and revise plans to address future occurrences. Actions such as updating zoning and building codes, providing additional training and education, or scheduling additional evacuation drills could be warranted based on the outcomes of the incident. The goal of any disaster management plan is to ensure that employees are prepared for various emergencies that could occur and have the knowledge and understanding to follow the appropriate procedures and protocols that provide for their safety and the safety of others.

When developing an emergency response plan, it is important to understand the three primary levels of responses: operational, communications, and management. Each is critical to ensuring a fully developed and effective response plan. **Operational responses** should focus on implementing the protocols and procedures when responding to an emergency with the ultimate goal to first protect all employees and second protect the business operations. Operational responses should assess the situation, determine the level of action appropriate and necessary, and brief leadership with the details. **Communications responses** should focus on ensuring that all employees, regardless of location or level, receive the messages and information necessary to follow the appropriate emergency response protocol. Additionally, Human Resources should ensure that data is available to contact employees and their families in case of an emergency.

Other elements of the communication plan should include messaging and information to the public, news media, government officials, and other appropriate parties as identified in the emergency action plan. Finally, **management responses** should include mobilizing and initiating crisis teams to assess the situation and determine the safety of employees. Management is responsible for engaging and advising senior leadership regarding the situation, response, and outcomes. If necessary, management should also begin assessing the action plans for future events and prepare for any additional external communications. Employees will need to know how to receive information if not at work due to particular emergencies. Many organizations use a phone tree or a local AM radio station to communicate information on a wide scale.

Once the disaster has concluded, it is necessary to assess the damage. First and foremost, all employees should be accounted for and an assessment of any injuries reviewed. Second, a review of the business operations should be conducted. Secondary operational locations may need to be set up and engaged to ensure that business operations and continuity of service can be continued. If a secondary location is not necessary, a full review of the facility should be conducted prior to returning employees to the facility. It is also important to understand that all individuals process emergencies differently. Having empathy and patience with employees as they process the disaster is important, and a best practice that many organizations employ is the utilization of counselors through an **Employee Assistance Program (EAP).**

Violence and Theft

Workplace violence happens when a verbal or physical act of violence occurs that threatens the safety of people who interact with the business. Employee theft is the stealing or misuse of a company's assets or property for personal use. Workplace theft is not limited to physical items; it also includes stealing or misusing company data or information. To prevent workplace theft and violence, employers can create zero-tolerance policies. **Zero-tolerance policies** state that the employer does not condone the behavior and establishes a strict standard for all individuals deemed to have broken the policy. To help ensure compliance, employers should require employees to read and understand the policy and agree to the terms of employment.

Business Continuity Plan

A business continuity plan is a document or system of preventative and recovery measures to avoid potential threats that could negatively interfere with a business's assets and personnel. Business continuity plans are part of an organization's risk-management strategy that help prevent disruption and threats from impacting the company in the face of an unplanned event. Business continuity plans should address the prevention of threats, critical information to maintain business integrity, and how to keep the business functioning properly should a threat occur. Effective communication is key to business continuity plans; businesses must educate their personnel on procedures and test the plan to ensure it is effective.

Intellectual and Employee Data Protection

Data security is defined as the security relating to the confidentiality, availability, and integrity of data. Data security focuses on the physical security of a premises as well as the logical security of data and digital information. Data security includes issues such as the confidentiality, integrity, and availability of data; network protection; and the physical security of facilities, equipment, transport, and employees. **Data privacy** is defined as the appropriate use and control of data. Data privacy focuses on protocols that employees have over their personal and work-related data and how to protect the data from unwanted or harmful uses. Data privacy includes issues such as how data are processed, where data is held, and how long data will be retained. Data security and privacy are vitally important, and although each is a separate concept, both relate to the protection of data and ensuring that information is safe and secure.

Data security and privacy are critically important to protect through robust policies and procedures, knowledge and training, and continued vigilance on an everyday basis. New efforts are constantly being identified to undermine and hack organizational systems to gain access to personal information such as social security numbers, dates of birth, health information, and banking information. Additionally, organizational information, such as account, access, credit card, and other sensitive and proprietary information, is also at risk with these security breaches. Security breaches can allow unauthorized individuals access to private information. Not only can this have an impact on the employees and the organization, but it can have a negative impact regarding publicity and social media, which can result in decreased customer loyalty and business. It is crucial for organizations to manage privacy and security issues effectively and as a core competency. Employees should have a feeling of security and not worry that their personal information could be stolen through a data breach.

Organizations can implement many best practices to ensure that data are safe and secure. First, organizations can fully evaluate, approve, and protect data. A great example is the compliance with procedures set in place for the **Health Insurance Portability and Accountability Act (HIPAA)** data, or medical information. A data breach of HIPAA data could be cause for serious concern as well as violate the legal statutes. This violation could include fees and fines for violating the law.

Second, organizations can control and limit access to data and the networks, ensuring that only authorized individuals can gain access. Encryption is an excellent practice that many organizations utilize. **Encryption** for emails ensures that only the sender and authorized recipient can access the email and

134

information included. If a recipient does not have the proper encryption software, the information cannot be accessed.

Third, organizations can secure devices and install privacy and control mechanisms such as compliance proof and identification software to ensure that only the authorized employee can gain access. Many organizations require a double authentication, or two-factor verification, to ensure the identity of the individual accessing the information. Employees' access to information can be aligned with their position and role within the organization to ensure access is only granted to the information necessary for the work being conducted.

Finally, organizations can ensure that all employees receive regular and frequent compliance training. Training programs should be included for all employees to understand how to create and update an appropriate password to ensure that if their computers are stolen, information is protected. Additionally, employees should be trained in how to identify malware, suspicious emails and requests, and viruses sent through emails. Reports should not include social security numbers, dates of birth, or other confidential information. In the case that this information is required to report, the report should be monitored to ensure that the hard copies are controlled and maintained.

While most data and security breaches are unintentional, there are very real consequences that can impact the employees and the organization. For example, consider that a full employee roster that includes social security numbers, home addresses, and dates of birth is printed and then disposed of in a regular trash receptacle. This report could easily be discovered in a garbage bin and identities stolen for illegal purposes. While this may have been a simple oversight, the consequences could be tremendous. Employees could now face having to monitor their credit and identity, and the organization could need to arrange to provide and fund credit monitoring for a period of time to ensure that the impact to employees is minimal. Procedures should be put in place to ensure that data is secure. Personnel files should be kept under lock and key, printed reports and documents should be disposed of in a confidential and private manner, and passwords should be strong.

If a data breach does occur, it is important to report the incident immediately so that appropriate responses and necessary actions can be deployed as soon as possible. Initiating immediate action can limit the exposure and liability of the organization. Executive leadership should be informed of the issue and corrective action taken. Additionally, a communication plan should be created and deployed to ensure that employees understand the breach and what it means on a professional, work-related basis and, if applicable, a personal basis. A best practice would be to incorporate an emergency management and action plan specific to a data breach that ensures appropriate actions are taken to address the issue.

Organizational Restructuring Initiatives

Organizations experience change often. Whether the change is due to restructuring, mergers and acquisitions, divestitures, expansions, or outsourcing, each change should be accompanied by a full due diligence process and a communications plan. **Due diligence** is an audit or investigation conducted by an organization of the changes being considered. Due diligence should include reviews of multiple facets including legal, financial, process, operations, products, consumers, information technology, human resources, and department functions. Each area will be impacted by a transition change, and it is important to understand the impacts prior to implementing any change. This will ensure that each impact is fully vetted, and liabilities can be minimized. A **communications plan** is the complete plan for all communications that should be delivered, including when and to whom. Multiple platforms may be appropriate including in-person meetings to deliver the same message to multiple employees, written memos or question and answer documents, and frequent updates via email. Each platform should be appropriate to the message and its importance.

Human resources has a key role in the due diligence process with the specific focus being the employees of the organization. Human resources serves as a business partner to senior leadership in the following areas:

- Identifying human resource management risks
- Establishing appropriate resolutions and options to mitigate the risks
- Determining costs associated with employment changes, such as severance
- Assessing the organizational structure
- Assessing the human resource management process

By fully vetting each of these areas during the due diligence process, senior leadership can make the best, most informed decision possible. Once the decision has been made, this information will also lead to a well-planned workforce transition strategy. This strategy should address all possible personnel actions, including changes in position, supervision and leadership, compensation and benefits, transfers, or layoffs.

Fully vetted and well-planned strategies will assist in the transition by providing the following:

- Fair treatment of all employees impacted by the change
- Strong commitment to the transition
- Transfer of critical knowledge and process
- Minimal disruption to the customer
- Stability to and a smooth transition for employees
- Effective training on new processes and procedures for employees

The goal of any transition is to minimize disruption, liability, and insecurity for employees, customers, investors, or vendors. In order to effectively accomplish this, it is vital that communications are accurate, timely, and targeted. This will assist the organization in keeping rumors, misunderstandings, and misperceptions to a minimum.

Mergers and Acquisitions

These are different means of combining two organizations into a single company. A **merger** takes place when two or more companies form a single entity with the goal of leveraging their assets to become more successful. An example of a merger occurred when Sirius merged with XM Radio. On the other hand, an **acquisition** takes place when one company purchases another company. An example of an acquisition occurred when Disney acquired Pixar. Acquisitions can take place under friendly or hostile conditions, and the organization that is purchasing the other company can do so with either stock or cash.

HR personnel assist management with the **due diligence** process that takes place prior to M&A. This process involves examining the following aspects to learn more about the worth of the company that may be purchased to ensure that no financial or nonfinancial aspects are questionable:

- EEO compliance records
- Employee handbook
- Collective bargaining agreements
- Employee relations practices

136

- Grievance history
- Compensation practices
- Employee contracts
- I-9 forms and visa documentation
- OSHA compliance
- Employees on leave
- Any pending legal exposure

HR personnel also assist management with integrating the workforces of the two companies following M&A. This may involve identifying gaps in employment, reducing or transferring staff, and efforts to assimilate the two cultures. Throughout the M&A process, continuous communication from HR is essential for maintaining employees' morale.

Divestitures

In an effort to eliminate redundancy or layers of bureaucracy, a company may engage in corporate restructuring activities. HR will assist management with looking at individual business units to reduce costs by removing management layers, offering employees early retirement buyouts, laying off employees (RIFs), or changing reporting relationships among staff. These actions will ultimately result in an increase in production.

Divestiture is another form of organizational restructuring where a company makes the decision to sell off some of its investments, business units, or subsidiaries. Divestitures occur when businesses are no longer in line with a company's core competencies, are redundant following a merger or acquisition, are experiencing financial duress, and are no longer profitable. For example, Nestlé sold its chocolate business because it was underperforming and the company wanted to focus on healthier products.

Integration

Shared service models are another form of organizational restructuring where a company's administrative staff positions in specific groups, such as HR or information technology, are consolidated and integrated across business groups so as not to be redundant. This allows for these types of overhead costs to be distributed across various geographic locations. For example, Bayer Group moved to an HR shared services model several years ago to allow their HRBPs to be more strategic in nature. By doing so, the HRBPs were able to focus on human capital development instead of on managing employee leaves of absence and administering tuition reimbursement. Benefits of an HR shared services model include the following:

- Internal resources placing focus on strategic tasks
- More efficient HR operations
- Greater continuity of HR operations
- Economies of scale gained from combining HR software and tasks
- Higher-quality HR services

Offshoring and Outsourcing

When a U.S.-based company wants to lower its production and manufacturing costs, **offshoring** is a process it can use to accomplish that goal by moving those parts of its organization to another country, such as Mexico, in order to experience a cost savings. For example, offshoring takes place when an

137

American automotive company shifts production of a certain passenger car to a factory in China to benefit from the lower cost of labor. When a company no longer wants to perform a particular function in-house, such as payroll, **outsourcing** can be used to contract a specific internal business service to a third party known for having expertise in a particular skill set. For example, a small business owner may outsource the payroll of its employees to Automatic Data Processing (ADP), which is well known for its payroll expertise. Both offshoring and outsourcing result in staff reductions at a company.

Downsizing and Furloughs

Downsizing and furloughs are ways companies can reduce operating costs or improve efficiency by reducing the workforce. **Downsizing** happens when a business terminates multiple employees to help cut costs during an organizational hardship. A **furlough**, while similar to downsizing, is a temporary leave of absence after which employees are expected to return to work. Businesses may choose to downsize or furlough their workforce by reducing the size of a workforce unit, departmental level, or entire plant. An employer may choose to downsize or furlough employees because of economic conditions, including recessions, crises in the industry, mergers or acquisitions, restructuring, and competitive forces.

Practice Quiz

1. Risks can be managed in one of four ways: elimination, mitigation, transfer, and _____.

2. _____ describes the situation when policies or practices affect one specific group of individuals.
   a. Nepotism
   b. Artificial recruitment barrier
   c. Disparate impact
   d. Recruitment

3. Which of the following relationships would be a potential violation of a standard nepotism policy? (Select all answers that apply.)
   a. Sibling
   b. Neighbor
   c. Spouse
   d. Parent

4. _____ prohibits discrimination in employment based on race, color, sex, religion, national origin, age, disability, pregnancy, or genetic information.
   a. Genetic Information Nondiscrimination Act (GINA)
   b. Age Discrimination in Employment Act (ADEA)
   c. Title VII of 1964
   d. Pregnancy Discrimination Act (PDA)
   e. Americans with Disabilities Act (ADA)

5. Which of the following statements about due diligence are true? (Select all answers that apply.)
   a. Due diligence is necessary to make the best and most informed decisions.
   b. Human resources plays a key role in the due diligence process.
   c. Due diligence only needs to focus on legal and financial implications.
   d. Due diligence is a complete audit or investigation conducted when assessing major changes.

6. Which of the following are objectives that collective bargaining seeks to achieve? (Select all that apply.)
   a. Resolve differences
   b. Agree to amicable terms
   c. Protect the organization's interests
   d. Maintain union and employee relationships
   e. Settle disputes or conflicts regarding wages, benefits, and other concerns

7. What are the five basic steps to the collective bargaining process?
   a. Stop, Think, Act, Review, Settlement (STARS Method)
   b. Prepare, Discuss, Propose, Bargain, Settlement
   c. Who, What, Where, When, Why (5 W's Method)
   d. Why, Why, Why, Why, Why (5 Why Method)

8. A construction employee is set to work forty hours per week. Which of the following situations is considered hours worked under the Fair Labor Standards Act (FLSA)?
    a. The employee travels from one job site to another site.
    b. The employee travels from work to home.
    c. The employee is on call at home.
    d. The employee chooses to attend a business conference after hours.

9. Which of the following people is NOT covered from discrimination and retaliation under the Uniformed Services Employment and Reemployment Rights Act (USERRA)?
    a. An employee interested in joining the military
    b. An employee who has applied to join the military
    c. An employee who is currently serving in the military
    d. An employee who previously served in the military

10. What is the main difference between downsizing and furloughs?
    a. Downsizing refers to a considerable reduction in the workforce; furloughs are a smaller volume.
    b. Downsizing is only used for reducing costs; furloughs are for restructuring.
    c. Employers are only required to provide notice when downsizing, not during furloughs.
    d. Downsizing is a permanent reduction in staff; furloughs are temporary.

11. _____ is a type of divestiture where a company creates a new subsidiary and distributes shares of the new company to the existing shareholders.
    a. Split-off
    b. Spin-off
    c. Sell-off
    d. Carve-out

See answers on the next page.

Answer Explanations

1. Acceptance: Once a company's risks are recognized and prioritized, they can be managed in one of the following four ways: elimination, mitigation, transfer, and acceptance.

2. C: Disparate impact occurs when policies or practices disproportionately affect a specific group of individuals. Nepotism occurs when favoritism is shown to certain applicants based on personal relationships. Artificial recruitment barriers are qualifications that are not necessary to perform the position, disqualifying applicants who would otherwise be qualified for consideration. Recruitment refers to the entire process involved in filling open positions.

3. A, C, & D: Nepotism policies concern the relationships that would be potential problems related to employment. Siblings, spouses, children, parents, and other familial relationships may be identified in this policy as disqualifiers for a position or to be reviewed regarding the specific circumstances. Neighbors are not generally included in a nepotism policy, although if favoritism is shown to an individual because of this relationship, it may be a violation of the nepotism policy.

4. C: Title VII of 1964 is the original federal law that prohibits discrimination in employment. Title VII has been updated throughout the years to increase protections to additional individuals. GINA, ADEA, PDA, and ADA are all laws that have been incorporated into Title VII or as civil rights laws to protect individuals from being discriminated against in the hiring process.

5. A, B, & D: Due diligence is necessary to make the best and most informed decisions, and human resources plays a key role in this process. Due diligence is a complete audit or investigation conducted by an organization when considering major changes. Due diligence needs to focus on various areas in addition to legal and financial implications. Areas such as process, operations, products, consumers, information technology, human resources, and departmental functions should also be reviewed.

6. A, B, E: Collective bargaining seeks to resolve differences, agree to amicable terms, and settle disputes or conflicts regarding wages, benefits, and other concerns. Collective bargaining seeks to protect the employees' interests while maintaining the employee and employer relationship.

7. B: The five basic steps to the collective bargaining process are: prepare, discuss, propose, bargain, and settlement. The STARS method is used to evaluate different situations and respond accordingly, such as in emergency situations. The 5 W's method is used to determine the full assessment of a situation before responding to address the concerns. The 5 Why method is used to determine the root cause of an issue before working to address the issue. The STARS, 5 W's, and 5 Why methods could be used to assess certain issues within the bargaining process during the preparation and discussion steps.

8. A: The Fair Labor Standards Act (FLSA) considers time and travel from one job site to the next as hours worked that should be paid accordingly. Choice *B* is incorrect; travel from work to home is not considered time spent working and is not counted as part of hours worked. Choice *C* is incorrect; on-call time is only considered hours worked if the employee is required to remain on the premises during the on-call hours. Choice *D* is incorrect; voluntarily attending a business conference is not required for the job or related to the position and is not considered hours worked.

9. A: All current and previous members of the armed service, or applicants to join the armed service, are covered under the Uniformed Services Employment and Reemployment Rights Act (USERRA). An employee who expresses interest but has not applied to join is not provided discrimination protections under the USERRA.

10. D: When a company furloughs employees, it expects them to return to work, whereas downsizing is a permanent reduction in the workforce. Choice *A* is incorrect; the volume for furloughs and downsizing is not necessarily different. Choice *B* is incorrect; employers can downsize or furlough their employees for multiple reasons, but the reason does not determine the choice of one over the other. Choice *D* is incorrect; companies should notify employees who are being downsized or furloughed.

11. B: Spin-offs are subsidiaries of an existing company where shares of the new company are distributed among the existing shareholders. Spin-offs are similar to split-offs, but a split-off does not distribute shares among the existing shareholders; instead, the shareholder determines where they would like to distribute their shares.

aPHR Practice Test #1

1. Which of the following statements is FALSE regarding employee engagement surveys?
   a. Surveys that focus on employee engagement are a best practice to implement.
   b. Conducting surveys often allows an organization to determine if employees are responding to new programs.
   c. Surveys that focus solely on gathering information are just as effective and productive as surveys that focus on actions and making changes.
   d. Survey messages should be clear, concise, and specific.

2. Which of the below statements is TRUE regarding medical benefits?
   a. Employees can change their medical benefits at any time they wish.
   b. Employees can only change their medical benefits if they experience a qualifying event.
   c. Employees can only change their medical benefits during the annual open enrollment.
   d. None of the above

3. Which of the following statements is INACCURATE regarding job analysis ranking methods?
   a. Human Resources professionals must be familiar with and completely understand a ranking method prior to applying it to analyze a job.
   b. Only one ranking method should be used when evaluating a job.
   c. Various ranking methods may be useful when analyzing different jobs.
   d. External reviews can ensure that an organization's analysis is aligned with current ranking methods

4. What is the correct structure for the STAR technique used during an applicant interview?
   a. Situation, Training, Assessment, Results
   b. Strengths, Task, Assessment, Reactions
   c. Situation, Task, Action, Results
   d. Strengths, Training, Action, Reactions

5. Which of the following is an example of a training opportunity that should be extended to all employees?
   a. Writing a request for proposal
   b. Diversity and inclusion
   c. General accounting practices
   d. Conducting investigations

6. Which of the following statements about the current market situation is true? (Select all answers that apply)
   a. The employment market will constantly evolve and change.
   b. Generational differences should not be a consideration that is taken into account.
   c. Incentives may be necessary to attract potential candidates into new fields.
   d. When recruiting, it is important to focus solely on the region and market that the organization is located.

7. An employee will report to a primary manager and a second manager for work on specified projects in an organizational structure known as a/an _____.

8. Which of the following liabilities could occur if an organization does NOT maintain compliance regarding recordkeeping? (Select all that apply.)
    a. Expensive fines
    b. Unorganized information
    c. Losing data
    d. There are no liabilities

9. When can an organization offer a benefit to employees that is different from the federal or state requirement?
    a. If the offered benefit is more lucrative, or greater than the requirement in the law
    b. Under no circumstances can a benefit be different from the requirement in the law
    c. If the offered benefit is less lucrative, or less than the requirement due to finances
    d. If the employee signs a release waiving their rights under the law

10. Employers can offer _____ benefits than the federal or state statutes require, as long as a policy is written to support it.
    a. the same
    b. greater
    c. lesser
    d. the same or greater

11. Which of the following is NOT a benefit of having a strong, robust EVP?
    a. Increased candidate referrals and talent pools
    b. Fewer job vacancies and lower absenteeism
    c. Trust in leadership and increased productivity
    d. Increased turnover and higher cost per hire

12. What term refers to the entire package that employees receive when joining an organization?
    a. Offer letter
    b. Employee value proposition
    c. Total rewards
    d. New employee orientation

13. What factors should organizations take into account when setting a salary for a position? (Select all that apply.)
    a. Minimum experience required
    b. The actual work being performed
    c. Internal equity
    d. Appropriateness
    e. Salary Range

14. Match the key term with the proper definition.
    a. Policies   1. Structured manuals that communicate employee expectations
    b. Procedures   2. Documents describing details to complete a task
    c. Employee handbook   3. Standards or guides to the philosophy, mission, and values
    d. Standard operating procedures   4. Targeted and specific action plans to meet established goals

144

15. Which of the following should an employee handbook strive to achieve? (Select all that apply.)
    a. Ensure compliance with laws
    b. Provide employees with their rights and responsibilities
    c. Provide forms and documents to complete for onboarding
    d. Introduce key senior leadership
    e. Define work schedules

16. Which of the following is NOT typically included in an offer letter?
    a. Scope of work
    b. Probation terms
    c. Growth and professional development opportunities
    d. Benefits and allowances

17. Which of the following components of a position should be reviewed and assessed while conducting a job analysis? (Select all that apply.)
    a. Impact of work
    b. Salary
    c. Work schedule
    d. Job title
    e. Minimum experience required
    f. Scope of work

18. What does a SWOT analysis evaluate?
    a. Strengths, Weaknesses, Opportunities, Threats
    b. Strengths, Workforce, Opportunities, Tasks
    c. Staffing, Weaknesses, Openings, Threats
    d. Staffing, Workforce, Openings, Tasks

19. Match the interviewing technique to its format.
    a. Focus groups   1. Formal, one-on-one conversations focusing on scope and range
    b. In-depth interviews 2. Consecutive interviews that allow a joint opinion of the applicant
    c. Dyads or triads   3. Moderator-led discussions focusing on specific work
    d. Paired interviews 4. Formal conversations with two or three interviewers

20. Match the key emergency management area to the specific activities within each.
    a. Preparedness 1. Establishing temporary workplaces, initiating claims, and providing counseling
    b. Response   2. Issuing public warnings, engaging emergency operations, and evacuations
    c. Recovery   3. Drafting plans, initiating evacuation drills, and training employees
    d. Mitigation   4. Reviewing the response, analyzing actions, and updating plans

21. What law is commonly referred to as the "wage and hour" law?
    a. Department of Labor
    b. Fair Labor Standards Act
    c. Affordable Care Act
    d. Family and Medical Leave Act

22. _____ encourage and nurture open communication between employees and managers.
   a. Strong and effective partnerships
   b. Multiple ways of communications
   c. Best practices
   d. Open door policies

23. Conflict resolution identifies which of the following? (Select all that apply.)
   a. Feelings, perceptions, and opinions regarding an issue
   b. Recommendations and actions to resolve the issue
   c. Communication techniques to deliver the plan
   d. Problems that cause the issue
   e. Potential impacts of the issue

24. William is looking over an offer letter that his organization will be making to a job candidate. He is concerned that the salary is lower than similar positions at other companies, but the offer letter includes a generous benefit program, and the company has extensive work-life programs and learning and development opportunities. He thinks these benefits make the offer an attractive one for the candidate. What is this entire package called?
   a. Compensation
   b. Pay structure
   c. Total rewards
   d. Job pricing

25. Which alternative dispute resolution method is a voluntary agreement that works out a solution directly between the two parties involved?
   a. Arbitration
   b. Negotiation
   c. Mediation
   d. Conciliation

26. Employee feedback gathered by _____ is a beneficial way to engage employees and enhances communication between the employer and employees.
   a. Exit interviews
   b. Surveys
   c. Ad hoc emails
   d. All of the above

27. Match the job analysis ranking method with its main feature:
   a. Ranking   1. Groups jobs to reflect levels of skill
   b. Classification/Grading   2. Reviews external data to compare jobs
   c. Point Factor   3. Identifies factors then groups them
   d. Factor Comparison   4. Ranks jobs in order based on value to each other
   e. Competitive Market Analysis   5. Identifies factors and then adds value and weight

146

28. Which of the following statements about candidate experience is true? (Select all answers that apply.)
   a. Candidate experience refers to the experiences and interactions during the interview process.
   b. Candidate experience is vital to an organization's recruitment efforts.
   c. Candidate experience has no effect on an applicant applying for future open positions with the organization.
   d. Candidates who experience a positive recruitment are more likely to refer others to apply for employment with the organization.

29. Which of the following is an example of bottom-up communication?
   a. Managers receiving an email from the board of directors
   b. Staff participating in an all-hands meeting
   c. Two employees on the same team sharing information to solve a problem
   d. Two managers in the same group working together on a project rollout

30. What is the one standard that should be adhered to regarding benefit plans, whether government mandated or voluntary?
   a. Clear and concise communication containing contact information
   b. Least expensive plans with the maximum benefit allowed
   c. Services with an online portal and customer service options
   d. Fully funded by the employer regardless of the cost for all dependents

31. The survey measurement calculating the _____ shows how effective a survey was in receiving feedback from employees.
   a. Satisfaction rate
   b. Response rate
   c. Communication plan
   d. Action items

32. _____ employees are not covered under the Fair Labor Standards Act, and therefore not eligible for overtime.
   a. Exempt
   b. Nonexempt
   c. Nonsupervisory
   d. Administrative

33. _____ is key to any initiative and can determine the ultimate success or failure of a program.
   a. Transformational leadership
   b. Organizational culture
   c. Cultural fit
   d. Communication

34. Which of the following types of information should be provided to employees during their separation, regardless of the type of termination? (Select all that apply.)
   a. Contact information
   b. Final paycheck details
   c. Employee handbook
   d. Leave balance payouts
   e. Unemployment insurance information
   f. Job flyers for other open positions in the area

147

35. What is the federal regulation that requires training in various safety and health areas?
    a. Fair Labor Standards Act (FLSA)
    b. Family Medical Leave Act (FMLA)
    c. Occupational Safety and Health Act (OSHA)
    d. Americans with Disabilities Act (ADA)

36. Employees must be employed for _____ months and work a minimum of _____ hours in the past year to be eligible for the Family and Medical Leave Act.
    a. 6/2,000
    b. 9/1,500
    c. 12/1,250
    d. 18/1,500

37. _____ is the required gear provided to employees to perform their job safely and effectively.
    a. Work boots
    b. A uniform
    c. A tool belt
    d. Personal protective equipment

38. Benchmarking is important to ensure that an organization knows which of the following:
    a. How an organization compares to competitors
    b. Potential reasons for employees leaving the organization
    c. A full perspective and understanding of the organization's total rewards
    d. All of the above

39. Which of the following is the accurate step sequence for the STAR technique used to address safety issues?
    a. Stop, Think, Act, Review
    b. Safety, Think, Act, Review
    c. Safety, Think, Avoid, Risk
    d. Stop, Train, Assess, Review

40. Which of the following long-term solutions could be implemented to address employee surpluses AND employee shortages? (Select all answers that apply.)
    a. Issuing recalls and limiting production
    b. Retraining employees
    c. Offering retirement incentives
    d. Permanently transferring employees to different positions
    e. Transferring work out of the department

41. The overall brand that an organization provides to its current and future workforce is referred to as what?
    a. Organizational branding
    b. Total rewards package
    c. Employee value proposition
    d. Compensation and benefits

148

42. What is the first step when implementing a change management process?
    a. Prepare for the change
    b. Implement the change
    c. Identify the need for change
    d. Reinforce the change

43. Which of the following statements regarding recordkeeping requirements are TRUE? (Select all that apply.)
    a. It is not necessary for recordkeeping to meet the needs of the business.
    b. Records should be kept in a manner that ensures privacy and confidentiality.
    c. Each type of record should have a policy and retention schedule.
    d. Training documents are not necessary to retain.

44. Which of the following statements is TRUE regarding employee and labor relations?
    a. Employee and labor relations is the sole responsibility of Human Resources.
    b. Employee and labor relations is the maintenance of effective working relationships with employees and the labor unions that represent them.
    c. Employee and labor relations manage themselves and require attention only as needed.
    d. The cornerstone of positive employee and labor relations is joint committees.

45. What do Key Performance Indicators (KPIs) of a training program show? (Select all that apply.)
    a. Progress toward a goal or objective
    b. Average training cost
    c. What matters and what needs attention
    d. A clear strategic picture
    e. Return on investment

46. What is the attrition rate of a hypothetical company if sixty-seven employees were working at the company at the start of the year, but twenty-three employees leave during the course of the year? Report your answer to two decimal places.

 %

47. What are the five components that make up the total rewards package?
    a. Offer letter, health insurance providers, supervisor information, training schedule, and policies
    b. Pay, health insurance providers, work-life, training schedule, and policies
    c. Offer letter, safety procedures, supervisor information, training schedule, and recognition
    d. Pay, benefits, work-life, learning and development, and performance and recognition

48. When should HR provide an employee with the handbook, policies, procedures, and expectations of employment?
    a. During new employee orientation, typically scheduled for the first day of employment
    b. When a situation arises, and the employee needs the information
    c. After applying for an open position
    d. The information should be accessible online for the employee to locate when needed

49. Which of the following types of organizational structures groups jobs according to industry or market?
    a. Division
    b. Geographic
    c. Product
    d. Functional

50. Which of the following statements is INACCURATE regarding talent acquisition?
    a. Talent acquisition is the entire process from when a vacancy occurs to the hiring of a new employee.
    b. Talent acquisition is a strategic process that includes assessing the workforce needs and recruiting talent.
    c. Talent acquisition aims to hire individuals with specific skills and abilities that align with the organization's needs.
    d. Talent acquisition deals only with the initial hiring of an employee and not the future opportunities.

51. Which element of adult learning refers to how participants apply the information to their job?
    a. Transference
    b. Reinforcement
    c. Orientation
    d. Motivation
    e. Retention

52. Match each step of the ADDIE process with its specific focus:
    a. Analyze   1. What should be included and the audience of the message
    b. Design   2. What the delivery of the training program will be
    c. Develop   3. How effective the training program was and validation for future use
    d. Implement   4. What is needed and the skills gaps in the organization
    e. Evaluate   5. What the actual content and materials will be

53. Which of the following is NOT a qualifying event that allows an employee to make changes to their medical insurance coverage outside of open enrollment?
    a. Marriage
    b. Birth of a child
    c. Divorce
    d. Adoption
    e. Diagnosis of a medical condition

54. Match the term to its definition.
    a. Collective bargaining   1. The duty of both parties to demonstrate sincere and honest intent
    b. Good faith bargaining   2. The process of voting to approve or deny proposed settlements
    c. Ground rules   3. The process of negation between management and unions
    d. Ratification   4. Items agreed upon by both parties to assist the process

55. _____ equity refers to the parity of salary between positions within the same organization; _____ equity refers to the parity of salary between positions in different organizations.
   a. External/Market review
   b. Aligned/External
   c. Internal/External
   d. Internal/Aligned

56. _____ is defined as fitting an employee's workplace conditions to the job demands and specific individual needs.
   a. Workplace security
   b. STAR technique
   c. Safety
   d. Ergonomics

57. _____ establish(es) the requirements and expectations of employees regarding reliability and stipulate(s) the consequences for not adhering to these requirements.
   a. Family Medical Leave Act (FMLA)
   b. Time and Attendance Procedures
   c. Disciplinary actions
   d. Employee handbooks

58. Why is communication in both an upward and downward direction important? (Select all that apply.)
   a. Increases success of a process
   b. Ensures achievements are met
   c. Places the responsibility on employees
   d. Allows for maximum engagement

59. A presentation from upper management to staff on the company's mission is an example of _____.

60. The tool that enables an employee to discuss future opportunities and the skills needed to achieve those opportunities is known as a(n) _____.
   a. Performance evaluation
   b. Individual development plan
   c. Training program
   d. Performance improvement plan

61. What actions should occur when a security breach happens? (Select all that apply.)
   a. Implement the emergency management action plan
   b. Report the incident immediately
   c. Inform leadership only when the issue has been resolved
   d. Communicate to employees the breach and any ramifications

62. Match the learning theory with its primary focus:
   a. Behaviorism   1. How an individual interprets and applies new information
   b. Cognitivism   2. What an individual does
   c. Constructivism   3. An individual being self-directed in learning
   d. Experiential   4. How an individual processes information
   e. Connectivism   5. How an individual learns from their own experiences

151

63. Which of the following is described as the strategic process that takes into account the holistic view of the workforce needs, both current and future?
    a. Recruitment process
    b. Talent acquisition process
    c. Onboarding process
    d. Workforce planning

64. What is the correct progression in evaluating the effectiveness of a training program?
    a. Results, Behavior, Learning, and Reaction
    b. Learning, Behavior, Results, and Reaction
    c. Reaction, Learning, Behavior, and Results
    d. Reaction, Results, Behavior, and Learning

65. The performance management process begins with _____ and concludes with employee _____.
    a. planning, recognition.
    b. coaching, evaluation.
    c. planning, evaluation.
    d. recognition, coaching.

66. Match the emergency response plan responses to their key focus.
    a. Operational   1. Ensuring employees receive the information necessary
    b. Communications   2. Implementing protocols to first protect employees and then operations
    c. Management   3. Engaging and advising senior leadership regarding the emergency

67. Match the term to its definition.
    a. Data security   1. Allowing unauthorized individuals access to private information
    b. Data privacy   2. Ensures only the sender and recipient of an email have access to information
    c. Encryption   3. Controlling the confidentiality, availability, and integrity of data
    d. Security breach   4. Appropriate use and control of data

68. Which teaching method has the lowest retention rate?
    a. Demonstration
    b. Practice
    c. Lecture
    d. Reading
    e. Teaching others

69. What is the ultimate goal of handling any complaint?
    a. Following a structure process to resolve the issues
    b. Informing leadership immediately of the issues
    c. Resolving the issue at the lowest level possible
    d. Being respectful and responsive

152

70. _____ examine how applicants process information, determine next steps, gather new information, formulate conclusions, and provide solutions.
    a. Reasoning tests
    b. Cognitive ability tests
    c. General intelligence tests
    d. Personality tests

71. The balanced scorecard contains metrics that span across four perspectives: customer, financial, employee learning and growth, and _____.

72. An organization has decided to conduct a market review to determine external equity regarding their supervisory positions. What is considered an acceptable salary range compared to the average market salary?
    a. Within 5 percent
    b. Within 10 percent
    c. Within 8 percent
    d. Within 7 percent

73. Which of the following statements are TRUE regarding recognition programs? (Select all that apply.)
    a. Recognition programs can be formal and structured.
    b. Recognition programs do not have an impact on employee morale.
    c. Recognition programs are unnecessary.
    d. Recognition programs can be informal and unplanned.

74. Match the culture type with the primary focus and foundation of each.
    a. Clan   1. Competition, built on a foundation of competitiveness and customer focus
    b. Adhocracy   2. Collaboration, built on a foundation of participation at all levels
    c. Hierarchy   3. Control and process, built on a foundation of control and efficiency
    d. Market   4. Creativity, built on a foundation of innovation, vision, and resources

75. Which of the following about a training program is true?
    a. When developing a training program, human resources does not need to ask anyone the needs of the organization.
    b. With regard to enrollment in training programs, all employees should attend every course offered.
    c. When creating a training program, increased structure results in increased participation and learning.
    d. It is not necessary for leadership to participate in or commit to training programs to ensure success.
    e. None of the above

76. Which of the following statements is TRUE regarding the goal of any disaster management plan?
    a. To ensure that employees are prepared for emergencies and have the knowledge to follow appropriate protocols that provide safety to all
    b. To review the responses and outcomes to provide insight in effective practices
    c. To ensure that work operations return to business as usual as quickly as possible
    d. To focus on any and all activities that occur during a disaster

77. Which of the following are flexible work schedules often offered under an alternate work schedule program? (Select all that apply.)
    a. 4X10
    b. 9X80
    c. 5X8
    d. None of the above

78. Which of the following are effects of a robust total rewards program? (Select all answers that apply.)
    a. Attracting the most qualified and experienced applicants
    b. Retaining the most qualified and experienced employees
    c. Maintaining high employee satisfaction and morale
    d. Having a highly qualified, well trained, and best-in-class workforce

79. Which of the following responsibilities are required by employers regarding workplace security? (Select all that apply.)
    a. Identify hazards and recommend alternate work processes as "workarounds"
    b. Evaluate, reduce, and control risks
    c. Work together with employees
    d. Inform supervisors about potential safety matters
    e. Handle issues informally and without creating a record

80. _____ are one of the most important and fundamental recordkeeping functions within Human Resources.
    a. New hire documents
    b. Offer letters
    c. Personnel files
    d. Timecards

81. Match the job analysis tool with its definition:
    a. Employee survey   1. A complete list of duties, responsibilities, and required skills
    b. Employee interview   2. A visual review of the actual work being performed
    c. Job description   3. A series of written questions to be completed by the individual
    d. On-the-job observation   4. A conversation to discuss the work to be performed

82. Which component of the employee value proposition (EVP) encourages employees to know and understand how their performance aligns with the expectations of the position and future opportunities?
    a. Culture
    b. Work environment
    c. Career
    d. Benefits

83. Which of the following statements is TRUE regarding the Family and Medical Leave Act? (Select all that apply.)
    a. The FMLA is paid leave and does not require vacation or sick leave to be taken.
    b. The FMLA is unpaid leave.
    c. Employees can use vacation or sick leave to receive pay during a protected FMLA leave.
    d. Because FMLA is a federal program, organizations do not need a policy regarding this program.

84. Which of the following is a way human resources can incorporate a company's vision into daily business activities?
   a. Develop a system to recognize and reward employees who demonstrate the values.
   b. Reinforce the values during employee exit interviews.
   c. Mention the values once a year during the annual holiday party presentation.
   d. Interview candidates only to ensure they have the right mix of skills and abilities.

85. Which of the following statements are TRUE regarding security breaches? (Select all that apply.)
   a. Security breaches can have a negative impact regarding publicity.
   b. Security breaches do not have an impact on customer loyalty and business, as they affect employees only.
   c. It is not necessary for employees to have a feeling of security regarding their personal information.
   d. It is crucial for organizations to manage privacy and security as a core competency of the business.

86. Drop and drag the short-term solutions to match them with the appropriate circumstance, either employee surplus or employee shortage.
   a. Offering additional overtime opportunities   Employee Surplus
   b. Offering vacation buybacks or leave buybacks
   c. Freezing hiring activity and managing headcount through attrition
   d. Transferring work out of the department   Employee Shortage
   e. Approving additional absences and time off
   f. Reducing the number of hours worked in the work week

87. Which of the following statements accurately characterize/s attrition? (Select all that apply.)
   a. Attrition is the process of visualizing current gaps in the organization.
   b. Attrition occurs when employees exit an organization, either voluntarily or involuntarily.
   c. Attrition is an organization's turnover rate.
   d. Attrition is an important metric that can enable an organization to make appropriate changes to retain employees.

88. The FLSA law determines whether a position is eligible for which of the following?
   a. Bilingual pay
   b. Overtime
   c. Merit increases
   d. All of the above

89. Which of the following items should be included on an employee's paycheck?
   a. All forms of salary including overtime, specialty pay, etc.
   b. Benefits deductions and contributions
   c. Retirement deductions and contributions
   d. All of the above

90. In John Kotter's Change Model, which step involves identifying the key stakeholders and true leaders in the organization who can guide the change effort with their influence and authority?

    a.   Create a clear vision for the change.

    b.   Communicate the vision.

    c.   Create short-term wins.

    d.   Form the change coalition.

Answer Explanations #1

1. C: Surveys are most effective and productive when the information gathered is used to affect change. Surveys that are initiated to solely gather information will not have the same level of support and participation. Surveys are a best practice that can be used to assess specific needs and concerns as well as overall satisfaction. Surveys also allow an organization to assess the effectiveness and utilization of new programs. Additionally, all communications regarding surveys should be clear, concise, and specific, with employees fully understanding how the survey results will be used.

2. D: Changes to medical benefits can only occur during open enrollment for the upcoming year or within a certain time frame during the year following a qualifying event. While Choices *B* and *C* are somewhat true, it is not true that they are the only times that medical benefits can be changed. Additionally, employees cannot change their medical benefits simply because they change their mind.

3. B: The inaccurate component of this statement is related to using only one ranking method. Human Resources professionals should be completely familiar with the tools being used before applying them to analyze a job, and various rankings methods should be used to fully understand a job and different jobs within an organization. This allows a holistic view of positions; by using multiple tools, it allows various perspectives to come through. To ensure that an organization's analysis is aligned with current ranking methods, external reviews can be performed.

4. C: Situation, Task, Action, Results is the correct structure for the STAR technique, which can be used to structure applicants' responses during an interview. While it is important for candidates to highlight strengths, training, assessments (such as performance reviews), and reactions to particular circumstances, the STAR technique is specific to Situation, Task, Action, and Results.

5. B: There are several training opportunities that should be extended to all employees, one of which is diversity and inclusion. Choices *A*, *C*, and *D* are incorrect as they are all specific areas of training for particular jobs or roles within an organization. Not all employees will need to know how to write a request for proposal nor will they work with accounting practices or conduct investigations.

6. A & C: The employment market will always be evolving and changing. Organizations may need to offer incentives to attract candidates and even create new talent pools depending on the recruitment needs and candidate availability. Generational differences are an important factor in the recruitment process and play a large role in the talent pool availability. Depending on the availability of talent, it may be necessary to expand outside of the region and market to source the most qualified candidates and have a robust and broad talent pool.

7. Matrix structure: An employee will report to a primary manager and a second manager for work on specified projects in an organizational structure known as a matrix structure.

8. A & C: Expensive fines and loss of data are liabilities that could occur if an organization does not maintain compliance regarding recordkeeping. While records could be unorganized and information hard to find, this is more a nuisance and concern than a liability.

9. A: An organization can offer a benefit to employees that is different from the federal or state requirement only if the offered benefit is more lucrative or greater than the requirements in the law. An example would be regarding FMLA and maternity leave. It would be possible for the agency to extend additional paid time off if they wanted to as long as the requirements within the laws are met. Choice *B* is

157

incorrect because an organization cannot offer a less lucrative benefit to employees. Choice *C* is incorrect because under no circumstances can an organization reduce a federal or state entitlement to an employee, even due to finances. Choice *D* is incorrect because employees cannot sign away their rights under the law with a waiver.

10. D: Employers can offer the same or greater benefits than what the federal or state statutes require, as long as a policy is written to support it. Employers cannot offer programs and benefits that are less generous than those afforded to them via federal and state law.

11. D: An organization that has a strong, robust EVP will NOT experience high turnover or a higher cost per hire. On the contrary, a strong EVP will allow an organization to see higher retention rates and lower costs per hire. Choices *A, B,* and *C* are incorrect because they are all benefits that an organization will experience with a strong EVP. Employees making referrals, larger and more qualified talent pools, fewer vacancies, lower absenteeism, increased productivity and trust in leadership are all benefits that an organization will see when having a strong EVP.

12. C: The term *total rewards* describes the entire package that an employee receives when joining an organization. The total rewards package includes the offer of employment, compensation details, benefits, work-life programs, learning opportunities, and recognition. Choice *A* is incorrect because the offer letter generally includes information related to the offered job, salary, supervisor information, and information specific to the position. Each organization will have a different way of communicating terms in the offer letter; however, this letter is only one component of the total rewards package. Choice *B* is incorrect because the employee value proposition, or EVP, is the overall brand that an organization provides to the workforce. The EVP communicates the programs that the organization offers to all employees but does not provide specifics to the individual employee. Choice *D* is incorrect because new employee orientation refers to the training an employee receives once hired into an organization. This training acclimates the new employee to the organization relative to the policies, procedures, standards, and expectations.

13. A, B, C, D, & E: Salary structures should consider the minimum experience required, the actual work being performed, internal equity, appropriateness, and salary range. All of these should be taken into account when setting a salary range.

14. A – 3, B – 4, C – 1, & D – 2: Policies are the standards or guides to the philosophy, mission, and values of an organization. Procedures are specific action plans to achieve goals. Employee handbooks are manuals that communicate employer expectations of employees. Standard operating procedures are documents that describe specific actions and instructions to accomplish a task.

15. A, B, & E: Employee handbooks are structured manuals that should ensure compliance with laws, provide employees with their rights and responsibilities, and define work schedules. Additionally, handbooks should strive to communicate expectations; introduce the culture, mission, values, and goals of the organization; and showcase the offered benefits. Forms and documents should be provided as separate paperwork during the onboarding process. Introducing new employees to key senior leadership should also be a part of the onboarding process; however, it is not a component of the employee handbook.

16. A: While the offer letter should include the job title and a summary of the position, the full scope of work is included in the job posting rather than in the offer letter. Choices *B, C,* and *D* are all typically included in an offer letter.

17. A, E, & F: An effective job analysis should include impact of work, scope of work, working conditions, supervisory roles, reporting relationships, internal and external relationships, leadership role, minimum experience requirements, and minimum qualifications. While salary, work schedule, and job title are important pieces of information, they are not used for a job analysis.

18. A: A SWOT analysis examines the following: Strengths, Weaknesses, Opportunities, Threats. While staffing, workforce, openings, and tasks may be items that need to be assessed, they can be reviewed within the SWOT categories.

19. A – 3, B – 1, C – 4, & D – 2: Focus groups are discussions led by a moderator that focus on specific work being done. In-depth interviews are formal, one-on-one conversations that focus on the scope and range of the position with specific questions to gauge the applicant's experience. Dyads or triads are formal conversations with two or three interviewers that focus on the candidate's ability to perform the job duties based on their previous experience. Paired interviews are consecutive interviews that allow for joint opinions and ratings of the applicant.

20. A – 3, B – 2, C – 1, D – 4: Preparedness activities include drafting plans and actions items, initiating evacuation drills, training employees, and providing opportunities to assess the plan's effectiveness. Response activities include issuing public warnings, engaging emergency operations and centers of operations, evacuating facilities, and communication. Recovery activities include establishing temporary workspaces, initiating and processing injury reports and claims, providing counseling services, and approving time off. Mitigation activities include reviewing the response and corresponding outcomes, updating zoning and building codes, providing additional training and education, or scheduling additional evacuation drills.

21. B: The Fair Labor Standards Act (FLSA) law determines whether a position is eligible for overtime compensation. The Department of Labor administers and enforces many laws, including the FLSA, while the Affordable Care Act and the Family and Medical Leave Act laws determine rights relative to medical insurance and protected leave.

22. D: Open door policies encourage and nurture open communication between employees and managers, which can result in a healthier workplace. Open door policies are a best practice that can ensure strong and effective partnerships. Best practices also include incorporating multiple ways of communication.

23. A, B, D, & E: Conflict resolution identifies feelings, perceptions, and opinions regarding an issue; recommendations and actions to resolve the issue; problems that are causing the issue; and potential impacts of the issue. While it is important to communicate the resolution with all parties as appropriate, communication techniques are not identified during a conflict resolution.

24. C: The entire package, including compensation, benefits, and other perks, is called the total rewards package. Compensation, Choice *A*, refers specifically to the financial pay that an employee receives, including salary and bonuses. Choice *B* refers to how an employee is paid, including salaries, bonuses, and consideration of equity between positions. Job pricing, Choice *D*, refers to the process of determining salaries for different jobs.

25. B: The process of negotiation is a voluntary agreement that works out a solution directly between the two parties involved. Choice *A* is incorrect because arbitration is a formal process in which an arbitrator considers evidence presented by each party and determines a solution that is binding and final. Choice *C* is incorrect because mediation is a facilitated negotiation process that works out a solution between the

159

two parties through a neutral third party. Choice *D* is incorrect because conciliation is a non-binding formal process in which a negotiator explains the law and provides the two parties with a non-binding recommendation to resolve the issue.

26. D: All of the above. Exit interviews, surveys, and ad hoc emails are all different and great ways to engage employees, gain feedback on programs, and enhance communication between employers and employees.

27. A – 4, B – 1, C – 5, D – 3, & E– 2: There are various ranking methods to use in conducting a job analysis, each having pros and cons. The ranking method ranks jobs in order based on value to each other. The classification/grading method groups jobs to reflect levels of skill. The point factor method identifies factors and then adds value and weight to each. The factor comparison identifies factors and then groups them. The competitive market analysis reviews external data to compare jobs.

28. B & D: Candidate experience is vital to an organization's recruitment efforts, and candidates who have a positive experience are more likely to refer others to apply for employment with the organization. Candidate experience includes more than the experiences and interactions during the interview process. The candidate experience encompasses the entire recruitment experience, from viewing a job posting, interviewing, and negotiating an offer to beginning employment. Furthermore, a positive candidate experience will have an impact on applicants applying for future open positions.

29. B: Staff participating in an all-hands meeting is an example of bottom-up communication. Managers receiving an email from the board of directors is an example of top-down communication. Two employees on the same team sharing information to solve a problem and two managers in the same group working together on a project rollout are examples of horizontal communication.

30. A: The one standard that should be applied and adhered to regarding any benefit plan, government mandated or voluntary, is to ensure clear and concise communications. Employees should be able to access this information, along with contact information and forms in a convenient and understandable manner. Choice *B* is incorrect because the best benefit plan should be selected based on the needs of the employees and organization as well as the costs and benefits provided; however, this may not mean that the least expensive plan is the best option. It may be in the best interest of the organization to offer employees multiple options for plans with varying cost and benefit levels. Choice *C* is incorrect because not all services are available online. By applying the general standard, an organization may eliminate excellent vendors with plans that would be beneficial to an employee. Choice *D* is incorrect because covering all costs for insurance may not be feasible, and typically, voluntary benefits are paid for fully by the employees.

31. B: The response rate shows how effective a survey was in receiving feedback from employees. Satisfaction rates calculate a specific metric for a specific question in the survey. Communication plans and action items are specific actions and proposed recommendations that occur before and after the survey has been established and completed.

32. A: Exempt employees are not covered under the FLSA and not eligible for overtime. Non-exempt employees are covered under the FLSA and eligible for overtime compensation. Non-supervisory and administrative employees are descriptions of the work an employee does within a certain position; these descriptions alone do not determine the FLSA status.

33. D: Communication is key to any initiative and can determine the ultimate success or failure of a program. Transformational leadership can reshape and change a culture as a response to an initiative or

160

program. Organizational culture refers to the shared beliefs, values, philosophies, and assumptions within an organization. Culture fit ensures that an individual's beliefs and work ethic align with the organizational culture.

34. A, B, D, & E: When an employee is separated from an organization, regardless of the reason, contact information, final paycheck details, leave balance payouts, and unemployment insurance information should be made available. An employee handbook is not necessary to be provided as this is usually provided when an employee begins employment, not ends employment. Additionally, providing job flyers for open positions within the area may be a nice gesture, but is not an accepted practice during the exiting process of an employee.

35. C: OSHA is the federal regulation that requires training in safety and health as well as all areas related to safety for specific jobs. FLSA is the law that sets the standards to determine overtime compensation. FMLA is unpaid leave that employees can be eligible to take in the case of a medical condition. ADA is the law protecting employees and applicants from discrimination due to having a disability.

36. C: Employees must work for an organization for 12 months and work a minimum of 1,250 hours in the past year to be eligible for the benefits of the Family and Medical Leave Act.

37. D: Personal protective equipment (PPE) is the required gear provided to employees to perform their jobs safely and effectively. Work boots, uniforms, and tool belts are all forms of PPE, and each job has its own required PPE that must be supplied by the organization.

38. D: Benchmarking allows an organization to understand how they compare to other organizations, reasons for attrition, and an understanding of the current total rewards programs, which can allow for focused changes to certain programs.

39. A: The STAR technique refers to Stop, Think, Act, Review. The STAR technique can be implemented to address safety and security through action, avoidance, training, and assessing prevention.

40. B & D: Retraining employees and permanently transferring employees to different positions are both solutions that can be implemented in either employee surplus or employee shortage situations. Issuing recalls and limiting production and transferring work out of the department are both solutions to address employee shortages only. Offering retirement incentives is a solution to address employee surpluses only.

41. C: The employee value proposition (EVP) is the organization's brand that is presented to both the current and future workforce. The EVP answers the question "what's in it for me?" to prospective candidates and allows current employees to be aware of their total rewards. Choice *A* is incorrect because organizational branding is specific to the product branding presented to customers, not to employees. Choice *B* is incorrect because the total rewards package is a component of the EVP and is comprised of compensation, benefits, policies, flexible work schedules, retirement, training, promotional opportunities, and more. Choice *D* is incorrect because compensation and benefits are a component of the total rewards package, which is a component of EVP.

42. C: The first step in a change management process, regardless of whether it is a simple or complex change, is to identify the need for change. Choice *A* is inaccurate because preparing for the change is the second step. Preparation for a change should only occur after first identifying the change needed. Choice *B* is inaccurate because implementation of change should occur after first identifying and then preparing for a change. Preparation is the third step in the change management process. Choice *D* is inaccurate because reinforcing the change is the final step in this process.

43. B & C: Records should be kept in a manner that ensures privacy and confidentiality, and each type of record should have a policy and retention schedule. Recordkeeping should meet the internal needs of the organization. Training records are absolutely necessary to maintain and retain for the required timeframe.

44. B: Employee and labor relations is the maintenance of effective working relationships with employees and the labor unions that represent them. Employee and labor relations is the responsibility of management, leadership, and Human Resources and requires frequent communication and attention for maximum success. Additionally, multiple best practices such as open door policies, joint committees, frequent meetings, and accurate information exchanges are all cornerstones of positive employee and labor relations.

45. A, C, & D: KPIs add value by showing a clear picture of the implemented strategy, what matters and needs attention, and the progress towards goals. The average training costs and return on investment are examples of actual KPIs that can be calculated to show the effectiveness of training.

46. 34.33%: To calculate attrition rate, divide the number of employees that left the company during the year by the total number of employees at the beginning of the year, and then multiply that amount by 100. In this example, the calculation is (23/67) x 100 = 34.33%.

47. D: The total rewards package is made up of five specific components: pay, benefits, work-life programs, learning and development, and performance and recognition. Choices *A, B,* and *C* are incorrect because they do not fully incorporate all of the components required for the total rewards package. Some of these items, such as the offer letter, training schedule, supervisor information, and health insurance providers, may be incorporated into the package. It is important to include all of the components to ensure a full awareness and understanding of all programs available to a new employee.

48. A: Employees should receive the employee handbook, policies, procedures, and expectations of employment on their first day with the organization. Typically, this information is provided during the new hire orientation. Choice *B* is incorrect in that employees should have this information before an issue arises; however, it may be a best practice to provide this information when a new issue is brought forward so that the employee can refamiliarize themselves with the policies. Choice *C* is incorrect because candidates are not usually provided with this level of information. The organization's vision, mission, and values can be made available, but an employee handbook and the policies, procedures, and expectations of an employee are for employees, not candidates. Choice *D* is incorrect because while this is a best practice for accessibility of information for employees to seek out when needed, it should be provided during an orientation session to allow for questions and not just available for an employee to find.

49. A: A division organizational structure groups jobs by industry or market. A geographic organizational structure groups jobs according to geographic location. A product organizational structure groups jobs by product line. A functional organizational structure groups jobs according to function.

50. D: Choice *D* is the correct answer because this statement is incorrect in defining talent acquisition. Talent acquisition does not only deal with the initial hiring of an employee, but it also looks beyond to the promotional opportunities and the future development of the workforce. Choices *A, B,* and *C* are incorrect answers because they are all accurate statements regarding talent acquisition. Talent acquisition is the entire process from when a vacancy occurs to when the new employee joins the organization. It is a strategic process that also includes assessing the needs of the workforce and recruiting the best talent to fill those needs. Additionally, talent acquisition works to acquire the talent needed to align with the needs of the organization.

162

51. A: Transference is one of the most important elements of adult learning; it is how a participant understands the information learned in training and relates it to their job. Reinforcement, orientation, motivation, and retention are all important components of adult learning, but transference is the component that specifically correlates how an individual "transfers" the knowledge to their work.

52. A – 4; B – 1; C – 5; D – 2; & E – 3: The ADDIE model follows the steps Analyze, Design, Develop, Implement, and Evaluate. Analysis focuses on what is needed. Design focuses on what should be included and the audience of the message. Development focuses on the actual content and material. Implement focuses on the delivery of the program. Evaluation focuses on the effectiveness and validation of the training program.

53. E: Only a qualifying event allows an employee to make changes outside of open enrollment. Qualifying events include marriage, divorce, birth or adoption of a child, or a spouse's loss or gain of a job. A diagnosis of a medical condition is not a qualifying event.

54. A – 3, B – 1, C – 4, D – 2: Collective bargaining refers to the process of negotiation between management and union representatives. Good faith bargaining refers to the duty of both parties to demonstrate a sincere and honest intent to reach agreement. Ground rules refer to a set of items agreed upon by both parties to assist the negotiations process. Ratification refers to the process in which represented employees vote to approve or deny a proposed settlement.

55. C: Internal equity refers to the parity of salary between positions within the same organization, and external equity refers to the parity of salary between positions between different organizations. While it is important to take into account market review information and ensure that the salary is aligned on various levels, internal and external equity refers to the parity of salary within the same organization and between different organizations. Both are important to utilize when referring to salary and pay structures.

56. D: Ergonomics is defined as fitting an employee's workplace conditions to the job demands and specific individual needs. Workplace security is the management of all personnel, equipment, and facilities, including ergonomics. The STAR technique can be used to assess a situation, including one for which ergonomics could be applied and solutions discovered. Safety is the responsibility of all employees and is an overarching theory in which ergonomics falls under.

57. B: Time and attendance procedures establish the requirements and expectations of employees regarding reliability as well as stipulate the consequences for not adhering to these requirements. FMLA is a type of medical leave that should be described and discussed within time and attendance procedures. Disciplinary actions may be warranted to address violations of time and attendance procedures and should be described and discussed within these procedures. Additionally, time and attendance procedures should be included in the employee handbook provided to new employees.

58. A, B, & D: Communication in both an upward and downward direction is important because this can increase the success of a process, help to ensure achievements are met, and allow for maximum engagement. It is the responsibility of all employees, managers, supervisors, and leadership to engage in open communication.

59. Top-down communication: A presentation from upper management to staff on the company's mission is an example of top-down communication.

60. B: An Individual Development Plan (IDP) is the tool used to engage employees in a discussion about future opportunities and skills needed to accomplish their goals. While performance evaluations, training programs, and performance improvement plans are important and are aligned with the IDP, they are different tools that assess specific performance and needs during a set time frame as well as identify courses to provide learning opportunities.

61. A, B, & D: When a security breach occurs, it is vital that organizations implement the emergency management action plan, report the incident immediately, and communicate to employees the breach and any ramifications. It is also important to inform leadership when the issue occurs and throughout the action plan, not only when the issue has been resolved.

62. A – 2; B – 4; C – 1; D – 5; E – 3: There are five common standard learning processes, each with a different focus. The focus of behaviorism is on what an individual does. Cognitivism focuses on how an individual processes information. The focus of constructivism is on how an individual interprets and applies new information. Experiential focuses on an individual's experiences and how they can learn from them. The focus of connectivism is on an individual being self-directed.

63. B: Talent acquisition is a strategic process that reviews the current and future needs of the workforce to ensure implantation of a holistic and complete process. Choice *A* is incorrect because recruitment is the tactical process of filling an open position. Recruitment is a component of talent acquisition. Choice *C* is incorrect because onboarding is the process of bringing a new employee into the organization and acquainting them with the day-to-day operations, training them in policies such as safety, and finalizing new paperwork. Choice *D* is incorrect because workforce planning is the practice of reviewing all positions within an organization and determining the needs to accomplish the work. Workforce planning feeds the talent acquisition process by identifying the jobs and positions needed first.

64. C: The correct progression in evaluating the effectiveness of a training program is Reaction, Learning, Behavior, Results. Each level builds on the previous level. Some programs need only the two lower levels of evaluation, depending on the scope and impact of the training.

65. A: The performance management process begins with planning and concludes with employee recognition. The standard performance management process includes the following steps: planning, coaching, evaluating, and rewarding.

66. A – 2, B – 1, C – 3: Operation responses focus on implementing protocols and procedures when responding to an emergency to protect employees first and the business second. Communications focus on ensuring that all employees, regardless of level or location, have all the information necessary to react safely and quickly in the event of an emergency. Management responses focus on engaging and advising senior leadership regarding the emergency, actions taken, and any necessary action plans.

67. A – 3, B – 4, C – 2, D – 1: Data security is defined as the security relating to controlling the confidentiality, availability, and integrity of data. Data privacy is defined as the appropriate use and control of data. Encryption is a best practice that ensures only the sender and recipients of an email have access to the information contained within the email. A security breach occurs when unauthorized individuals gain access to private and sensitive information.

68. C: The method with the lowest retention rate is Lecture at 5 percent, and the method with the highest retention rate is Teaching Others at 90 percent. Demonstration has a 30 percent retention rate; Practice is 75 percent; Reading is 10 percent.

69. C: The ultimate goal of handling any complaint is to resolve the issue at the lowest level possible. While it is important to follow a structured process to resolve issues and inform leadership of the issues,

164

effective resolution of the issue with the lowest amount of intervention is the goal. Resolving complaints does require being respectful and responsive, but this is not the ultimate goal when handling complaints. Please note that some complaints must proceed directly to a formal and escalated response due to the complaint.

70. C: General intelligence tests show how quickly an applicant processes complex problems with the information provided and then formulates a solution based on the steps taken. Reasoning tests assess how applicants determine the right answers to a problem after receiving set pieces of information. Cognitive ability tests assess mental abilities in verbal and non-verbal skills, memory, and information processing. Personality tests show the general personality type of applicants and provide insight into how they will work with others.

71. Internal business processes: The balanced scorecard contains metrics that span across four perspectives: customer, financial, employee learning and growth, and internal business processes.

72. A: Ideally, an organization should offer salaries that are within 5 percent of the average market salary. If the salary is outside of this range, as with Choices *B, C,* and *D,* HR should assess why and make recommendations to address the disparity, especially if the offered salaries are below the market average, as that could affect employee retention.

73. A & D: Recognition programs should be common and frequent, and can be formal or informal and structured or unplanned. Formal programs are important but informal programs are just as important and may even have a bigger impact with employee morale. Recognition programs definitely have an impact on employee morale and are necessary for an organization to offer.

74. A – 2, B – 4, C – 3, & D – 1: The clan culture focuses on collaboration with leaders and is built on a foundation of employee development and participation at all levels of the organization. The adhocracy culture focuses on creativity with leaders and is built on a foundation of innovation, vision, and new resources. The hierarchy culture focuses on control and process with leaders and is built on a foundation of control and efficiency through the use of stable and consistent processes. The market culture focuses on competition with leaders and is built on a foundation of aggressive competitiveness and customer focus.

75. E: None of these statements are true. When developing a training program, many resources should be used to consider the needs of the organization. When delivering a training program, employees should be selected based on their individual needs and growth opportunities. The exception to this is that some training programs are mandatory; therefore, all employees must attend. When creating a training program, structure is important, but flexibility should be added in where appropriate to encourage discussion and dynamic learning. It is vital for leadership to participate and commit to training programs to ensure success.

76. A: The goal of any disaster management plan is to ensure that employees are prepared for emergencies and have the knowledge to follow appropriate protocols that provide safety to all. Reviewing the responses and outcomes to provide insight into effective practices is the focus of the mitigation step within an emergency management plan. Ensuring that work operations return to business as usual as quickly as possible is the focus of the recovery step within an emergency management plan. Focusing on any and all activities that occur during a disaster is the focus of the preparedness step within an emergency management plan.

77. A & B: Alternate work schedules offered to employees can allow flexibility for employees. The 4X10 schedule allows employees to only work four days a week, ten hours a day. The 9X80 schedule allows employees to work nine out of ten days within a two-week period, nine hours a day for eight days and eight hours a day for one day. The 5X8 schedule is a standard schedule working five days a week, eight hours a day; therefore, it is not considered an alternate work schedule.

78. A, B, C, & D: A robust total rewards program has many benefits, including attracting and retaining the most qualified and experienced individuals, maintaining a high employee satisfaction and level of morale, and having highly qualified personnel.

79. B, C, & D: Evaluating, reducing, and controlling risks are required responsibilities by employers regarding workplace security. Additionally, employers need to work together with employees and inform supervisors about any potential safety matters. It is necessary for employers to identify hazards and remove these risks, not create workarounds; therefore, Choice *A* is incorrect. It is also necessary for employers to document and record any and all issues identified, along with the specific actions taken to address these issues; thus, Choice *E* is incorrect.

80. C: Personnel files are one of the most important and fundamental recordkeeping functions within Human Resources. New hire documents and offer letters are components of the personnel file and timecards are generally retained within Payroll.

81. A – 3, B – 4, C – 1, & D – 2. An employee survey is a series of written questions to be completed by the individual performing the work that is being analyzed. An employee interview is a conversation to discuss the work being performed and ask additional follow-up questions that may arise after reviewing the survey. A job description is the complete list of duties, responsibilities, and required skills that may need to be updated to reflect an accurate picture of the work being performed. An on-the-job observation is a visual review of the actual work being performed. All of the above job analysis tools should be used together to complete a thorough assessment.

82. C: The career component of the EVP encourages employees to know and understand how their performance aligns with the expectations of the position and future opportunities. Additionally, the career component includes the stability, training, education, coaching, evaluation, and feedback. Choice *A* is incorrect because the culture component of the EVP encourages the entire organization to understand the overarching goals and objectives, including the values of trust, support, teamwork, collaboration, and social responsibility. Choice *B* is incorrect because the work environment component of the EVP includes the recognition of performance, balancing work life and home life, and encouraging engagement and involvement across all levels of the organization. Choice *D* is incorrect because the benefits component of the EVP includes the retirement programs, health insurance programs, time off, holiday schedule, telecommuting options, and educational reimbursements.

83. B & C: The FMLA is unpaid leave (so Choice *A* is incorrect), but employees can take vacation and sick leave to receive pay during a protected FMLA leave; thus, Choices *B* and *C* are correct. The FMLA is not a paid leave, and organizations should have a policy regarding this leave that includes the responsibilities of the employer and employee, the entitlements afforded to taking this leave, and the process to request FMLA.

84. A: Human resources can incorporate a company's vision into daily business activities through all of the following activities:

- Training hiring managers to interview candidates to determine if they are going to be the best cultural fit based on the company's values.

- Reinforcing the values during a new hire orientation presentation.

- Reinforcing the values in company communications.

- Developing a system to recognize and reward employees for demonstrating the company's values.

- Integrating the company's values into the performance review process.

- Deciding to terminate employees who ultimately fail to follow the company's values.

85. A & D: Security breaches can have a negative impact regarding publicity, and it is crucial for organizations to manage privacy and security as a core competency of the business. Security breaches can absolutely have an impact on customer loyalty and business, as they affect both employees and customers. Additionally, it is absolutely necessary for employees to have a feeling of security regarding their personal information.

86. Employee Surplus – C, E, & F; Employee Shortage – A, B, & D: When organizations face an employee surplus, it may be necessary to implement short-term solutions to attempt to remedy the situation. These solutions include freezing all hiring activity and using attrition to manage the headcount, approving additional absences, and reducing the number of hours worked each week. When organizations face an employee shortage, short-term solutions may include offering additional overtime opportunities, offering vacation or leave buybacks, and transferring work out the department.

87. B, C, & D: Attrition occurs when employees leave an organization. Attrition can be broken down into voluntary and involuntary attrition; it is the data representation of an organization's turnover. Attrition is an important metric that can enable an organization to make appropriate changes to retain employees and minimize turnover. The process of visualizing gaps in an organization, Choice *A*, is called succession planning.

88. B: The FLSA law sets the standards to determine if a position is eligible for overtime compensation. An organization determines within their policies whether bilingual pay is offered as well as if and when merit increases will be awarded to an employee.

89. D: As much information as possible regarding compensation should be included on an employee's paycheck and communicated to them so there is an understanding of how the paycheck is arranged. All forms of salary including overtime, specialty pay, etc.; benefits deductions and contributions; and retirement deductions and contributions should all be included on an employee's paycheck.

90. D: In John Kotter's Change Model "form the change coalition" step, key stakeholders and true leaders in the organization who will be able to lead the change effort with their influence and authority are identified. The coalition should be made up of a mix of individuals from various levels and departments throughout the organization.

aPHR Practice Test #2

1. Minh was injured and will need to be out of work for about a month to recuperate. She has contacted her HR department regarding filing a claim with her disability insurance. Which policy will she need to file against to cover her time out of work?
   a. LTD
   b. PPO
   c. STD
   d. HMO

2. Which of the following is a drawback to the ADDIE instructional design model?
   a. It does not allow for handling unexpected questions.
   b. It does not include a variety of information delivery methods.
   c. It does not work well if changes and continual evolution are happening.
   d. It requires an evaluation person to sit in on the training courses.

3. Organization A pays its middle management employees a relatively high salary and enjoys a high retention rate as a result. Organization B pays significantly below the going rate for their middle management employees, while Organization C pays well, but not quite as much as Organization A. What is the term for Organization C?
   a. Market leader
   b. Market follower
   c. Market lagger
   d. Market sub

4. There are many benefits of hiring an outside, third-party investigator when handling employee issues. All BUT which of the choices below is one of these benefits?
   a. It enhances credibility and trust in HR.
   b. It allows for a quicker and speedier investigation.
   c. It ensures a fair and unbiased investigation.
   d. It provides an accurate representation of the issue.

5. What is a long-term solution for an employee surplus?
   a. Reducing the work week to under forty hours
   b. Permanently transferring employees to different positions
   c. Reducing overtime
   d. Approving absences without pay

6. Which of the following resolutions could be initiated to resolve a complaint? (Select all that apply.)
   a. Changing policy
   b. Creating a training program
   c. Conflict resolution between employees
   d. Discipline

7. Match the Act to the proper regulation that was enacted with its passing.
   a. Norris-LaGuardia Act
   b. National Labor Relations Act
   c. Taft-Hartley Act
   d. Landrum-Griffin Act

   1. Increased reporting requirements, regulated union affairs, and protected union members from inappropriate practices
   2. Governs relations between unions and employees, allowing the right to organize and bargain
   3. Endorses collective bargaining as public policy
   4. Provides employers with additional rights and protections

8. The Family Medical Leave Act provides an employee how much time of protected leave to care for a family member or for the birth of a child?
   a. Six months
   b. Twelve weeks
   c. Six weeks
   d. Four months

9. Which of the following is NOT a benefit of a critical skills gap analysis?
   a. Making better decisions in training
   b. Analyzing the qualification and skills requirements for a job
   c. Allowing employees to understand how to be successful and progress their careers
   d. Assist hiring managers with evaluating applicants

10. Which talent sourcing technique involves using keywords with Applicant Tracking System technology?
   a. Job postings
   b. Resume mining
   c. Employee referrals
   d. Educational candidate pipelines

11. Which of the following benefits is government mandated to be offered to employees?
   a. Long-term care coverage
   b. Health care coverage
   c. Legal protection coverage
   d. Pet insurance coverage

12. Which of the following is a standard, efficient, and effective method to identify employee needs, wants, or concerns?
   a. Comment cards
   b. Individual meetings
   c. Employee surveys
   d. Market research

13. Which part of the employee value proposition includes retirement programs, insurance coverage options, and paid time off?
    a. Compensation
    b. Work Environment
    c. Culture
    d. Benefits

14. Which of the following statements about confidentiality is FALSE?
    a. Confidentiality and privacy should be provided for all employees, including those reporting bad behavior and those who may have engaged in the behavior.
    b. Confidentiality should be protected at all costs and under no circumstance compromised.
    c. Confidentiality is vital to an employee reporting unethical or inappropriate behavior.
    d. Confidentiality allows for an unbiased and fair investigation to occur.

15. Which of the following benefits are realized when an organization practices and maintains strong employee relations? (Select all that apply.)
    a. Engaged employees
    b. Increased budgets
    c. Enhanced employee rights
    d. Increased productivity

16. Darnell needs to assess the recent training program that his company provided to the employees. What are good sources of information that he can use to assess and report on the training program's effectiveness?
    a. Participant surveys and pre/post-testing
    b. Management input on the training program
    c. HR studies on similar past programs
    d. Employee participation rates

17. How should the information on paychecks, such as salary, overtime, taxes, etc., be listed?
    a. Itemized by payments and deductions
    b. Grouped according to payments and deductions
    c. Grouped by income and itemized deductions
    d. Itemized income and grouped deductions

18. Why is it important for internal investigations to be independent and impartial? (Select all that apply.)
    a. Allows for a fair and accurate investigation, conclusion, and recommendation
    b. Allows for a broad investigation, identifying new resources with information
    c. Avoids allegations or the perception of conflicts of interest
    d. Affects cultural change and promotes appropriate and respectful behavior

19. Which of the following statements about alternative dispute resolution (ADR) is NOT accurate?
    a. ADR processes progress from more formal to less formal.
    b. ADR processes include negotiation, mediation, conciliation, and arbitration.
    c. ADR processes include both formal and informal methods to resolve concerns.
    d. ADR processes work to expedite the exchange of information and decision-making processes.

20. Susan needs to analyze a job at her company to write an updated job description. What are the three job analysis methods she should use?
    a. Observation, evaluation, characterization
    b. Interview, observation, questionnaire
    c. Characterization, responsibilities, scope of work
    d. Interview, evaluation, questionnaire

21. Which term refers to an organization's ability to implement changes in a diligent and comprehensive manner?
    a. Change agents
    b. Change model
    c. Change initiatives
    d. Change management

22. Which term refers to the process of filling an open position at an organization?
    a. Advertisement
    b. Recruitment
    c. Screening
    d. Onboarding

23. Organization A is looking to hire a new employee. Their budget does not allow them to pay as high a salary as their competitor across town, but they would really like to attract high-caliber, high-performing candidates for the position. What can they do to make their position more attractive to potential employees?
    a. Advertise at upscale locations in high-end parts of town.
    b. Offer bonus pay and monetary performance awards.
    c. Post the position on social media.
    d. Promote the position at local college campuses to attract recent graduates.

24. Which of the following is NOT a mandatory subject of a collective bargaining agreement (CBA)?
    a. Employee wages
    b. Overtime earnings
    c. Union dues
    d. Employee termination

25. What is the term for an unstructured interview during which an applicant meets with multiple people at once, such as an entire work group or department?
    a. Candidate experience
    b. Open-ended panel interview
    c. STAR interview
    d. Triads

26. How can companies encourage current employees to assist in the recruitment process?
    a. By offering referral bonuses
    b. By letting employees directly hire their coworkers
    c. By allowing employees to sit in on interviews
    d. By asking employees to post job openings on social media

171

27. Once a new employee has begun working, when is the best time to schedule NEO follow-up discussions?
   a. After thirty, sixty, and ninety days
   b. After forty-five, ninety, and 180 days
   c. On an as-needed basis
   d. Only when the new employee is having trouble with something

28. An organization that wants to ensure that an employment candidate would be a good fit for the existing team should consider incorporating what type of interview during the hiring process?
   a. Triads
   b. Focus groups
   c. Paired interviews
   d. In-depth interviews

29. Which of the following is a good definition of job pricing?
   a. The parity of salary between positions within the same organization
   b. The comparison of salaries between positions at different organizations
   c. The salary range that compensates for various levels of experience
   d. The process by which an organization determines the salary of positions

30. A cafeteria-style benefit plan is dictated by which section of the Internal Revenue Code?
   a. 125
   b. 135
   c. 145
   d. 155

31. Which of the following is NOT a qualifying event in regard to benefits enrollment?
   a. Birth or adoption of a child
   b. Death of a spouse
   c. Marriage and/or divorce
   d. Loss or gain of a spouse's job

32. What type of communication strategy is used when the leader of an organization issues a communication to their direct reports, who then relay this message to the next level of the organization until the message has been relayed to all employees?
   a. Pyramid Method
   b. Triangle Method
   c. Cascading Method
   d. Top-Down Method

33. Which organizational expert devised a change theory that included unfreezing, changing, and refreezing?
   a. John Kotter
   b. Peter Senge
   c. Kurt Lewin
   d. Joseph Kowalski

34. When forecasting the personnel needs of an organization, it is important to consider which of the following?
    a. Scope of work, working conditions, and minimum job requirements
    b. Qualifications, experience, and skills needed for the position
    c. Sales, market opportunities, company demographics
    d. Observation, questionnaire, and interview

35. A(n) _____ is a neutral third party that helps resolve disputes by hearing both parties and making a final, binding decision.
    a. facilitator
    b. arbitrator
    c. mediator
    d. fact finder

36. When would mediation be the best method for resolving a dispute?
    a. When both parties want a binding decision
    b. When one party has more power/authority over the other
    c. When a dispute requires an expert to make a decision
    d. When both parties want to preserve the relationship

37. Which of the following statements is NOT correct regarding risk management within the HR department?
    a. HR policies and practices should always support a workplace that minimizes risk.
    b. HR should identify risks only when a specific incident occurs, or in a reactive setting.
    c. HR can be proactive in minimizing risk by establishing strong documentation and process.
    d. HR should conduct regular audits to ensure compliance with laws and updates.

38. There are many benefits when working with a group of diverse employees. Which of the following do organizations NOT typically face when there is diversity among employees?
    a. Recruiting and retention
    b. Turnover and attrition
    c. Growth and development
    d. Creativity and innovation

39. Which of the following are benefits resulting from establishing a commitment to diversity and inclusion? (Select all that apply.)
    a. Increased innovation
    b. Stronger performance
    c. Expansion in market share
    d. Enhanced engagement
    e. Greater motivation

40. Thomas is working on his company's policies and practices regarding appropriate behavior expectations, and he wants to be proactive. He has already posted labor law posters in the break rooms and scheduled training sessions for all of the employees. What else could he do?
    a. Address issues as they arise.
    b. Speak to each employee individually about expectations.
    c. Have a plan in place in the event of a lawsuit.
    d. Provide handbooks to new employees during orientation.

41. Of the five market analysis methods for analyzing a job, which would be the best method for considering individual factors and allowing for more objectivity?
    a. Ranking method
    b. Point factor method
    c. Factor comparison method
    d. Classification/grading method

42. An employee is involuntarily terminated from a company for poor performance. How long does the employee have to elect Consolidated Omnibus Budget Reconciliation Act (COBRA) continuation coverage?
    a. Involuntary separations are not eligible for COBRA continuation coverage.
    b. Thirty days
    c. Sixty days
    d. There is no time limit for electing coverage.

43. A supervisor approached LaShonda with a complaint that one of the employees has not been performing well on the job and has missed several days of work over the last few weeks. LaShonda reviewed the employee's records and employment history with the company. Until now, the employee has always done an exceptional job, though the current issues are causing problems within the department. How should LaShonda handle the situation?
    a. Let the HR manager know that the employee is being fired.
    b. Tell the supervisor to fire the employee and let HR know when it is done.
    c. Meet with the employee and tell them that their job is at risk, and they need to improve their performance.
    d. Speak with the employee and see if the employee counseling and employee assistance programs offered by the company would help them resolve the problems affecting their work.

44. Delores is working on revising the salary structure for a position at her company. Management has approved three classifications: minimum, middle, and maximum. They want a minimum salary of $40,000 and will allow a 30 percent range. Given that information, what would be the midpoint salary offering and the maximum salary for the position?
    a. $52,000 and $64,000
    b. $46,000 and $52,000
    c. $45,000 and $50,000
    d. $48,000 and $56,000

45. Human Resources should be structured in a way that provides the best customer service to the organization, departments, and employees. The two most common forms of structure are decentralized and centralized models. What is the difference between these two models?
    a. A decentralized model allows for HR staff to report to the HR department, while a centralized model allows for HR staff to report to external department leaders.
    b. Both models allow for HR staff to report to the HR department, with a decentralized model providing services to external customers.
    c. A decentralized model allows for HR staff to report to external department leaders, while a centralized model allows for all HR staff to report to the HR department.
    d. Both models allow for HR staff to report to the HR department, with a centralized model providing services to internal customers.

174

46. Under Title VII of the Civil Rights Act of 1964, which of the following is NOT prohibited from workplace discrimination?
    a. Discrimination based on race.
    b. Discrimination based on gender.
    c. Discrimination based on age.
    d. Discrimination based on national origin.

47. Which of the following categories includes deferred compensation and retirement programs, direct deposit forms, and the I-9?
    a. Application and resume
    b. Benefits paperwork
    c. Intranet and self-service portal
    d. ATS

48. Which term describes the intentional planning to engage all employees in the achievement of objectives that align with the overall success of an organization?
    a. Diversity
    b. Strategic planning
    c. Inclusion
    d. Business acumen

49. Maya's company is looking at offering a retirement program to its employees. The company is a nonprofit organization with more than three hundred employees and has been in business since 2018. The company is headquartered in Missouri. Which retirement plan would be appropriate for this company?
    a. 401(k)
    b. 403(b)
    c. 457(b)
    d. 425(a)

50. Which of the following statements regarding internal investigations are TRUE? (Select all that apply.)
    a. It is a best practice to always escalate issues and complaints to a third-party investigation.
    b. Investigations should be conducted with good-faith efforts.
    c. Investigations should be conducted by professionals who have been properly and formally trained.
    d. It is best practice to interview only the individual making the complaint and the individual the complaint is against.

51. _____ refers to the honest attempt made by both an employer and union to reach an agreement.
    a. Mandatory subjects of bargaining
    b. Good faith bargaining
    c. Collective bargaining
    d. Labor relations

52. Under the employment-at-will doctrine, how much notice must an employee or employer provide to terminate the working relationship?
    a. Employees and employers must provide two weeks' notice.
    b. Employees must provide two weeks' notice; employers are not required to provide notice.
    c. Employees do not need to provide notice; employers are required to provide two weeks' notice.
    d. Neither employees nor employers need to provide notice.

53. There are numerous ways to communicate policies, programs, and changes to practices. Employees should have multiple ways of accessing this information so that they are informed, educated, and aware. Which of the following is the easiest way for misunderstandings and inaccuracies to occur?
    a. Town halls and employee meetings with leadership
    b. Formal handbooks and brochures
    c. Printed webpages and electronic documents
    d. Word of mouth and employee-to-employee communication

54. Strategic planning is dependent on which of the following?
    a. HR professionals who are proficiently trained in process mapping and assessment
    b. Robust and thorough recruitment, selection, hiring, and onboarding practices
    c. Knowledge and awareness of the organizational and departmental goals and objectives
    d. Outsourced HR staff who are unbiased and separate from the organizational culture

55. Patrick's company follows the eight-step change model with regard to large organization-wide changes. Patrick is working on devising a plan to manage an overhaul of his company's management system using this eight-step model. Management has already created urgency around the need for this change, and they have formed a change coalition, putting Patrick in charge of it. What is the next step Patrick needs to take?
    a. Empower action.
    b. Create a clear vision.
    c. Create short-term wins.
    d. Build on the change.

56. Which of the following is NOT a circumstance allowing for a hardship withdrawal from a retirement account?
    a. Medical expenses
    b. Educational tuition
    c. Spousal job loss
    d. Funeral expenses

57. What are the current deductible thresholds for a plan to be considered an HDHP?
    a. $1,400 for individuals and $2,800 for families
    b. $1,400 for individuals and $2,000 for families
    c. $2,800 for individuals and $3,600 for families
    d. $2,800 for individuals and $5,400 for families

58. A candidate's first look at how an organization behaves and what is expected from employees is presented in what?
    a. Job description brochure
    b. Benefits overview
    c. Vision, mission, and values statements
    d. Company background

59. What is the complete process of forecasting an organization's current and future workforce needs and determining the most effective way to fill these needs called?
    a. Critical skills gap analysis
    b. Succession planning
    c. Recruitment
    d. Workforce planning

60. _____ can assist employees with their transition out of an organization and can include compensation, extension of benefits, transition services, and other services.
    a. Employee Assistance Programs
    b. Severance packages
    c. Reductions in force
    d. Performance management

61. Which statements below are TRUE regarding diversity and inclusion? (Select all that apply.)
    a. Diversity and inclusion foster an inclusive environment in which differences are valued and respected.
    b. Diversity and inclusion strategies have an impact solely in the workplace.
    c. Diversity is the mixture, and inclusion is making the mixture work.
    d. The impacts of a strong diversity and inclusion strategy are seen within the organization but do not have an external impact.

62. Which of the following are items that ground rules should address? (Select all that apply.)
    a. Where, when, and how long the parties will meet
    b. Ratification process
    c. Communications plan regarding media
    d. Cut-off date for new proposals
    e. Employee interests

63. Elise is writing up all the information that should be included in her organization's benefit programs policy. So far, she has notes about how and when premiums are paid, eligibility terms and waiting periods, opt-out options and mandatory participation details, and how to make changes when needed. What else should she include?
    a. CEO emails regarding a new program the company is considering adding
    b. Information about why one of the providers was replaced, if necessary
    c. Details about how employees can sign up for benefits on their own
    d. Contact information for service providers

64. Drop and drag the separation reason with the termination type.
    a. Poor performance
    b. Failure of probation   Voluntary Termination
    c. Retirement
    d. Resignation to accept another job   Involuntary Termination
    e. Discipline
    f. Resignation to relocate with spouse

65. Which of the following is NOT a use of an LMS?
    a. Create training materials and delivery methods.
    b. Activity and learning tracking
    c. Incorporate the five P's.
    d. Assess teaching and learning performance.

66. You are working on filling a position at your company. Currently, you are in the process of scheduling interviews. Which step of the recruitment process are you in?
    a. Two
    b. Three
    c. Four
    d. Five

67. Angelina is preparing for the arrival of a new employee and wants to make sure she has everything ready to go when the employee arrives. She has the orientation set up to review paychecks, benefits, holidays, and the retirement package. She also has onboarding in place with the employee's new laptop and phone. The employee is going to be a supervisor, so Angelina has prepared a package with information on all the employees the new person will be supervising. She knows there is a fourth area that she needs to include but can't remember what it is. What is she forgetting?
    a. Connecting the new employee with a buddy or mentor
    b. Showing the new employee around the building, break rooms, and workstations
    c. Worker's compensation, personal medical leaves, and safety protocol
    d. Introducing the new employee to everyone around the office

68. Match the inclusive workplace pillar with its description.
    a. Awareness   1. Set up the policies and procedures that allow for accountability
    b. Mobilization   2. Analyze, review, and revise policies and procedures
    c. Action   3. Implement strategies through specific actions and plans
    d. Alignment   4. Raise the understanding of employees toward diversity initiatives

69. Which alternative dispute resolution method is a non-binding formal process in which a negotiator explains the law and provides the two parties with a non-binding recommendation to resolve the issue?
    a. Arbitration
    b. Negotiation
    c. Mediation
    d. Conciliation

70. The ADDIE model is a generic instructional design model that can be used to create effective training programs. ADDIE stands for analyze, design, develop, implement, evaluate. What should be included in the design step of this program?
    a. Assessing the needs of the organization, departments, teams, and individuals
    b. Deciding what should be included and who will deliver the program
    c. Determining the content of the training and the materials that will be used
    d. Running trial sessions to resolve any issues

71. An employee recently approached Gordon to ask about potentially increasing the company's paid maternity leave policy. When Gordon approached the CEO about it, the CEO said that this was not possible because it would not conform with federal laws. Is this correct?
    a. No, each company can choose whether or not they want to offer maternity leave, and if so, how much.
    b. No, the law allows for adding more than the minimum benefit requirements.
    c. Yes, companies must only offer what the federal and state laws provide.
    d. Yes, federal law says that the maximum maternity leave a company can offer is twelve weeks.

72. Which of the following workplace accommodations would be considered UNREASONABLE?
    a. Installing a sit/stand ergonomic desk to allow for wheelchair access
    b. Approving a telecommuting arrangement to work from home due to an injury
    c. Modifying the work schedule to allow for unlimited paid breaks
    d. Providing additional breaks and a secure, private area to allow nursing mothers to lactate

73. Which of the following is a detailed risk assessment that provides insight and information regarding a specific concern or issue?
    a. Due diligence investigation
    b. Policy audit
    c. Workplace safety investigation
    d. Benefit audit

74. When must an employer have filed an I-9 document for a new employee?
    a. On the employee's first day
    b. Within the first three days of employment
    c. Within the first week of employment
    d. The employer is not required to file an I-9; that is the employee's responsibility.

75. Sections on confidentiality, conflicts of interest, and reporting code violations should be included in which company document?
    a. Code of conduct
    b. Anti-sexual harassment posters
    c. New employee orientation handbook
    d. Onboarding procedures manual

76. Which of the following is NOT one of the skills assessments organizations may use during the hiring process?
    a. Background check
    b. Personality
    c. Cognitive ability
    d. Reasoning

77. Which of the following agencies enforces the laws regarding employee privacy?
    a. Occupational Safety and Health Administration (OSHA)
    b. Equal Employment Opportunity Commission (EEOC)
    c. Department of Justice (DOJ)
    d. Department of Labor (DOL)

78. Which of the following examples would be an INAPPOPRIATE reason to enter into a contract with an outside legal service?
    a. To negotiate a new contract with a union, and the team currently does not have this experience
    b. The current staff does not want to audit the safety practices because they find it uninteresting.
    c. To resolve a conflict between two employees after multiple attempts with the current staff
    d. To review and update leave administration policies based on updated state legislation

79. Which of the following is an INACCURATE statement about strategic planning?
    a. Strategic planning is critical to ensure that employees are working toward the goals and objectives of the organization.
    b. Strategic planning is the formal assessment of available resources, work force, knowledge, and skills within an organization.
    c. Strategic planning ensures that the organization is aware of and in possession of the resources necessary to succeed.
    d. Strategic planning plays a vital role in the success of an organization at all levels, including each individual department.

80. If your company began the year with ninety-two employees and ended the year with eighty-six employees, what is the attrition rate?
    a. 0.93 percent
    b. 93.5 percent
    c. 0.065 percent
    d. 6.5 percent

81. Tatiana is developing her company's organizational learning strategy. What are the five elements she should include in the training classes?
    a. Onboarding, motivation, retention, video learning, and transference
    b. Orientation, motivation, reinforcement, retention, and transference
    c. Orientation, written and auditory lessons, reinforcement, and training
    d. Onboarding, retention, auditory and video learning, and training

82. What term below includes the establishment, negotiation, and administration of bargaining agreements and policies as well as managing grievances and disagreements?
    a. Labor relations
    b. Workforce planning
    c. Employee relations
    d. Mediation

180

83. Which of the following options is NOT a program that can be uniquely tailored to enhance employee engagement?
    a. Safety and security protocols
    b. Training and learning opportunities
    c. Recognition and achievement programs
    d. Telecommuting and alternate work schedules

84. What are the five primary components that make up the EVP?
    a. Compensation, benefits, overtime pay, work environment, and culture
    b. Compensation, vacation and sick time, career, and culture
    c. Compensation, benefits, career, work environment, and culture
    d. Compensation, benefits, career, advancement opportunities, and culture

85. Which of the following workplace accommodations would be considered UNREASONABLE?
    a. Purchasing interpretation software
    b. Creating a new job and role for the employee
    c. Reassigning the employee to a new job
    d. Acquiring new office equipment and special devices

86. What is an employee surplus?
    a. When there is not enough work for all of the employees
    b. When there are not enough employees for all of the work
    c. When there is more work than expected, and employees cannot take time off
    d. When too many employees are taking time off during busy times of the year

87. Which of the following is a best practice regarding employee surveys?
    a. Committed leadership is not necessary for an effective survey.
    b. Surveys should require employees to identify themselves to ensure appropriate actions are taken.
    c. Commit to surveying employees every six to twelve months.
    d. Share data consistently at all levels of the organization.

88. What data point calculates how many employees are absent from work?
    a. Attrition
    b. Human capital
    c. Presenteeism
    d. Absenteeism

89. An employee moves from full-time employment to part-time status and elects COBRA continuation coverage. How long can the employee maintain their coverage under the Consolidated Omnibus Budget Reconciliation Act (COBRA)?
    a. Twelve months
    b. Eighteen months
    c. Twenty-four months
    d. Thirty-six months

90. Sammy's organization has several trainings sessions that it needs to provide to employees, covering annual legal and compliance updates, a new safety protocol, written communication guidelines and policies, and some teambuilding activities. Which training sessions can likely be provided in-house, and which ones should be outsourced to an external training service?

  a. The legal and safety topics should be in-house; the communication and teambuilding should be done by external training services.

  b. The legal topics and teambuilding should be done by external training providers; the safety and communication protocols should remain in-house.

  c. The legal topics and communications should be in-house; the safety and communication protocols should be outsourced.

  d. The legal and safety topics should be outsourced; the communication and teambuilding should be done in-house.

Answer Explanations #2

1. C: Short-term disability (STD) is insurance coverage that helps maintain an employee's income for a short duration. Long-term disability (LTD), Choice *A*, is insurance coverage for disabilities that keep the employee from working for an extended period. Choices *B* and *D* both refer to types of medical provider organizations, a preferred provider organization (PPO) and a health maintenance organization (HMO), respectively.

2. C: Because the ADDIE model is linear, each step builds on the last. This may not work well when there are continual changes and evolutions in the program. While handling unexpected questions, Choice *A*, can be difficult, the instructor should be ready for those situations regardless of the training methods. Choice *B*, a variety of delivery methods, such as the use of visual aids, can be included in a training program during the development stage of ADDIE. The evaluation step of ADDIE can involve having an evaluator sit in on the course, Choice *D*, but this is not required if it would be inconvenient or distracting to the participants.

3. B: Organization C would be considered a market follower. They do not pay as well as Organization A, which is a market leader, Choice *A*. They do not pay as low as Organization *B*, the market lagger, Choice *C*. Choice *D* is a made-up term.

4. B: Hiring a third-party investigator will most likely not allow for a quicker and speedier investigation. A proper and thorough investigation should take the amount of time needed to process all of the information and interview all potential witnesses or others who may have information in relation to the complaint. Choices *A*, *C*, and *D* are incorrect because they are all items that can be accomplished when an outside investigator is hired to handle complaints. These include enhanced credibility and trust in the HR department, a fair and unbiased investigation, and an accurate representation of the issues and concerns.

5. B: Permanently transferring employees to different positions is one of the possible long-term solutions to an employee surplus. Choices *A*, *C*, and *D* are all short-term solutions to this problem.

6. A, B, C, & D: Potential resolutions that could be initiated to resolve a complaint include changing policy, creating a training program, conflict resolution between employees, discipline, and/or various combinations of these four resolutions. Each concern should have a resolution(s) that is appropriate and supported based on the evidence and conclusions from the investigation.

7. A – 3, B – 2, C – 4, & D – 1: The Norris-LaGuardia Act endorses collective bargaining as public policy. The National Labor Relations Act governs relations between unions and employees, allowing the right to organize and bargain. The Taft-Hartley Act provides employers with additional rights and protections. The Landrum-Griffin Act increased reporting requirements, regulated union affairs, and protected union members from inappropriate practices.

8. B: An employee is eligible to receive twelve weeks of protected leave under the Family Medical Leave Act (FMLA) to care for a family member or for the birth of a child. There are additional eligible circumstances for an employee to take FMLA. Choices *A*, *C*, and *D* are incorrect because the FMLA allows for only twelve weeks of leave. While there are other circumstances that may allow for additional leave, such as caring for a service member, the standard leave time is twelve weeks.

9. B: Analyzing the qualifications and skills needed for a job is part of a job analysis rather than a critical skills gap analysis. A critical skills gap analysis helps an organization achieve its goals by making better decisions in training and recruitment, Choice *A*; assisting managers with evaluating applicants for hire, Choice *D*; and allowing employees to understand the skills required for success within the company, Choice *C*.

10. B: HR personnel can use technology such as the Applicant Tracking System to search for potential candidates. This is known as resume mining. Choices *A, C,* and *D* are all other ways to source talent and recruit potential employment candidates.

11. B: The Affordable Care Act (ACA) requires that all employers that meet certain standards provide health care coverage to their employees. Choices *A, C,* and *D* are incorrect because there is no government regulation that requires an employer to provide long-term care, legal protection, or pet insurance coverage. These benefits are considered voluntary, and employers may offer these benefits to employees at their own cost. Organizations may be able to offer discount pricing to employees on these programs, but there is not a requirement to provide them to employees.

12. C: Employee surveys are a standard, efficient, and effective method used to identify employee needs, wants, or concerns. These surveys can provide an opportunity for employees to communicate what the organization is doing well, what needs to be improved or changed, and any ideas or concerns they may have. Choice *A* is incorrect because comment cards are not effective, and employees may not feel a sense of confidence when utilizing this old-school method. Choice *B* is incorrect because meeting individually with every employee is not efficient, and employees may not want to communicate their true feelings to Human Resources. Choice *D* is incorrect because market research does not indicate the specific needs of the internal employees. This information may be beneficial when benchmarking new ideas and what the competition offers, but it will not provide insight into the needs of the current employees.

13. D: An employee benefits package includes retirement programs, insurance coverage options, and paid time off. Choices *A, B,* and *C* cover other aspects of the EVP, such as pay and bonuses, work-life balance, and organizational goals and objectives, respectively.

14. B: The correct answer is Choice *B*, as confidentiality may need to be broken due to information received. In cases in which a law has been broken or abuse has been reported, HR professionals may need to involve law enforcement or a legal advisor. Employees should understand this during the process of reporting to HR. Choice *A* is an incorrect answer, as providing confidentiality and privacy to all employees involved is true and should be extended to all individuals, including those who have allegedly engaged in the behavior. Choice *C* is an incorrect answer, as confidentiality is in fact vital to employees who may need to report unethical behavior. Choice *D* is also incorrect because confidentiality does allow for a fair and unbiased investigation.

15. A & D: Engaged employees and increased productivity are benefits that an organization will realize when practicing and maintaining strong employee relations. Indirect benefits may also include increased budgets and enhanced employee rights; however, there are many other factors in addition to employee relations that will affect the benefits being realized.

16. A: Participant surveys and pre- and post-testing are great ways to get feedback on the overall effectiveness of a training program. While management input, Choice *B*, might be helpful when creating the program, it cannot provide information about a program's effectiveness. Similarly, while reviewing the outcomes of past programs, Choice *C*, can help with planning, past results are not an indication of future success. Employee participation rates, Choice *D*, can show interest (in the case of optional trainings) but are not an indication of effectiveness.

17. A: Pay statements should include itemized lists of the types of income and the specific deductions. This gives employees a clear, detailed record of their pay for tax purposes, wage garnishment situations, pension contribution calculations, and so on. Simply grouping by payment and deduction, Choice *B*, or itemizing one category but not another, Choices *C* and *D*, do not give enough detail.

18. A & C: It is important for internal investigations to be independent and impartial because this allows for a fair and accurate investigation, conclusion, and recommendation and avoids allegations or the perception of conflicts of interest. Being proactive allows for a broad investigation, identifying new resources with information. Aligning recommendations with policies and procedures as well as making updates to these items based on investigation results affects cultural change and promotes appropriate and respectful behavior.

19. A: ADR processes progress from less formal to more formal. Choice *A* is the correct answer because it presents the process backwards. Choices *B, C,* and *D* are incorrect answers because they are all accurate statements about the alternative dispute resolution processes. ADR includes negotiation, mediation, conciliation, and arbitration. ADR includes both formal and informal processes to resolve issues. ADR works to expedite the exchange of information and decision-making for both parties.

20. B: When analyzing a job, it's beneficial to interview the employees in that position, observe them doing the work, and have them complete a questionnaire about the position. Choices *A, C,* and *D* are all incorrect.

21. D: Change management refers to an organization's ability to implement changes in a diligent and comprehensive manner. Change agents, Choice *A,* are the people tasked with implementing organizational changes. Choice *B* refers to the different theories around organizational change, and Choice *C* is a made-up term.

22. B: *Recruitment* refers to the entire process of filling a job opening. Choices *A, C,* and *D* are all parts of the recruitment process.

23. B: Offering bonus pay and monetary performance awards is a great way of adding to an employee's compensation package without committing to a higher regular salary. This way, if the company does better, the employee also does better. While advertising the position on social media, Choice *C,* and at local colleges, Choice *D,* can attract applicants, that does not help the organization be more competitive with regard to salary. Advertising in upscale parts of town, Choice *A,* is irrelevant to the situation.

24. C: Choice *C* is correct. Mandatory subjects that must be covered in a collective bargaining agreement include wages, hours, and conditions of employment. Union dues are permissive, as they do not pertain to any of the mandatory subject criteria. All other choices are mandatory subjects for a CBA.

25. B: An open-ended panel interview is one where an applicant is interviewed by a group of people. The applicant is given time to explain why they are the best candidate for the position. Candidate experience, Choice *A,* refers to the feelings, behaviors, and attitudes a job candidate faces when interacting with interviewers. STAR, Choice *C,* refers to a particular type of interview technique, and Choice *D,* triads, refers to structured interviews with three people.

26. A: Many organizations offer a financial reward or bonus program as an incentive for current employees to promote the company and recruit potential candidates. Employees are not usually permitted to sit in on interviews or conduct the actual hiring, Choices *C* and *B*. Organizations also generally do not ask employees to post job openings on social media, Choice *D*, because job postings have specific requirements that HR personnel need to oversee.

27. A: New employee orientation (NEO) follow up discussions should be scheduled after thirty, sixty, and ninety days to give the employee the opportunity to ask any questions or address any concerns they may have as they settle into their new position. Choices *B*, *C*, and *D* are not the correct intervals for a follow-up.

28. C: Paired interviews are usually conducted by current employees who would be working with the new recruit, so they can provide especially beneficial feedback as to how a new recruit might fit in and work with existing employees. Choices *A*, *B*, and *D*, while they are all interview techniques, do not specifically focus on how the potential employee fits in with the team.

29. D: Job pricing is the process by which an organization determines the salary of positions. Choice *A* refers to internal equity, and Choice *B* refers to external equity. Choice *C* refers to salary structure.

30. A: Section 125 of the Internal Revenue Code dictates a cafeteria-style benefit plan. Choices *B*, *C*, and *D* are incorrect.

31. B: The death of a spouse is not one of the qualifying events that allows an employee to make changes to their benefits enrollment selections outside of the open enrollment period. Choices *A*, *C*, and *D* are all qualifying events.

32. D: When a leader issues a communication that is then relayed to each level of the organization by the next level, they are using the Top-Down Method of communication. Choices *A*, *B*, and *C* are incorrect, as they are fictitious terms to create an image of how the message is relayed. Creating a picture of the Top-Down Method would look like a pyramid or triangle and could be synonymous with the term *cascading*.

33. C: Kurt Lewin was a social psychologist who devised a theory of organization change that included unfreezing, changing, and refreezing. John Kotter, Choice *A*, expanded on Lewin's ideas. Peter Senge, Choice *B*, advocates for systems thinking, and Choice *D* is a made-up answer.

34. C: Forecasting involves determining which positions must be filled and how. This involves reviewing sales and market opportunities as well as the company's current demographics. Choice *A* refers to the job description, which is part of the next stage of workforce planning: job analysis. Choice *B* lists some of the job specifications to consider during job analysis. Choice *D* refers to three methods of job analysis.

35. B: Choice *B* is correct. In arbitration, both parties dispute an issue and share their side. However, it is the responsibility of the arbitrator to decide on the subject and how the dispute will be resolved, forming a binding decision. Choices A, C, and *D* are all incorrect; while facilitators, mediators, and fact finders may intervene to help resolve a dispute, they do not make binding decisions.

36. D: Choice *D* is correct. Mediation is best suited for cases where the employees have a working relationship that they want to preserve, despite the dispute. Choice *A* is incorrect; mediation does not result in a binding decision. Choice *B* is incorrect because when one party in a dispute has a power advantage over the other, it can make mediation unfair or biased. Choice *C* is incorrect; a mediator does not have to be an expert and will not make a decision for the parties involved.

37. B: HR should identify risks when a specific incident occurs, or in a reactive setting. However, HR should also identify risks in a proactive manner. Choice *A* is incorrect because it is a factual statement;

186

every policy and practice within an organization should focus on supporting the workplace and minimizing risk. Choice *C* is an incorrect answer because HR should work to be proactive in minimizing and eliminating risk with strong documentation and process. This can include job descriptions, policies, safety procedures, complaints procedures, and investigations. Choice *D* is an incorrect answer because HR should conduct regular audits to ensure compliance with laws and updates. Being proactive is vital in ensuring a solid and robust risk management process.

38. B: Turnover and attrition are not usually issues in an organization that encourage and maintain a diverse workforce. The primary benefits of diversity include better recruitment, retention, growth, development, creativity, and innovation, Choices *A*, *C*, and *D*. More candidates will want to join the organization; employees will want to stay with the organization; employees will seek growth and development; and employees will engage with each other with creativity and innovation to resolve issues and seek out new solutions.

39. A, B, C, D, & E: Increased innovation, stronger performance, expansion in market share, enhanced engagement, and greater motivation are all benefits that an organization may gain from establishing a commitment to diversity and inclusion.

40. D: Providing new employees with a code of conduct handbook during orientation is a great way to make sure every employee is aware of the organization's policies and procedures from the beginning of their employment. Issues certainly need to be addressed as they arise, Choice *A*, but that would not be proactive. Speaking to each employee, Choice *B*, is not necessarily a feasible option, particularly in very large organizations. While it is good to have a plan in place in the event of an issue, Choice *C*, that is also not a proactive way of preventing problems.

41. B: The point factor method considers the individual factors of a job and adds value and weight to each factor, allowing for more objectivity in the analysis. The ranking method, Choice *A*, is easy to implement but does not consider individual job factors. Choice *C*, the factor comparison method, groups specific factors, but it is a difficult system and contains more subjectivity than the point factor method. Choice *D*, the classification/grading method, is straightforward but may force jobs into a particular grade that does not truly reflect the nature of the work.

42. C: Choice *C* is correct. The Consolidated Omnibus Budget Reconciliation Act (COBRA) allows employees sixty days after a qualifying event to elect continuation of their healthcare coverage.

43. D: Employee counseling and employee assistance programs are good ways of offering assistance to an otherwise good employee who may be having some temporary personal problems that are impacting their work. Simply telling the employee to improve, Choice *C*, is not an effective solution to whatever is causing the problem. While the employee may need to be fired, Choices *A* and *B*, it is often a good idea to try to fix the issues and retain a good employee first.

44. B: If the minimum salary is $40,000, and a 30 percent range is allowed, then the midpoint salary would be $46,000 (the minimum salary plus half of the range, or 15 percent, which is $6,000). The maximum salary would be $52,000 (the minimum salary plus the full 30 percent, or $12,000). Choice *A* reflects a 60 percent range (30 percent at the midpoint and another 30 percent at the maximum). Choices *C* and *D* are likewise incorrect.

45. C: The difference between a decentralized and centralized organizational structure is that a decentralized model allows for HR staff to report to external department leaders while a centralized model allows for all HR staff to report to the HR department. Both structures have positive and negative attributes, and organizations should select the model most appropriate for the customers being served. Choice *A* is incorrect because the definitions of the models are backwards. Choices *B* and *D* incorrectly state that both models allow for HR staff to report to the HR department. Additionally, these structures do not indicate an external or internal customer, but rather where the staff reports to and the departments being served by each position.

46. C: Choice *C* is correct. While age is a protected class of employees (under ADEA), Title VII of the Civil Rights Act of 1964 does not prohibit workplace discrimination based on age.

47. B: Benefits paperwork includes information and paperwork necessary for the employee to enroll in the organization's health insurance, deferred compensation and retirement programs; to sign up for direct deposit; and to complete the required I-9 form. The application and resume, Choice *A*, are usually part of the pre-employment process. Choice *C* refers to the technology an employee might use to review their benefits, payroll, and other relevant information. An ATS, Choice *D*, is software used to manage an organization's recruitment process.

48. C: Inclusion is the specific and intentional planning that engages every employee in the achievement of the organization's success by aligning individual objectives to the overall goals. Choice *A* is not the correct answer because diversity is the actual inclusion of individuals who are different—backgrounds, educations, perspectives, experiences, and more. Choice *B* is not the correct answer because strategic planning is the holistic and overarching planning that incorporates inclusion within the overall plan. Choice *D* is not the correct answer because business acumen is the ability to identify, understand, and resolve situations that result in positive outcomes.

49. C: 457(b) plans are typically for nonprofit employees. Choice *A*, 401(k) plans are for private sector employees. Choice *B*, 403(b) plans are for public education employees, and Choice *D* is a made-up answer.

50. B & C: Investigations should be conducted with good-faith efforts and by professionals who have been properly and formally trained. While an investigation may need to be escalated to a third-party investigation, it is a best practice to attempt to resolve the issue at the lowest level possible. Additionally, as many witnesses as possible should be interviewed to fully gain understanding of the situation and provide support to any proposed recommendation.

51. B: Good faith bargaining refers to the honest attempt made by both an employer and union to reach an agreement. Mandatory subjects of bargaining include the specific items, such as benefits and wages, that must be negotiated. Collective bargaining is the entire process by which negotiations take place. Labor relations is the management of relationships between the organization, employees, and the union representatives.

52. D: Choice *D* is correct. While most employees provide two weeks' notice when leaving a position, under the employment-at-will doctrine, neither the employee nor employer is required to provide notice when terminating an employee or when an employee is exiting a position.

53. D: While there are numerous communications methods and techniques, it is important to remember that consistent communication should always be the goal. Employees should not learn about policies, programs, and changes from word of mouth and one-on-one communication as the primary means of learning. Choices *A*, *B*, and *C* are incorrect answers because town halls, employee meetings, formal handbooks, brochures, webpages, and electronic documents are all best practices to ensure that employees receive the same message and information. Consistency, clarity, and specific information are vital to ensure that all employees understand and are aware of the organization's policies.

54. C: Strategic planning is dependent on the knowledge and awareness of the goals and objectives that have been developed for both the organization and the department. Aligning these two is vital to the strategic planning process. Choice *A* is incorrect because while having HR professionals trained in process mapping and assessment is beneficial and considered a resource in the process, strategic planning is not dependent on this. Choice *B* is incorrect because strategic planning is not dependent on strong recruitment and selection processes. Strong recruitment and hiring practices may actually be dependent on strategic planning, as this process clarifies the needs of the department and areas for improvement. Choice *D* is incorrect because, once again, strategic planning is not dependent on staff location or the actual employer, whether within or outside an organization. Strategic planning may actually be more productive with internal staff members than with an outsourced resource; staff members are aware of the history, culture, information, and organizational specifics.

55. B: The third step in Kotter's eight-step change model involves creating a clear vision for the change, including identifying the reasons and purpose for the change. The fourth step is to communicate the vision, followed by the fifth step, empowering action, Choice *A*. Choice *C* is the sixth step, and building on the change, Choice *D*, is the seventh step. The eighth step involves rooting the change, or making it stick.

56. C: A spouse's job loss is not one of the hardship criteria set forth by the IRS for early retirement withdrawal. Choices *A*, *B*, and *D* all qualify.

57. A: The current deductible thresholds for a plan to be considered a high-deductible health plan (HDHP) are $1,400 for individuals and $2,800 for families. Choices *B*, *C*, and *D* are incorrect.

58. C: A candidate can learn about an organization, its behavior toward process, and expectations regarding employees from the vision, mission, and values statements usually presented on the website. While Choices *A*, *B*, and *D* all provide information about the position, benefits, and company, they do not necessarily identify how work is done and how employees should conduct themselves. This information is usually contained with the vision, mission, and values statements.

59. D: Workforce planning refers to the process that forecasts an organization's current and future workforce needs, determines the most effective practices and processes to fill these needs, and implements the plans to deliver results. Choices *A*, *B*, and *C* are all parts of the workforce planning process.

60. B: Severance packages can assist employees with their transition out of an organization and can include compensation, extension of benefits, transition services, and other services. Employee assistance programs can be—and usually are—included in a severance package. Reductions in force are actions that occur when downsizing is necessary and severance packages are a response to these actions. Performance management is the process by which an organization plans, coaches, evaluates, and rewards an employee.

61. A & C: Diversity and inclusion foster an inclusive environment in which differences are valued and respected. Diversity is the mixture, and inclusion is making the mixture work. Diversity and inclusion

189

strategies have an impact not only in the workplace, but also with the workforce, in the marketplace, and within the community. The effects of a strong diversity and inclusion strategy are seen within the organization and have a far-reaching external impact, including social commitment and responsibility.

62. A, C, & D: Ground rules should address where, when, and how long the parties will meet; a communications plan regarding media; and a cutoff date for new proposals. The ratification process and employee interests are components within the collective bargaining process, but they are not included in the ground rules.

63. D: A benefits program policy should include contact information for any third-party service providers. While Choices *A*, *B*, and *C* are not often shared with employees company-wide, this type of information could be provided on an as-needed basis if the organization so chooses. These things are not, however, typically included in written benefits program policies.

64. Voluntary Termination – C, D, & F; Involuntary Termination – A, B, & E: Examples of a voluntary termination are retirement and resignation to accept another job or relocate to another location. Examples of an involuntary termination are poor performance, failure of probation, and disciplinary actions. Involuntary terminations are based on inappropriate actions by the employees or failure to perform at the appropriate standard, causing the employer to end the employment relationship.

65. C: The five Ps are "proper preparation prevents poor performance," which is associated with salary negotiation techniques rather than a learning management system (LMS). Choices *A*, *B*, and *D* are all good uses of an LMS.

66. C: There are five steps in the recruitment process, and interviewing is the fourth step. Step one is to assess the need and create a job posting. Step two, Choice *A*, involves sourcing candidates and assessing the candidate pool. Step three, Choice *B*, is screening for appropriately qualified candidates. Step five, Choice *D*, is making an offer of employment and completing orientation.

67. C: Health and safety, including worker's compensation, personal medical leaves, and safety protocol, is an important part of the orientation process. Choices *A*, *B*, and *D* may be part of the company culture and might be included in an orientation process, but they are not one of the four main areas: orientation, onboarding, health and safety, and supervisory information (if needed).

68. A – 4, B – 1, C – 3, & D – 2: Awareness is the pillar that raises the understanding of diversity initiatives. Mobilization is the pillar that sets up the policies and procedures that allow for accountability. Action is the pillar that implements strategies through specific actions and plans. Alignment is the pillar that analyzes, reviews, and revises policies and procedures.

69. D: The process of conciliation is the alternative dispute resolution technique that is a non-binding formal process. In the conciliation process, a negotiator explains the law and provides the two parties with a non-binding recommendation to resolve the issue. Choice *A* is incorrect because arbitration is a formal process in which an arbitrator considers evidence presented by each party and determines a solution that is binding and final. Choice *B* is incorrect because negotiation is a voluntary agreement that works out a solution directly between the two parties involved. Choice *C* is incorrect because mediation is a facilitated negotiation technique that works out a solution between the two parties through a neutral third party.

70. B: The design stage of ADDIE includes deciding what will be included and who will deliver the training. Choice *A* refers to analysis, the first step of ADDIE. Choices *C* and *D* both refer to the third step, develop.

190

71. B: While employers must comply with all federal and state laws and regulations, they are permitted to offer more than the minimum benefits. Offering extended maternity leave would be allowed under federal law, so Choice *C* is incorrect. Employers do not have the choice, however, to not offer federal benefits, such as the maternity leave granted under FMLA, so Choice *A* is incorrect. Federal law says that companies must allow up to twelve weeks, but it does not specify that this is the maximum benefit, which makes Choice *D* incorrect.

72. C: An employer should make every effort to provide reasonable accommodations for an employee; however, modifying the work schedule to allow for unlimited paid breaks would be considered unreasonable. Employees still have a responsibility to complete their work and adhere to the work schedules and legal standards regarding breaks. Allowing an employee to take as many paid breaks as possible would not be appropriate. If there is medical documentation that substantiates this request, it may be appropriate to discuss a limited work schedule or a different position versus allowing the employee to take unlimited paid breaks.

Choice *A* is incorrect because providing access to the workplace for an employee who is utilizing a wheelchair is a completely reasonable and appropriate request under the ADA. It may be necessary to discuss options to ensure cost is not prohibitive. Choice *B* is incorrect because a telecommuting arrangement for an injured employee would be considered reasonable and appropriate. This arrangement could be temporary until the employee can return to work with no restrictions and have specific deliverables and expectations outlined as well. Choice *D* is incorrect because providing additional breaks and private areas for nursing mothers to lactate is not only reasonable and appropriate but also mandated by law in several states.

73. A: A due diligence investigation is a detailed risk assessment that provides insight and information regarding a specific concern or issue. Due diligence investigations provide insight into the issues and root cause of the concern as well as a direction for recommendations. They should be thorough, extensive, and fully assess the situation. Choice *B* is incorrect because a policy audit is a process to specifically review and assess a policy and make recommendations to update it. Choice *C* is incorrect because a workplace safety investigation is a process to specifically investigate a safety issue or an incident in which an injury occurred. Choice *D* is incorrect because a benefit audit is a process to specifically review and assess the benefits being offered to employees or to ensure that the appropriate paperwork is completed and filed with HR.

74. B: Choice *B* is correct. Employers should attempt to complete and file I-9 forms as soon as possible; however, an employee must complete an I-9 form within their first three days of employment. If a form is not completed within the employee's first three days on the job, the employer can terminate the employee for not providing employment verification.

75. A: The code of conduct details a company's ethical standards and should include sections on confidentiality, conflicts of interest, reporting code violations, and ownership of intellectual property. Choices *B, C,* and *D* are made-up terms.

76. A: While many companies do include background checks as part of the hiring process, these are not skills assessments. Choices *B, C,* and *D* are all types of skills assessments that organizations may use in their hiring process.

77. C: The Department of Justice (DOJ) is responsible for enforcing the laws regarding employee privacy. Choice *A* is incorrect because the Occupational Safety and Health Administration (OSHA) is responsible for enforcing the laws regarding workplace safety. Choice *B* is incorrect because the Equal Employment Opportunity Commission (EEOC) is responsible for enforcing the laws regarding discrimination. Choice *D* is incorrect because the Department of Labor (DOL) is responsible for enforcing the laws regarding compensation.

78. B: The current staff not wanting to audit the safety practices just because they find it uninteresting would not be an appropriate reason to contract with an outside legal service. Choice *A* is incorrect because negotiating a contract with a union can be a difficult and consuming process. Additionally, if the staff does not have this experience, it would be in the organization's best interest to bring in expertise to assist with this task. Choice *C* is incorrect because resolving conflict by a third party may be appropriate based on the previous attempts. This would be another good example of when to bring in an outside legal service. Choice *D* is incorrect because bringing in legal experts to review and update policies is a vital component to ensuring that the policies comply with any new regulations.

79. B: While strategic planning includes the formal assessment of available resources, workforce, knowledge, and skills within an organization, strategic planning also encompasses much more. Strategic planning includes reviewing the mission, goals, and objectives of the organization and departments; assessing the resources available; forecasting the gaps and needs; and developing a plan. Choices *A, C,* and *D* are incorrect because they are all accurate statements about strategic planning. Strategic planning is critical to ensure that employees are all working together to accomplish the goals and objectives defined by the department and organization. Strategic planning ensures that the organization, department, and individual employees are aware of the resources needed to succeed. Strategic planning plays a vital role in the success of individual employees, departments, and an organization.

80. D: The attrition rate is calculated by dividing the number of employees that left during the year by the number of employees at the beginning of the year and multiplying that number by 100. Using this formula, HR can come up with a percentage for the attrition rate. For this problem, if a company had eighty-six employees at the end of the year, and they began the year with ninety-two, that means they lost six employees during the year. The attrition rate would be $6 \div 92 = 0.065 \times 100 = 6.5$ percent. A high attrition rate would be indicative of a problem. Choice *C* is missing the step of multiplying by one hundred to translate the decimal into a percentage. Choice *B* divided the number of employees at the end of the year by the number of employees at the beginning of the year and then multiplied by one hundred, and Choice *A* did this but did not multiply by one hundred.

81. B: Organizational learning should include orientation, motivation, reinforcement, retention, and transference to effectively engage all participants and ensure the best learning opportunities. Choices *A, C,* and *D* are incorrect.

82. A: Labor relations includes establishing, negotiating, and administering bargaining agreements and policies. Labor relations also includes managing grievances and disagreements. Choice *B* is incorrect because workforce planning is the process used to align an organization's needs and priorities with the available workforce and skills. Choice *C* is incorrect because employee relations is defined as the organization's commitment to foster a positive working relationship with its employees. Choice *D* is incorrect because mediation is a facilitated negotiation that works out a solution between two parties with a neutral third party.

83. A: Safety and security protocols are a necessary and vital requirement for an organization. They are not considered a unique program because there are many specific regulations that must be adhered to in order to achieve compliance. Choices *B, C,* and *D* are incorrect as they are all examples of programs that

192

can be uniquely tailored to the organization and employees to increase engagement and satisfaction. Training and learning opportunities, recognition and achievement programs, and telecommuting and alternate work schedules are all examples of programs that can be developed and tailored to maximize employee satisfaction and the employee experience within an organization.

84. C: The employee value proposition (EVP) refers to the value an employee gains from working for any given company. The five key components of that are compensation, benefits, career, work environment, and culture. Choices *A*, *B*, and *D* are not correct.

85. B: Creating a new job and role for an employee as a workplace accommodation would be considered unreasonable. The Americans with Disabilities Act (ADA) requires employers to make reasonable accommodations to support employees in the workplace; however, these accommodations should not create an undue hardship on the organization. Creating a role that has not existed before would be considered an unreasonable accommodation. Choice *A* is incorrect because interpretation software, while having a cost associated, could be considered reasonable based on the need of the employee. Choice *C* is incorrect because reassigning the employee to a new job is an appropriate request; if it does not displace or negatively affect another employee, then it should be considered a viable option. Choice *D* is incorrect because workplace accommodations often include acquiring new office equipment and special devices. As long as the cost is not substantial, employers should consider these options to assist an employee in the workplace.

86. A: An employee surplus occurs when there is not enough work for all employees or when there are more employees than the company needs. Choice *B* is the opposite; it refers to an employee shortage. Choices *C* and *D* are not correct.

87. D: Survey data should be shared consistently with all levels of the organization. Committed leadership is essential for an effective survey. Surveys should always ensure confidentiality and anonymity for employees. There is no set timeline for administering employee surveys; however, a standard recommendation is at least once per year.

88. D: Absenteeism is the data point that calculates how many employees are absent from work. Choice *A* is incorrect because attrition is the data point that calculates how many employees are leaving an organization. Choice *B* is incorrect because human capital is the data point that compares the costs of employees to the organization's revenues. Choice *C* is incorrect because presenteeism is the data point that calculates how many employees are not absent from work. Presenteeism is the data point used to calculate perfect attendance awards.

89. B: Choice *B* is correct. When an employee's hours are reduced, they are eligible to elect COBRA continuation coverage for up to eighteen months. The policyholder and their dependents may choose continuation coverage when an employee reduces their hours.

90. D: In-house training staff can most effectively provide training for organization-specific topics, such as internal written communication protocols and company teambuilding exercises. External training specialists are particularly helpful for more complex topics such as legal and compliance issues and health and safety matters. Choices *A*, *B*, and *C* are incorrect in one or more of those respects.

aPHR Practice Tests #3-#5

The 3rd, 4th, and 5th practice tests are available as digital tests along with the first two tests. Go to apexprep.com/bonus/aphr or scan the QR code below to access them. Many customers find this more convenient as it keeps this book to a manageable size and allows you to take the tests on your phone, tablet, or computer.

After you go to the website, you will have to create an account and register as a "new user" and verify your email address before you begin.

If you need any help, please contact us at info@apexprep.com.

Greetings!

First, we would like to give a huge "thank you" for choosing us and this study guide for your aPHR exam. We hope that it will lead you to success on this exam and for years to come.

Our team has tried to make your preparations as thorough as possible by covering all of the topics you should be expected to know. In addition, our writers attempted to create practice questions identical to what you will see on the day of your actual test. We have also included many test-taking strategies to help you learn the material, maintain the knowledge, and take the test with confidence.

We strive for excellence in our products, and if you have any comments or concerns over the quality of something in this study guide, please send us an email so that we can improve.

As you continue forward in life, we would like to remain alongside you with other books and study guides in our library. We are continually producing and updating study guides in several different subjects. If you are looking for something in particular, all of our products are available on Amazon. You can also send us an email!

Sincerely,
APEX Publishing
info@apexprep.com

FREE

Free Study Tips Videos/DVD

In addition to this guide, we have created a FREE set of videos with helpful study tips. **These FREE videos provide you with top-notch tips to conquer your exam and reach your goals.**

Our simple request is that you give us feedback about the book in exchange for these strategy-packed videos. We would love to hear what you thought about the book, whether positive, negative, or neutral. It is our #1 goal to provide you with quality products and customer service.

To receive your **FREE Study Tips Videos**, scan the QR code or email freevideos@apexprep.com. Please put "FREE Videos" in the subject line and include the following in the email:

      a. The title of the book

      b. Your rating of the book on a scale of 1-5, with 5 being the highest score

      c. Any thoughts or feedback about the book

Thank you!

Made in United States
Troutdale, OR
01/11/2024